THE COMPLETE BOOK OF
BABYCRAFTS

ARCO PUBLISHING COMPANY, INC.
New York

Published in the United States of America by
Arco Publishing, Inc.
219 Park Avenue South
New York, N.Y. 10003
U.S.A.

First impression 1981
© Marshall Cavendish Limited 1981

Library of Congress Cataloging in Publication Data
Eleanor Van Zandt
The Complete Book of Babycrafts
1. Non-fiction
2. Needlecrafts

LCCN 81-67322
ISBN 0-668-05342-9

Produced by Marshall Cavendish Books Limited
58 Old Compton Street
London W1V 5PA

Consultant Editor: Eleanor Van Zandt
House Editor: Mary Lambert

Printed in Belgium

INTRODUCTION

There's a special pleasure in making things for babies. If you're
an expectant mother you'll enjoy creating with your own
hands some of the many items that will be needed by the
new arrival. And if you're a doting aunt or grandmother, or a
friend, you can find few better ways to please a busy mother
than by contributing a hand-made garment every now and
then as the little one grows up.

In this book you'll find projects for every taste and talent:
things to knit, sew and crochet; cuddly toys; sturdy, practical
garments for playtime and exquisite outfits for special
occasions, including a lace-trimmed christening gown. There's
a layette to knit and one to crochet and a set of pretty and
practical nursery accessories. The projects have been specially
chosen to provide a good balance between clothes for hot
and cold weather, for infants and toddlers and for boys and
girls. In the front of the book you'll find useful information,
such as knitting and crochet abbreviations, how to enlarge a
graph pattern, how to straighten fabric, as well as a glossary of
sewing terms including illustrations of embroidery stitches.

Hand-made baby clothes are not only better quality than
most mass-produced ones, they're also less expensive – an
important factor in these economy-conscious times. So why
not start now to make something pretty for someone special?

CONTENTS

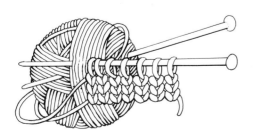

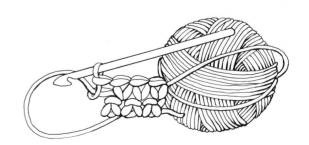

BASIC INFORMATION

Enlarging a pattern

Most of the sewing projects in this book use patterns that have been reduced to fit the page. To use the pattern you must first enlarge it to the correct size – in some cases a choice of size is indicated by different-colored lines – using graph paper, which can be purchased in notions departments. Usually this paper is ruled in inches. Most of the patterns in this book are printed on a grid corresponding to 2 inches, though in some cases a 1 inch grid is used. An alternative to enlarging the pattern yourself is to take it to a photostat service and have it enlarged to the desired size.

Before enlarging the pattern onto graph paper it is a good idea to darken the grid lines you will be using – for example, those at 2in intervals. Now copy the pattern pieces so that their outlines relate to the large grid just as the smaller pieces relate to the small grid – that is, so that they follow and cross the same number of grid lines in the same relative positions. For curved lines you may find it helpful to use a flexible curve, a length of pliable plastic that you can bend to the desired shape and use as a guide.

Straightening fabric

Often fabric becomes distorted in being wound onto the bolt. Make sure before you cut out a garment that the fabric is straight, so that the pieces can be cut on the straight grain.

If the length has been cut, rather than torn, you must first even the ends. Pull a crosswise thread and then cut carefully along the puckered line produced. If the fabric is loosely woven it may be possible to pull out a long length of thread and cut along the space created.

When the ends are even, check to see whether or not they are at right angles to the selvage. You can check this with a right-angled triangle, if you have one. Otherwise, fold the fabric in half lengthwise and pin the selvages together. If the fabric lies flat the grain is straight; if not, you must straighten it. Enlist the aid of another person and pull the fabric on its true bias – at a 45° angle to the

selvages – along the entire length, pulling in the direction shown below.

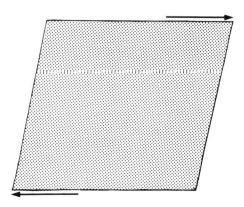

Testing for shrinkage

With washable fabrics there is sometimes a possibility of shrinkage, unless the fabric label says that it is pre-shrunk. Before cutting out the garment, cut a small square of fabric and draw around it on a sheet of paper. Immerse the swatch in warm water for a few minutes, let it dry, and iron it. Place it on the drawn outline. If it does not fill the outline you should shrink the fabric.

Clip the selvages at intervals of about 3in. Immerse the fabric, folded crosswise, in a basin of warm water for about half an hour. Then gently squeeze the water out of it and hang it up to dry, keeping it as straight and smooth as possible. When it is nearly dry, press it on the wrong side.

Marking the fabric

There are several ways of transferring pattern markings onto the fabric. Those used most often are tailor's tacks, tailor's chalk and a tracing wheel with dressmaker's carbon paper.

To make tailor's tacks, thread a needle with a double strand of thread – do not knot the ends – make a small stitch through the pattern and both thicknesses of fabric at the point to be marked – leaving a thread end about 1in long, then make another small stitch across the first – leaving a loop about 2in long. Cut off the thread, leaving a 1in end. Repeat for the other markings. Cut the loops, then

lift the pattern off gently. Carefully raise the top fabric piece slightly and clip the threads between the two layers.

If you are using tailor's chalk you should fold the fabric with the right side inside before cutting, so that you can mark the pieces on the wrong side. After cutting out the pieces, insert pins through the pattern at the places to be marked. Carefully slip the pattern over the pins. Then mark the fabric on both – wrong – sides over the pins.

To use the tracing wheel and dressmaker's carbon you must also fold the fabric with right sides together and mark the wrong sides. Cut two pieces of the carbon; place one right side up under the bottom fabric piece and the other wrong side up between the pattern and the upper fabric piece. Run the wheel once, firmly, over the marking. For darts or other line markings use a ruler to keep the wheel straight.

If a marking transferred with chalk or dressmaker's carbon needs to be visible on the right side, run a line of basting through the marking.

Fabric amounts

In most cases the fabric amounts specified in this book have been rounded up where necessary to purchasable amounts. In the standard system of measurement used in the United States, the smallest unit a store will cut is an eighth of a yard.

Gauge

Before beginning to knit or crochet any item you must obtain the same gauge obtained by the designer of the pattern. To do this, make a swatch using the suggested needles or hook and working the specified number of stitches and rows over the specified stitch pattern. Pin the swatch flat on an ironing board, taking care not to stretch it in either direction, and measure it with a ruler (not a tape-measure). If the swatch is larger than the measurements given in the instructions, make another swatch using smaller size needles or hook. If the square is too small, try a larger size needles or hook.

It is absolutely essential to obtain the correct gauge; otherwise the finished article will not be the correct size. Check the gauge occasionally while working to make sure you are neither tightening nor loosening up.

Substituting yarns

It is sometimes possible to substitute one yarn for another, but not recommended, as you may have difficulty obtaining the correct gauge and a fabric similar to the original. However, if you do wish to use another yarn you should first buy one ball of the substitute and make a sample, adjusting needle or hook size if necessary until you achieve the correct gauge. The label on some yarns will state the normal gauge on the recommended needles; by comparing this with the pattern gauge you can tell whether or not your chosen yarn is likely to be an acceptable substitute. But you must still check this by making one or more samples.

Note also that the length of yarn contained in a ball will often vary from one brand or type to another, even where the weight is the same, owing to variation in thickness. It is advisable to buy a little extra of the substitute yarn so that you do not run the risk of having to buy extra from a different dye lot.

A list of manufacturers of the imported yarns used in this book is given on page 184. By writing to them you can obtain information on your nearest stockist and mail order outlets.

Making a twisted cord

To make a twisted cord, first cut the required number of strands – usually specified in the pattern – making them three times the length of the finished cord. Knot the strands together at both ends and insert a pencil in each knot.

Preferably, enlist the aid of another person. Each of you should take hold of one end and turn the pencils clockwise until the strands are very tightly twisted – so that they kink up tightly if you loosen the tension. (If you are working alone, secure one end around a hook or drawer pull and twist the other end only.) Holding the strands taut, fold them in half at the center and knot the two ends together.

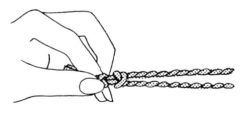

Then, holding the knotted ends, give the cord a sharp shake and smooth it down toward the folded end to even out the twists. Make another knot at the folded end and cut the strands at both ends.

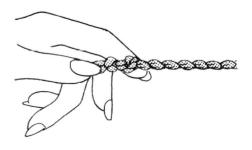

Knitting and crochet abbreviations			
alt	alternate(ly)	RS	right side
approx	approximate(ly)	sc	single crochet
beg	begin(ning)	sl	slip
ch	chain	sl st	slip stitch in knitting
cont	continu(e)(ing)	sp	space(s)
dec	decrease	ss	slip stitch in crochet
dc	double crochet	st(s)	stitch(es)
dtr	double triple	st st	stockinette stitch (one row
foll	follow(ing)		knit, one row purl)
g st	garter stitch (every row knit)	tbl	through back of loop(s)
gr(s)	group(s)	tog	together
hdc	half double crochet	tr	treble, triple
inc	increase	tr tr	triple triple
K	knit	WS	wrong side
K up	pick up and knit	yo	yarn over
K-wise	knitwise	yib	yarn in back
psso	pass slipped stitch over	yif	yarn in front
pat	pattern		
P	purl		
P up	pick up and purl		
P-wise	purlwise		
rem	remain(ing)		
rep	repeat		

Asterisks * indicate that the instructions within should be repeated as often as specified.

In patterns given for more than one size the figures given in brackets [] refer to the larger sizes.

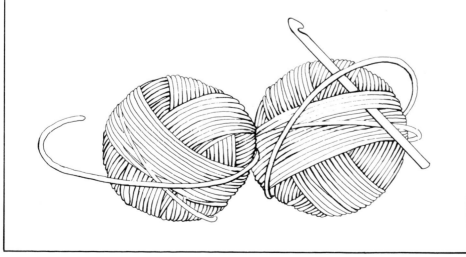

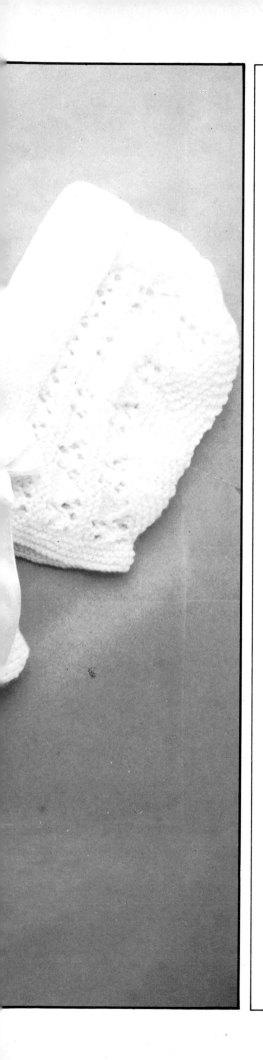

KNITTING

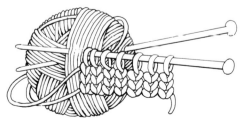

Lacy Layette

A delicate lacy pattern is combined with garter stitch in this beautiful layette, which includes a shawl, jacket, dress, cardigan, leggings, undershirt, bonnet, bootees and mittens. In short a miniature wardrobe for your child.

Size
The garments will fit a baby up to 6 months old, or chest size 19in.

Materials
Bernat Berella 3 ply Fingering in the amounts specified for the individual garments one pair each of sizes 0, 2, 4 and 6 needles.

Shawl
9 1oz balls of yarn

Jacket

4 1oz balls of yarn
4 small buttons

Dress

3 1oz balls of yarn
4 small buttons

Cardigan

2 1oz balls of yarn
5 small buttons

Leggings

2 1oz balls of yarn
shirring elastic

Undershirt

2 1oz balls of yarn
1yd of narrow ribbon

Bonnet

1 1oz ball of yarn
1½yd of narrow ribbon

Bootees and mittens

1 1oz ball of yarn
1yd of narrow ribbon

Gauge

30 sts and 38 rows to 4in over pat worked on size 2 needles

Shawl

Using size 6 needles cast on 225 sts. Work in g st, dec one st at each end of 2nd and every alt row until 197 sts rem. Commence pat.
1st row Using size 4 needles, K1, *yo, sl 1 P-wise, K2 tog, psso, yo, K5, rep from * to last 4 sts, yo, sl 1 P-wise, K2 tog, psso, yo, K1.
2nd row K1, P to last st, K1.
3rd–4th rows As 1st–2nd rows.
5th row K1, *K3, yo, sl 1 P-wise, K1, psso, K1, K2 tog, yo, rep from * to last 4 sts, K4.
6th row As 2nd.
7th row K1, *yo, sl 1 P-wise, K2 tog, psso, yo, K1, rep from * to end.
8th–12th rows Change to size 6 needles; work 5 rows g st.
These 12 rows form the pat. Cont in pat until 7th row of 24th pat has been worked. Change to size 6 needles. Cont in g st, inc one st at each end of 2nd and every alt row to 225 sts. Bind off.
Side borders
Using size 6 needles and with RS of work facing, K up 197 sts evenly along one side of shawl. Work 28 rows g st, inc one st at each end of 2nd and every alt row. Bind off. Work along other side to match.

Finishing

Press center of shawl very lightly under a dry cloth with a cool iron. Join corners.

Jacket

Using size 2 needles cast on 247 sts and work in one piece to underarm. Work 7 rows g st. Cont in pat as given for shawl using size 2 needles throughout and keeping 5 sts at each end of every row in g st, until work measures 7in from beg, ending with a 12th pat row, and dec one st at end of last row. 246 sts.
Divide for armholes
Next row K6, pat 58 sts, bind off 2 sts, pat 114 sts, bind off 2 sts, pat 58 sts, K6. Complete left front first. Keeping pat and g st border correct, dec one st at armhole edge on next 7 rows. 57 sts. Break off yarn and leave sts on holder.
With WS of work facing, rejoin yarn to back sts and work 7 rows in pat, dec one st at each end of every row. 100 sts. Break off yarn and leave sts on holder. With WS of work facing, rejoin yarn to right front sts and complete to match left front, reversing shaping. Do not break off yarn but leave sts on holder.

Sleeves
Using size 0 needles cast on 32 sts. Work 5 rows g st.
Next row K1, *K2, inc in next st, K1, inc in next st, rep from * to last st, inc in last st. 45 sts.
Change to size 2 needles. Cont in pat as given for jacket until sleeve measures 5½in from beg, ending with a 12th pat row, and inc one st at end of last row.
Shape top
Keeping pat correct, dec one st at beg of next 8 rows. 38 sts. Break off yarn and leave sts on holder.

Yoke
Using size 2 needles and with RS of work facing, work across all sts on holders as foll :
Next row K6, (K2 tog) 24 times, K3 across right front ; K2 tog, K34, K2 tog across right sleeve ; K4, (K2 tog) 46 times, K4 across back ; K2 tog, K34, K2 tog across left sleeve ; K3, (K2 tog) 24 times, K6 across left front. 192 sts.
**Next row K to end.
Next row (buttonhole row) K1, K2 tog, yo, K to end.
Work 7 rows g st.
Next row (buttonhole row) K1, K2 tog, yo, K3, *K2 tog, K1, rep from * to last 6 sts, K6. 132 sts.
Work 7 rows g st.
Next row (buttonhole row) K1, K2 tog, yo, K3, *K2 tog, K1, rep from * to last 6 sts, K6. 92 sts.
Work 7 rows g st.
Next row K7, *K2 tog, K1, rep from * to last 7 sts, K7. 66 sts. ******
Next row K to last 11 sts, turn, sl 1, K to

last 11 sts, turn.
Next row Sl 1, K to last 18 sts, turn, sl 1, K to last 18 sts, turn.
Next row K to end.
Change to size 0 needles. Work 4 rows g st making buttonhole as before at beg of first row. Bind off loosely.

Finishing

Press each piece lightly under a dry cloth with a cool iron. Join sleeve and underarm seams. Sew on buttons.

Dress

Using size 2 needles cast on 239 sts and work in one piece to underarm. Work 7 rows g st. Work in pat as given for jacket, using size 2 needles throughout, but K one more st before and after pat rows, until work measures 8½in from beg, ending with a 12th pat row and inc one st at each end of last row.

Divide for armholes
Next row Pat 62 sts, bind off 2 sts, pat 113 sts, bind off 2 sts, pat 62 sts. Complete right back first. Keeping pat correct, dec one st at armhole edge on next 7 rows. 55 sts. Break off yarn and leave sts on holder.
With WS of work facing, rejoin yarn to front sts ; keeping pat correct dec one st at each end of next 7 rows. 99 sts. Break off yarn and leave sts on holder. With WS of work facing, rejoin yarn to rem sts and complete to match right back, reversing shaping. Do not break off yarn but leave sts on holder.

Sleeves
Using size 0 needles cast on 39 sts. Work 3 rows g st.
Next row *K5, inc in next st, rep from * to last 3 sts, K3. 45 sts.
Change to size 2 needles. Work 12 rows pat, inc one st at end of last row.
Shape top
As given for jacket sleeve.

Yoke
Using size 2 needles and with RS of work facing, work across all sts on holders as foll :
Next row K7, (K2 tog) 24 times across left back ; K2 tog, K34, K2 tog across left sleeve ; K4, (K2 tog) 45 times, K5 across front ; K2 tog, K34, K2 tog across right sleeve ; (K2 tog) 26 times, K3 across right back ; cast on 6 sts for under flap. 192 sts. Work from ** to ** as given for jacket yoke.
***Next 2 rows K18, turn, sl 1, K to end.
Next 2 rows K11, turn, sl 1, K to end. *******
Next row K to end.
Rep from *** to *** once more. Change to

size 0 needles. Work 4 rows g st making buttonhole as before at beg of first row. Bind off loosely.

Finishing
Press as given for jacket. Join sleeve and underarm seams. Join back to underflap. Sew down underflap. Sew on buttons. Press seams.

Cardigan
Using size 0 needles cast on 133 sts and work in one piece to underarm.
1st row K1, *P1, K1, rep from * to end.
2nd row P1, *K1, P1, rep from * to end.
Rep these 2 rows 6 times more. Change to size 2 needles. Commence pat.
1st row K1, *yo, sl 1 P-wise, K2 tog, psso, yo, K5, rep from * to last 4 sts, yo, sl 1 P-wise, K2 tog psso, yo, K1.
2nd, 4th and 6th rows K1, P to last st, K1.
3rd row As 1st.

5th row K1, *K3, yo, sl 1 P-wise, K1, psso, K1, K2 tog, yo, rep from * to last 4 sts, K4.
7th row K1, *yo, sl 1 P-wise, K2 tog, psso, yo, K1, rep from * to end.
8th–12th rows Work 5 rows g st. Rep 1st–7th rows once more. Cont in g st until work measures 5½in from beg, ending with a WS row.
Divide for armholes
Next row K30, bind off 6 sts, K61, bind off 6 sts, K30.
Complete left front first. K 1 row. Dec one st at armhole edge on next and every alt row until 25 sts rem. Cont without shaping until armhole measures 2¼in from beg, ending at neck edge.
Shape neck
Bind off 4 sts at beg of next row. Dec one st at neck edge on every row until 16 sts rem. Cont without shaping until armhole measures 3½in from beg, ending at armhole edge.

Shape shoulder
Bind off 8 sts at beg of next and foll alt row.
With WS of work facing, rejoin yarn to back sts and K to end. Dec one st at each end of next and every alt row until 51 sts rem. Cont without shaping until armholes measure same as left front to shoulder, ending with a WS row.
Shape shoulders
Bind off 8 sts at beg of next 4 rows. Leave rem sts on holder for center back neck.
With WS of work facing, rejoin yarn to rem sts and complete right front as given for left front, reversing shaping.

Sleeves
Using size 0 needles cast on 45 sts. Work 12 rows Kl, P1 rib as given for cardigan. Change to size 2 needles. Cont in g st, inc one st at each end of 5th and every foll

10th row until there are 55 sts. Cont without shaping until sleeve measures 5½in from beg.

Shape top
Bind off 3 sts at beg of next 2 rows. Dec one st at each end of next and every alt row until 23 sts rem. Bind off 3 sts at beg of next 4 rows.
Bind off rem sts.

Button band
Using size 0 needles cast on 8 sts. Work in K1, P1 rib until band fits from cast-on edge to neck shaping of left front, when slightly stretched. Leave sts on holder. Baste band to left front. Mark positions for 5 buttons, first to come ½in above cast-on edge and last to come in neckband with 3 more evenly spaced between.

Buttonhole band
Work as given for button band making buttonholes as markers are reached, as foll:
1st row Rib 3 sts, bind off 2 sts, rib 3 sts.
2nd row Rib 3 sts, cast on 2 sts, rib 3 sts.

Neckband
Baste buttonhole band to right front. Using size 0 needles and with RS of work facing, rib across buttonhole band, K up 66 sts evenly around neck and rib across button band. Work 6 rows K1, P1 rib, making buttonhole as before on 4th and 5th rows.
Bind off in rib.

Finishing
Press each piece lightly under a dry cloth with a cool iron. Join sleeve seams. Set in sleeves. Sew on button and buttonhole bands. Press seams.
Sew on buttons.

Leggings right leg
Using size 0 needles cast on 89 sts. Work 12 rows K1, P1 rib as given for cardigan. Change to size 2 needles. K 2 rows g st.

Shape back
***1st row** K11 sts, turn.
2nd and every alt row Sl 1, K to end.
3rd row K18 sts, turn.
5th row K25 sts, turn.
Cont in this way until row K 46, turn, has been worked. Work 63 rows g st across all sts, inc one st for back edge at beg of 4th and every foll 6th row. 99 sts.
Cont without shaping until work measures 8in from beg. Dec one st at each end of next and every alt row until 47 sts rem. Cont without shaping until work measures 7in from beg of dec, ending at back edge ***

Shape instep
1st row K40, sl rem 7 sts onto holder, turn.
2nd row K18 sts.
Work 16 rows g st on these 18 sts for instep. Break off yarn. With RS of work facing, K up 16 sts evenly along side of instep, K across instep sts, K up 16 sts from other side of instep and K across 7 sts on holder. 79 sts. Work 9 rows g st.

Shape foot
1st row K5, K3 tog, K4, K3 tog, K22, K3 tog, K14, K3 tog, K22.
2nd and 4th rows K to end.
3rd row K4, K3 tog, K2, K3 tog, K20, K3 tog, K12, K3 tog, K21.
5th row K3, (K3 tog) twice, K18, K3 tog, K10, K3 tog, K20.
6th row As 2nd.
Bind off loosely.

Leggings left leg
Work as given for right leg from ** to ** K1 row. Work as given for right leg from *** to ***, inc one st at end of 4th and every foll 6th row instead of at beg.

Shape instep
1st row K25, sl rem 22 sts onto holder, turn.
2nd row K18 sts, turn.
Work 16 rows g st on these 18 sts. Break off yarn. With RS of work facing, K up 16 sts along side of instep, K across instep sts, K up 16 sts from other side of instep and K across sts on holder. Work 9 rows g st.

Shape foot
1st row K22, K3 tog, K14, K3 tog, K22, K3 tog, K4, K3 tog, K5.
2nd and 4th rows K to end.
3rd row K21, K3 tog, K12, K3 tog, K20, K3 tog, K2, K3 tog, K4.
5th row K20, K3 tog, K10, K3 tog, K18, (K3 tog) twice, K3.
6th row As 2nd.
Bind off loosely.

Finishing
Press as given for cardigan. Join front, back and leg seams. Beg at center of toe, join foot seam. With WS of work facing, thread shirring elastic through every K st on first and every alt row of rib at waist edge.

Undershirt
Using size 2 needles cast on 64 sts. Work 5 rows g st. Beg with a K row cont in st st until work measures 5in from beg, ending with a P row. Inc one st at each end of next and every alt row until there are 72 sts, ending with a P row.

Shape sleeves
Cast on 10 sts at beg of next 2 rows. 92 sts.
Next row K to end.

Next row K4, P to last 4 sts, K4.
Rep last 2 rows until work measures 9in from beg, ending with a K row.
Next row K4, P29, K26, P29, K4.
Next row K to end.
Rep last 2 rows twice more.

Divide for neck
Next row K4, P29, K4, turn and leave rem sts on holder.
Next row K4, inc in next st, K to end.
Next row K4, P to last 4 sts, K4.
Cont in this way inc one st at front edge inside border on 11th row, then on every alt row until sleeve edge measures 6in, ending at side edge. Bind off 10 sts at beg of next row for sleeve. Cont to inc at front edge as before, *at the same time* dec one st at armhole edge on next and every alt row 4 times in all. Keeping armhole edge straight, cont to inc at front edge until there are 45 sts. Cont without shaping, keeping front border correct, until work measures same as back to top of welt, ending with a K row. Work 5 rows g st. Bind off.
With WS of work facing, rejoin yarn to rem sts, bind off 18 sts for center neck, pat to end. Complete to match first side, reversing shaping.

Finishing
Press lightly under a dry cloth with a cool iron. Join side and sleeve seams. Overlap right front over left front and sew on ribbons to last shaping and 2in below.

Bonnet
Using size 2 needles cast on 93 sts. Work 1in g st.
Next row K1, *P1, K1, rep from * to end.
Next row P1, *K1, P1, rep from * to end.
Rep these 2 rows 3 times more then first of them again. Commence pat.
1st row K1, *yo, sl 1 P-wise, K2 tog, psso, yo, K5, rep from * to last 4 sts, yo, sl 1 P-wise, K2 tog, psso, yo, K1.
2nd, 4th and 6th rows K1, P to last st, K1.
3rd row As 1st.
5th row K1, *K3, yo, sl 1 P-wise, K1, psso, K1, K2 tog, yo, rep from * to last 4 sts, K4.
7th row K1, *yo, sl 1 P-wise, K2 tog, psso, yo, K1, rep from * to end.
8th–12th rows Work 5 rows g st.
These 12 rows form pat. Cont in pat until work measures 5in from beg, ending with an 8th row. Work 4 rows g st, dec 3 sts evenly across last row.

Shape crown
1st row *K7, K2 tog, rep from * to end.
2nd and every alt row K to end.
3rd row *K6, K2 tog, rep from * to end.
Cont dec in this way until 10 sts rem. Break off yarn, thread through rem sts, draw up and fasten off.

Finishing

Press as given for undershirt. Join back seam to beg of shaping.

Neck edge Using size 0 needles and with RS of work facing, K up 80 sts around neck, leaving g st brim free. Work 6 rows g st. Bind off.

Turn back brim. Make 2 ribbon rosettes, leaving rem ribbon free to tie, and sew one to each side of bonnet.

Bootees

** Using 2 needles cast on 45 sts.
Work 5 rows g st. Work 18 rows pat as given for bonnet, dec 3 sts evenly across last row.

Next row *K2, yo, K2 tog, rep from * to last 2 sts, K2. **.

Next row K to end.

Next row K6, (K2 tog, K7) 4 times. 38 sts.

Next row K to end.

Divide for instep

1st row K25, turn.

2nd row K12, turn.

Work 20 rows g st on these 12 sts for instep. Break off yarn. With RS of work facing, K up 12 sts along side of instep, K across instep sts, K up 12 sts up other side of instep and K across 12 sts on left hand needle. 62 sts. Work 9 rows g st.

Shape foot

1st row K2 tog, K23, K2 tog, K8, K2 tog, K23, K2 tog.

2nd and every alt row K to end.

3rd row K2 tog, K22, K2 tog, K6, K2 tog, K22, K2 tog.

5th row K2 tog, K21, K2 tog, K4, K2 tog, K21, K2 tog.

7th row K2 tog, K20, K2 tog, K2, K2 tog, K20, K2 tog.

8th row As 2nd.
Bind off loosely.

Finishing

Press as given for undershirt. Join foot and leg seams. Thread ribbon through eyelet holes.

Mittens

Work as given for bootees from ** to **.

Cont in g st until work measures 2in from eyelet hole row.

Shape top

1st row *K2, K2 tog, rep from * to last 2 sts, K2.

2nd and 4th rows K to end.

3rd row *K1, K2 tog, rep from * to last 2 sts, K2.

2nd and 4th rows K to end.

3rd row *K1, K2 tog, rep from * to last 2 sts, K2.

5th row *K2 tog, rep from * to end.
Break off yarn, thread through rem sts, draw up and fasten off.

Finishing

Press as given for undershirt. Join seams. Thread ribbon through eyelet holes.

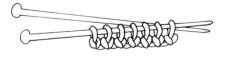

Dress and Jacket

A wide rib pattern and contrasting trim are featured in this pretty little dress and matching jacket.

Sizes

The pattern is given in three sizes :
0–3 months, 1 year and 3 years, or chest sizes 18in, 20in and 22in respectively.

dress

length from shoulder, 11[12½ :14]in
sleeve seam, 1½in

jacket

length from shoulder, 8[9[:10]in
sleeve seam, 5[6½ :8]in

Materials

5[6 :7] 1oz balls of Bernat Berella 3 ply
 Fingering in main color A
1[1 :1] ball of yarn in contrast color B
1 pair each of sizes 0, 2 and 3 needles
3 small buttons for dress
2 medium buttons for jacket
1yd of narrow ribbon for dress

Gauge

32 sts and 40 rows to 4in over rib pat worked on size 2 needles

Dress

Front

Using size 0 needles and A, cast on 100[110 :120] sts. Beg with a K row work 8 rows st st, ending with a P row. Join in B. Using B, K one row.
Next row K5 to end to form hemline. Change to size 2 needles. K one row. Break off B. Using A and beg with a P row work 3 rows st st.
Next row *K5, (K into front and back of next st) twice, then K into front of same st once more, turn and beg with a P row work 4 rows st st on these 5 sts, then using point of left-hand needle, lift 2nd, 3rd, 4th and 5th sts over first st and off right-hand needle – called "bobble 5" or B5 – K4, rep from * to end.
Beg with a P row work 3 rows st st. Join in B. Using B, K 2 rows. Break off B. ** Change to size 3 needles. Using A and beg with a K row cont in st st until work measures 7[7½ :8]in from hemline, ending with a K row. Change to size 0 needles.
Shape bodice
Next row P5, *P2 tog, P3, rep from * to

end. 81[89 :97] sts.
Next row (eyelet hole row) K1, *K1, yarn twice over – called y2o – K2 tog, K1, rep from * to end.
Next row K1, *P7, K1, dropping extra loops, rep from * to end.
Next row P1, *K7, P1, rep from * to end
Change to size 2 needles. Cont in rib pat

as now set until work measures 8[9 :10]in from hemline, ending with a WS row.
Shape armholes
Keeping rib pat correct, bind off 4 sts at beg of next 2 rows. *** Dec one st at each end of next and every foll row 5[7 :9] times in all and on foll alt row once. 61[65 :69] sts. Cont without shaping until

armholes measure 2[2½:3]in from beg, ending with a WS row.

Shape neck

Next row Pat 18[19:20] sts, K2 tog, turn and leave rem sts on holder.

Complete this side first. Dec one st at neck edge on next and foll alt rows until 16[17:18] sts rem, ending at armhole edge.

Shape shoulder

Bind off at beg of next and foll alt rows 5 sts twice and 6[7:8] sts once.

With RS of work facing, sl first 21[23:25] sts onto holder for center front neck, rejoin yarn to rem sts, K2 tog, pat to end. Complete to match first side, reversing shaping.

Back

Work as given for front to ***. 73[81:89] sts.

Divide for back opening

Next row K2 tog, pat 32[36:40], turn and leave rem sts on holder.

Complete this side first. Keeping center back edge straight cont in pat, dec one st at armhole edge on next and every foll row 4[6:8] times in all and on foll alt row once. 28[30:32] sts. Cont without shaping until back measures same as front to shoulder, ending at armhole edge.

Shape shoulder

Bind off at beg of next and foll alt rows 5 sts twice and 6[7:8] sts once. Leave rem 12[13:14] sts on holder.

With RS of work facing, sl first 5 sts onto holder and leave for buttonhole band, rejoin yarn to rem sts and pat to last 2 sts, K2 tog. Complete to match first side, reversing shaping.

Button band

Using size 0 needles and A, cast on 5 sts. Work in g st until band, slightly stretched, fits up back opening to neck edge. Bind off 2 sts, break off yarn and sl rem 3 sts onto holder at right back neck. Sew band in place along back opening. Mark positions for 3 buttons on button band, first to come in above lower edge, last to come just below top with one more spaced evenly between.

Buttonhole band

Using size 0 needles, A and with RS of work facing, rejoin yarn to 5 sts on holder and work as given for button band, making buttonholes as markers are reached as foll:

Next row (buttonhole row) (RS) K2, yo, K2 tog, K1.

When buttohole band fits up back opening to neck edge, ending at outside edge, bind off 2 sts, break off yarn and sl rem 3 sts onto holder at left back neck.

Sew band in position.

Sleeves

Using size 0 needles and A, cast on 31[37:43] sts. Work as given for front to **, *at the same time* making bobbles on 5th row above hemline as foll:

Next row K10[13:16], B5, K9, B5, K10[13:16].

Shape sleeves

Next row K1, *K twice into next st, K2, rep from * to end. 41[49:57] sts.

Change to size 3 needles.

Next row K1, *P7, K1, rep from * to end. Cont in rib pat as now set until sleeve measures 1½in from hemline, ending with a WS row.

Shape top

Bind off at beg of next and every foll row 4 sts twice and 2 sts 8[12:14] times. Bind off rem 17[17:21] sts.

Neckband

Join shoulder seams. Using size 0 needles, A and with RS of work facing, beg at left back opening edge, K across left back neck sts on holder, K up 10 sts down left front neck, K across center front neck sts on holder, K up 10 sts up right front neck and K across right back neck sts on holder. 71[75:79] sts.

Next row (WS) K3, P0[4:4], *P2 tog, P2, rep from * to last 4[4:8] sts, P1[1:5], K3. 55[59:63] sts.

Join in B. Using B, K 2 rows.

Next row Using A, K to end.

Next row Using A, K3, P to last 3 sts, K3.

Next row Using A, K6[8:7], *K into front, back and front of next st, turn and beg with a P row work 2 rows st st on these 3 sts, then using point of left-hand needle, lift 2nd and 3rd sts over first st and off right-hand needle – called B3 – K5, rep from * to last 1[3:2] sts, K1[3:2].

Using A, work 3 rows st st, keeping g st border at each end correct.

Next 2 rows Using B, bind off 3 sts, K to end.

K 1 row. Using A and beg with a P row, work 7 rows st st. Bind off loosely.

Finishing

Press each piece under a dry cloth with a cool iron, avoiding ribbing. Set in sleeves. Join side and sleeve seams. Turn lower and sleeve hems and neckband in half to WS and sl st in position. Thread ribbon through eyelet holes at waist and tie in a bow at front. Sew on buttons. Press seams.

Jacket

Using size 0 needles and A, cast on 161[177:193] sts and work in one piece to underarm. Work as given for dress front

to **, making bobbles on 5th row from hemline as foll:

Next row K5[3:6], *K5, B5, K4, rep from * to last 6[4:7] sts, K6[4:7].

Change to size 2 needles.

Next row P1, *K7, P1, rep from * to end. Cont in rib as now set until work measures 4½[5:5½]in from hemline, ending with a WS row.

Right front

Next row Pat 38[42:46], turn and leave rem sts on holder.

Complete this side first.

Next row Bind off 4 sts, pat to end. Keeping pat correct, dec one st at armhole edge on next 5[7:9] rows and foll alt row. 28[30:32] sts. Cont without shaping until armhole measures 2½[3:3½]in from beg, ending at armhole edge.

Shape neck

Next row Pat 18[19:20] sts, K2 tog, turn and leave rem 8[9:10] sts on holder for front neck.

Keeping armhole edge straight, dec one st at neck edge on next and foll 2 alt rows, ending at armhole edge. 16[17:18] sts.

Shape shoulder

Bind off at beg of next and foll alt rows 5 sts twice and 6[7:8] sts once.

Back

With RS of work facing, rejoin yarn to rem sts, bind off 4 sts, pat until there are 81[89:97] sts on right-hand needle, turn and leave rem sts on holder.

Next row Bind off 4 sts, pat to end. Keeping pat correct, dec one st at each end of next and every foll row 5[7:9] times in all, and at each end of foll alt row. 65[69:73] sts. Cont without shaping until back measures same as front to shoulder, ending with a WS row.

Shape shoulders

Bind off at beg of next and every row 5 sts 4 times and 6[7:8] sts twice. Leave rem 33[35:37] sts on holder.

Left front

With RS of work facing, rejoin yarn to rem sts, bind off 4 sts, pat to end. Complete to match right front, reversing shaping.

Sleeves

Using size 0 needles and A, cast on 31[37:43] sts. Work as given for dress front to ** making bobbles on 5th row above hemline as foll:

Next row K10[13:16], B5, K9, B5, K10[13:16].

Shape sleeves

Next row K1, *K twice into next st, K2, rep from * to end. 41[49:57] sts.

Change to size 2 needles.

Next row (WS) K1, *P7, K1, rep from * to end.

Keeping pat correct, inc one st at each

end of 3rd and every foll 6th row until there are 49[57 :65] sts.
Cont without shaping until work measures 5[6½ :8]in from hemline, ending with a WS row.

Shape top
Bind off at beg of next and every row 4 sts twice, 2 sts 8[12 :14] times and 3 sts twice. Bind off rem 19[19 :23] sts.

Buttonhole band
Using size 0 needles, A and with RS of work facing, K up 56[64 :72] sts up right front from hemline to beg of neck shaping. Join in B.
1st-2nd rows Using B, P to end.
3rd row Using A, P to end.
4th row Using A, K to last st, K twice into last st.
5th row (buttonhole row) P3, (bind off 4, P5) twice, P to end.
6th row As 4th, casting on 4 sts above those bound off in previous row.
7th row As 3rd.
8th row As 4th.
9th row As 3rd.
10th-12th rows Using B, K to end.
13th row Using A, P to end.
14th row Using A, K to last 2 sts, K2 tog.
15th row As 13th. 58[66 :74] sts.
16th row (buttonhole row) Using A, K40[48 :56], bind off 4, K5, bind off 4, K1, K2 tog.
17th row P to end, casting on 4 sts above those bound off in previous row.
18th row As 14th.
19th row P to end.
Bind off rem sts.

Button band
Work as given for buttonhole band, omitting buttonholes and reversing shaping.

Neckband
Join shoulder seams. Using size 0 needles, A and with RS of work facing, K across 8[9 :10] sts of right front neck on holder, K up 10 sts up right front neck, K across 33[35 :37] sts of back neck on holder, K up 10 sts down left front neck and K across 8[9 :10] sts of left front neck on holder. 69[73 :77] sts.
1st row P to end. Join in B.
2nd-3rd rows Using B, K to end.
4th row Using A, K to end.
5th row Using A, P twice into first st, P to last st, P twice into last st. 71[75 :79] sts.
6th row K2[1 :3], *B3, K5, rep from * to last 3[2 :4] sts, B3, K2[1 :3].
7th row As 5th.
Rep 4th and 5th rows once more. 75[79 :83] sts.
10th-12th rows Using B, K to end.
13th row Using A, P to end.
14th row Using A, K2 tog, K to last 2 sts, K2 tog.
Rep 13th-14th rows twice more. 69[73 :77] sts. P 1 row. Bind off.

Finishing
Press as given for dress. Join sleeve seams. Set in sleeves. Join mitered edges of neckband and front bands. Turn hems at neck, front and lower edges in half to WS and sl st down. Finish double buttonholes. Sew on buttons. Press seams.

Pants and Top

Snug pants, worn over a matching diaper cover, are teamed with a smart two-color jacket to make an ensemble that is ideal for outings

Sizes
The pattern is given in two sizes:
0–3 months and 3–6 months, or chest, size 16 [18]in.
length from center-back neck, 8½[9½]in
sleeve seam, 5½[6]in

Materials
Jacket
3[3] 1oz balls of Bucilla Perlette in main color A
1 [1] ball of contrast color B

Diaper cover
2 [2] balls of A

Pants
2[3] balls of A

one pair each of sizes 0 and 2 needles
2 small buttons for jacket
2 snap fasteners for jacket
4 small buttons for diaper cover
waist length of elastic for pants

Gauge
28 sts and 38 rows to 4in over st st worked on size 2 needles

Jacket
Back and fronts
Using size 0 needles and A, cast on 131 [149] sts and work in one piece to underarm.
1st row (RS) Using A, K1, *P1, K1, rep from * to end.
2nd row Join in B, P1, *K1, P1, rep from * to end.
3rd row Using B, as 1st.
4th row Using A, as 2nd.
Rep these 4 rows once more, inc one st at end of last row. 132[150] sts.
Change to size 2 needles. Using A only and beg with a K row, work 6 rows st st.

Commence spot pat.
1st row K2 A, *K2 B, 4 A, rep from * to last 4 sts, K2 B, 2A.
2nd row P2 A, *P2 B, 4A, rep from * to last 4 sts, P2 B, 2 A.
Using A only and beg with a K row, work 6 rows st st.
9th row K5 A, *K2 B, 4 A, rep from * to last 7 sts, K2 B, 5 A.
10th row P5 A, *P2 B, 4 A, rep from * to last 7 sts, P2 B, 5 A.
Note The two spot rows are repeated alternately on every foll 7th and 8th row

throughout.
Using A only and beg with a K row, work 2[4] rows st st.

Vertical belt slot for a boy
Next row Using A only, K94[107] sts, turn and leave rem 38[43] sts on holder.
Keeping pat correct throughout, work 9 rows pat. Leave sts on holder. Break off A and B.
With RS of work facing and A, rejoin yarn to rem sts and K to end. Complete to match first side. Work 18[20] rows pat

across all sts.

Vertical belt slot for a girl

Next row Using A only, K38[43] sts, turn and leave rem 94[107] sts on holder. Work as given for boy's version.

Both versions

Divide for armholes

Keeping pat correct throughout, pat across first 38[43] sts for right front, turn and leave rem sts on holder.

1st row Bind off 3 sts, pat to end.

2nd row Pat to last 3 sts, K2 tog, K1.

3rd row Pat to end.

Rep 2nd and 3rd rows until 20[23] sts rem. Leave sts on holder.

With RS of work facing, rejoin yarn to sts on holder, Bind off 3 sts for back armhole, pat 53[61] sts, turn and leave rem sts on holder.

1st row Bind off 3 sts, pat to end.

2nd row K1, sl 1, K1, psso, pat to last 3 sts, K2 tog, K1.

3rd row Pat to end.

Rep last 2 rows until 20[24] sts rem. Leave sts on holder.

With RS of work facing, rejoin yarn to rem sts on holder, bind off 3 sts for left front armhole, pat to end. Complete to match right front, reversing shaping.

Sleeves

Using size 0 needles and A, cast on 33[39] sts. Work 8 rows rib as given for body, inc one st at end of last row. 34[40] sts. Change to size 2 needles. Beg with a K row and using A only, work 6 rows st st. Commence spot pat.

Next row K4 A, *K2 B, 4 A, rep from * to end.

Next row P4 A, *P2 B, 4 A, rep from * to end.

Beg with a K row and using A only, work 6 rows st st, inc one st at each end of first row.

Next row K2 A, *K2 B, 4 A, rep from * to last 4 sts, K2 B, 2A.

Next row P2 A, *P2 B, 4 A, rep from * to last 4 sts, P2 B, 2 A.

Beg with a K row cont in st st and spot pat, inc one st at each end of next and every foll 9th row and working extra sts into pat, until there are 44[48] sts. Cont in pat without shaping until sleeve measures 5[6]in from beg, ending with a P row.

Shape top

Bind off 3 sts at beg of next 2 rows.

Next row Keeping pat correct, K1, sl 1, K1, psso, pat to last 3 sts, K2 tog, K1.

Next row Pat to end.

Rep last 2 rows until 8 sts rem. Leave sts on holder.

Neckband

Using size 0 needles, A and with RS of work facing, K20[23] sts of right front, 8 sts from first sleeve top, 20[24] sts from back neck, inc one st at center, 8 sts from 2nd sleeve top and 20[23] sts from left front. 77[87] sts. Beg with a 2nd row work 7 rows rib as given for body. Bind off in rib.

Bands

Using size 0 needles, A and with RS of work facing, K up 63[71] sts along right front edge. Beg with a 2nd row work 7 rows rib as given for body. Using A, bind off in rib.

Complete left front edge in same way.

Belt

Using size 0 needles and A, cast on 11 sts. Using A, work 1 row K1, P1 rib. Cont in rib, working 2 rows B and 2 rows A throughout until belt measures 4in from beg.

Next row (buttonhole row) Rib 5, yo, K2 tog, rib 4.

Work 6 more rows rib, then work 2nd buttonhole as before. Work 2 more rows rib. Bind off in rib.

Make another belt in same way, omitting buttonholes.

Finishing

Do not press. Join raglan and sleeve seams. Sew on belts to correspond with openings at side. Sew buttons onto belt. Sew one snap fastener to neck and the other 3in below.

Diaper cover

Using size 0 needles and A, cast on 93[97] sts and work in one piece, beg at back waist edge.

Next row K1, *P1, K1, rep from * to end.

Next row P1, *K1, P1, rep from * to end.

Rep last 2 rows twice more. Break off yarn. Change to size 2 needles. Sl first 7 sts of row onto holder, rejoin yarn to rem sts, K1, sl 1, K1, psso, K to last 10 sts, K2 tog, K1, sl last 7 sts onto holder.

Next row K1, P to last st, K1.

Cont to dec one st at each end of next and every alt row, keeping one st at each end in g st throughout, until 17[19] sts rem, ending with a WS row. Work 6 rows without shaping. Inc one st at each end of next and every alt row until there are 57[61] sts, ending with a WS row.

Leg bands

Using size 0 needles, work in K1, P1 rib across 7 sts left on holder until band fits around edge of cover then transfer 7 sts onto size 2 needle. Work 2nd leg band to match.

Next row Work in K1, P1 rib across 7 sts of leg band, then across 57[61] sts on size 2 needle, then across 7 sts of other leg band. 71[75] sts.

Next row (buttonhole row) Rib 4 sts, bind off 2 sts, rib 6 sts, bind off 2 sts, rib to last 14 sts, bind off 2 sts, rib 6 sts, bind off 2 sts, rib to end.

Next row Rib to end, casting on 2 sts above those bound off in previous row. Work 4 rows K1, P1 rib. Bind off in rib.

Finishing

Do not press. Sew leg bands to edges of cover. Sew on buttons to back waist edge to match buttonholes.

Pants

Using size 0 needles and A, cast on 75[81] sts and beg at front waist. Work 2in K1, P1 rib as given for diaper cover, ending with a 2nd row. Change to size 2 needles. Beg with a K row cont in st st until work measures 6[7]in from beg, ending with a P row.

Shape legs

Cont in st st, dec one st at each end of next and every row until 19[21] sts rem. Work 6 rows without shaping.

Work back

Inc one st at each end of next and every row until there are 75[81] sts. Cont in st st without shaping until back measures same as front to beg of waist ribbing, less 2 rows, ending with a P row.

Shape back

1st row K to last 12 sts, turn.

2nd row Sl 1, P to last 12 sts, turn.

3rd row Sl 1, K to last 18 sts, turn.

4th row Sl 1, P to last 18 sts, turn.

5th row Sl 1, K to last 24 sts, turn.

6th row Sl 1, P to last 24 sts, turn.

7th row Sl 1, K to end.

8th row P to end.

Change to size 0 needles. Work 2in K1, P1 rib. Bind off in rib.

Leg bands

Using size 0 needles, A and with RS of work facing, K up 85[89] sts around leg. Work in K1, P1 rib. Bind off in rib.

Finishing

Do not press. Join side seams. Fold waistband in half to WS and sl st down. Thread elastic through waistband.

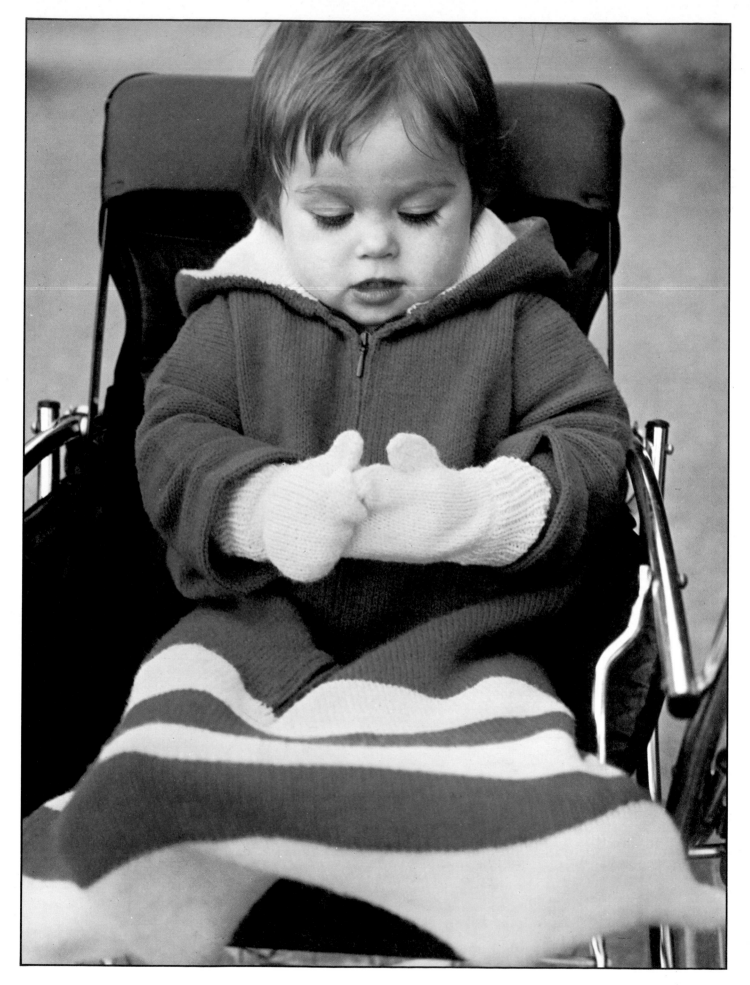

Bunting and Mittens

On chilly days keep baby warm with this cozy bunting and matching mittens.

Size
The bunting is sized to fit a baby approximately 6 to 18 months old.

Materials
Brunswick Nylamb in the amounts specified below

Bunting
4 40g balls of yarn in main color A
3 40g balls of yarn in contrast color B
a pair of size 3 needles
a 14in zipper

Mittens
1 40g ball of yarn in contrast color B
a set of 4 size 3 needles pointed at both ends

Gauge
28 sts and 36 rows to 4in over st st on size 3 needles

Bunting
Using size 3 needles and B, cast on 92 sts for front. Beg with a K row cont in st st, working (20 rows B and 16 rows A) twice, then 20 rows B. Break off B. Cont using A only.

Divide for front opening
Next row K46 sts, turn and leave rem sts on holder.
Complete this side first. Beg with a P row cont in st st for a further 11¾in, ending with a P row.

Shape sleeve
Next row Cast on 46 sts, K to end. 92 sts.
Beg with a P row work a further 2in st st, ending with a K row.

Shape neck
Bind off at beg of next and every alt row 7 sts once, 3 sts twice, 2 sts twice and one st twice. 73 sts. Cont without shaping until work measures 4in from beg of sleeve, ending with a K row. Break off yarn and leave this piece for time being. With RS of work facing, rejoin yarn to rem sts and complete to match first side, reversing shaping and ending with a K row. Do not break off yarn.

Join work for back
Next row P73 sts, cast on 38 sts, P73 sts of

other piece. 184 sts.
Beg with a K row cont without shaping for a further 4in, ending with a P row.

Shape sleeves
Bind off 46 sts at beg of next 2 rows. 92 sts. Cont in st st without shaping for a further 11¾in, ending with a P row. Join in B. Work (20 rows B and 16 rows A) twice, then 20 rows B. Bind off.

Hood
Using size 3 needles and B, cast on 32 sts for back piece. Beg with a K row work in st st, inc one st at each end of 7th and every foll 8th row until there are 38 sts. Cont without shaping until work measures 3½in from beg, ending with a P row. Dec one st at end of next and foll alt row. Bind off 2 sts at beg of next 8 rows. Bind off rem 18 sts. Work another back piece in same way.

Front piece
Using size 3 needles and A cast on 99 sts. Beg with a K row work in st st, inc one st at each end of 7th and every foll 8th row until there are 107 sts. Cont without shaping until work measures 4½in from beg, ending with a P row, 40 rows in all.
Next row K to last 4 sts, turn.
Next row P to last 4 sts, turn.
Next row K to last 8 sts turn.
Next row P to last 8 sts, turn.
Cont working 4 sts less in this way on every row until 27 sts rem in center, ending with a P row. Break off A. Join in B.
Next row K31 sts, turn.
Next row P35 sts, turn.
Cont working 4 sts more in this way on every row until all sts are in work. Work 8 rows st st without shaping. Dec one st at each end of next and every foll 8th row until 99 sts rem.
Work 7 rows without shaping. Bind off.

Finishing
Press each piece under a damp cloth with a warm iron. Join side and underarm seams. Sew in zipper. Turn in in hem on sleeve edges and sl st down. Fold front piece of hood in half and join the cast-on and bound-off edges to form face edge. Place 2 back pieces tog with WS inside, then join shaped edge of front to 2 back pieces. Sew on hood around neck edge. Press all seams.

Mittens
Using set of 4 size 3 needles and B, cast on 36 sts. Work 18 rounds K 1, P1 rib. Cont in st st and work 9 rounds.

Shape thumb
Next round K17 sts, K up 1, K2 sts, K up 1, K17 sts.
Next round K to end.
Next round K17 sts, K up 1, K4 sts, K up 1, K17 sts.
Next round K to end.
Cont inc in this way on next and every alt round 3 times more. 46 sts.

Divide for thumb
Next round K17 sts, sl next 12 sts onto a holder, cast on 2 sts, K17 sts. 36 sts. Work 8 rounds st st.

Shape top
Next round *K1, K2 tog, K13 sts, sl 1, K1, psso, rep from * once more.
Next round K to end.
Next round *K1, K2 tog, K11 sts, sl 1, K1, psso, rep from * once more.
Next round K to end.
Cont dec in this way on next and every alt round until 8 sts rem, ending with a dec round. Break off yarn, thread through rem sts, draw up and fasten off.

Thumb
Sl 12 thumb sts onto 3 needles, cast on 2 sts and join into a round. Work 6 rounds st st.

Shape top
Next round *K2 tog, rep from * to end. Break off yarn, thread through rem sts, draw up and fasten off.

Finishing
Press as given for bunting.

Embroidered Dresses

From one basic pattern you can make these two pretty dresses : one in stockinette stitch with rabbit motifs in duplicate stitch embroidery and one in a lacy stitch embroidered with daisies.

Sizes
The pattern is given in two sizes : 1 year and 3 years, or chest sizes 20in and 22in respectively.
length, 14[16]in
short sleeve seam, 2in
long sleeve seam, $5\frac{1}{2}$ [$6\frac{1}{4}$]in

Materials
Brunswick Bambini in the amounts specified for the individual garments
1 pair each of sizes 2 and 3 needles

Dress with rabbits
3[4] 40g balls of yarn in main color
small amounts of yarn in 4 colors for embroidery
a 4in zipper

Patterned dress

3[3] 40g balls of yarn in main color
small amounts of yarn in two colors for
embroidery
a 4in zipper

Gauge

28 sts and 36 rows to 4in over st st on size
3 needles

Pattern stitch

1st row K to end.
2nd row P to end.
3rd row K to end.
4th row P3, *K3, P5, rep from * to last 6 sts,
K3, P3.
5th row K3, *P1, yo, P2 tog, K5, rep from *
to last 6 sts, P1, yo, P2 tog, K3.
6th row As 4th.
7th-9th rows As 1st-3rd.
10th row K2, *P5, K3, rep from * to last 7
sts, P5, K2.
11th row P2, *K5, P1, yo, P2 tog, rep from *
to last 7 sts, K5, P2.
12th row As 10th.

Front

Using size 3 needles cast on 129 [145] sts.
K4 rows. Beg with a K row, cont in st st or
pat, work 18 rows.
19th row K3, K2 tog, *K26[30], sl 1, K1,
psso, K1, K2 tog, rep from * twice more,
K26[30], sl 1, K1, psso, K3. Work 17 rows.
37th row K3, K2 tog, *K24[28], sl 1, K1,
psso, K1, K2 tog, rep from * twice more,
K24[28], sl 1, K1, psso, K3.
Cont to dec in this way on every 18th
row twice more, then on every 12th row
until 89[97] sts rem. Work 7[5] rows. * *
92[102] rows in all.
Shape raglans
Bind off 6 sts at beg of next 2 rows.
Next row K1, sl 1, K1, psso, pat to last 3
sts, K2 tog, K1.
Next row P2, pat to last 2 sts, P2. Rep last
2 rows until 57[61] sts rem, ending with a
RS row.
Shape neck
Next row P2, work 16, bind off 21 [25],
work to last 2 sts, P2.
Cont on last 18 sts.
Next row K1, sl 1, K1, psso, work to end.
Next row Bind off 2, work to last 2 sts, P2.
Rep last 2 rows 4 times more, then first of
them again. Bind off rem 2 sts.
Rejoin yarn to rem 18 sts and complete to
match first side of neck.

Back

Work as given for front to * *
Shape raglans and divide for opening
Next row Bind off 6, work to end.
Next row Bind off 6, work 36 [40], K2, K2
tog, K1, work to end.
Next row K1, sl 1, K1, psso, work 33[37],

K2, turn and leave rem sts on spare
needle.
Next row K2, work to last 2 sts, P2.
Keeping 2 sts at inside edge in g st
throughout, cont to dec at armhole edge
on every alt row until 22[24] sts rem,
ending with a WS row. Bind off. Rejoin
yarn to rem 38[42] sts and complete to
match first side.

Short sleeves

Using size 3 needles cast on 65[73] sts.
Work 18 rows st st or pat.
Shape raglans
Bind off 6 sts at beg of next 2 rows.
1st row K1, sl 1, K1, psso, work to last 3
sts, K2 tog, K1.
2nd row P1, P2 tog, work to last 3 sts, P2
tog tbl, P1.
3rd row As 1st.
4th row P2, work to last 2 sts, P2.
Rep last 4 rows 7[8] times more. Bind off
rem 5[7] sts.

Long sleeves

Using size 3 needles cast on 65[73] sts.
Work in st st or pat for 5½[6¼]in, ending
with a WS row.
Shape raglans
Work as given for short sleeves.

Neckband

Using size 2 needles cast on 6 sts.
1st row K into front and back of first st, K
to last 2 sts, K2 tog.
2nd row P to end.
Rep these 2 rows until work measures
about 11[11¾]in. Bind off.

Sleeve edges

Using size 2 needles cast on 6 sts. For
short sleeves make strips as given for
neckband about 5½[6]in long and about 4¾
[5]in long and about 4¾[5]in long for long
sleeves.

Finishing

Press over a dry cloth with a cool iron.
Patterned dress Embroider around some
of the holes at random, working blanket
stitch (see page 182) in one color around
hole, then working 8 lazy daisy (see page
183) stitches in another color around the
outside of the blanket stitches.
Dress with rabbits Duplicate stitch motif
from chart, centering pat and beg on 14th
row of st st on lower part of front. Make 2
small pompoms – about ¾-1⅛in in
diameter – in white for rabbits' tails.
Join raglan seams. Join side and sleeve
seams. With RS tog, sew neckband to
neck edge, gathering neck to fit. Fold
neckband in half to WS and slipstitch in
position. Sew on sleeve edges in the same
way. Sew in zipper. Press seams.

Duplicate stitch

Thread the yarn into a tapestry needle
and begin at the lower right-hand corner
of the design, first securing the yarn on
the wrong side with a few stitches in the
knitted stitch to be embroidered first.
Bring the needle up at the base of this
stitch and draw yarn through, insert the
needle from right to left under the two
loops of the stitch immediately above and
draw yarn through, insert needle back
into the base of the first stitch and up
through the base of the next stitch to the
left and draw yarn through. Continue
along the row for as many stitches as are
required.
   At the end of the row, insert the needle
into the base of the last stitch worked,
then up in the center of this same stitch,
which is the base of the stitch
immediately above it. Now insert needle
from left to right behind the two loops of
the stitch immediately above and
continue working as before, but from left
to right.

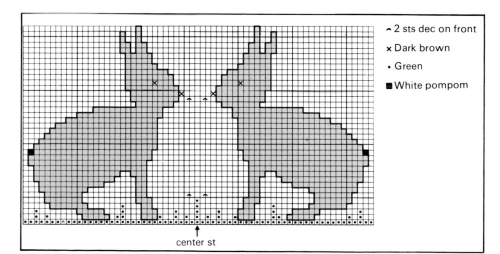

Key:
⌃ 2 sts dec on front
x Dark brown
• Green
■ White pompom

center st

One-piece suit

Perfect for playtime, this one-piece suit zips up the front. Striped sleeves and patch pockets provide color contrast.

Sizes
The pattern is given in three sizes: 0–3 months, 1 year and 3 years, or chest sizes 18in, 20in and 22in respectively.
length from shoulder 23 [25½:28] in
sleeve seam 7 [8:9]in

Materials
4 [4:5] 1oz balls of Brunswick Nylamb in main color A
1 [1:1] ball of yarn in contrast color B
1 pair each of sizes 1 and 2 needles
a 10 [12:14]in zipper

Gauge
30 sts and 40 rows to 4in over st st on size 2 needles

Right half
Using size 1 needles and A cast on 93 [99:105] sts. Beg with a K row work 1in st st, ending with a K row.
Next row K all sts tbl to form hemline. Change to size 2 needles. Beg with a K row cont in st st until work measures 1¼in from hemline, ending with a P row. Dec one st at each end of next and every foll 8th row until 81[87:93] sts rem. Cont without shaping until work measures 6[6½:7]in from hemline, ending with a P row. Inc one st at each end of next and every foll 8th row until there are 89[97:105] sts. Cont without shaping until work measures 9[10½:12]in from hemline, ending with a P row. Inc one st at each end of next and every alt row until there are 105[113:121] sts, ending with a P row.
Shape gusset
Bind off at beg of next and every foll row, 2 sts once, 5 sts once and 2 sts 3 times. P 1 row. Dec one st at each end of next and foll 1[2:3] alt rows, then at end (back edge) only on foll 5 alt rows ending with a P row. 83[89:95] sts.
Next row K to end.
Next row P to last 2 sts, K2
Rep last 2 rows until work measures 8½[9½:10½]in from beg of gusset shaping ending with a WS row.
Divide for armhole
Next row K38[41:44], bind off 7 sts, K to end.

Cont on last 38[41:44] sts for back.
Next row P to end.
Next row K3, K2 tog, K to end.
Rep last 2 rows until 18[19:20] sts rem, ending with a P row. Bind off.
With WS of work facing rejoin yarn to rem sts, P to last 2 sts, K2.
Next row K to last 5 sts, sl 1, K1, psso, K3
Next row P to last 2 sts, K2.
Rep last 2 rows until 26[27:28] sts rem ending with a WS row.
Shape neck
Next row Bind off 9[10:11], K to last 5 sts, sl 1, K1, psso, K3.
Next row P to end.
Next row Bind off 2 sts K to last 5 sts sl 1, K1, psso, K3.
Rep last 2 rows once more, then first of them again.
Next row K2 tog, K to last 5 sts, sl 1, K1, psso, K3.
Next row P to end.
Rep last 2 rows once more, 6 sts.
Next row K3 tog, K3.
Next row P to end.
Next row K2 tog, K2.
Next row P to end.
Next row K2 tog, K1.
Next row P2. Bind off.

Left half
Work as given for right half, reversing all shaping.

Sleeves
Using size 1 needles and A, cast on 47[49:51] sts.
1st row K1, *P1, K1, rep from * to end.
2nd row P1, *K1, P1, rep from * to end.
Rep these 2 rows for 1½in, ending with a 2nd row. Change to size 2 needles.
Next row K to end.
Next row P2[3:4], *K1, P5, rep from * to last 3[4:5] sts, K1, P2[3:4].
Rep the last 2 rows throughout, *at the same time* working in striped pat of 4 rows A and 4 rows B throughout, inc. one st at each end of every 10th row until there are 57[61:65] sts, working extra sts into pat. Cont without shaping until sleeve measures 7[8:9]in from beg, ending with a WS row.
Shape top
Keeping rib and striped pat correct, bind off 4 sts at beg of next 2 rows. Dec one st at each end of next and every alt row

until 9 sts rem, ending with a WS row. Bind off.

Pocket
Using size 1 needles and A, cast on 31 sts. K 4 rows g st. Change to size 2 needles.
Next row K3, sl these 3 sts onto holder, K to last 3 sts, turn and leave rem 3 sts on holder. 25 sts.
Next row K1, *P5, K1, rep from * to end. Cont in rib and striped pat as given for sleeves for 26 more rows, ending with 4 rows in A. Break off yarn and leave sts for time being.
Return to 2 sts of 3 sts which were left; using size 1 needles and A, work in g st until bands are same length as pocket ending with a WS row, noting that yarn is not broken off on the band at beg of RS rows.
Top edge
Using size 1 needles and A, cont across all sts in g st for 3 rows.
Bind off K-wise.

Neckband
Join raglan seams, Using size 1 needles, A or B as required and with RS of work facing, K up 81[87:93] sts around neck.
Next row K2, *P1, K1, rep from * to last st, K1.
Next row K3, *P1, K1, rep from * to last 2 sts, K2.
Rep last 2 rows for 1½in. Bind off in rib.

Finishing
Press each piece under a damp cloth with a warm iron. Join back seam. Join sleeve seams. Join leg seams. Join front seam as far as beg of opening. Fold neckband in half to WS and sl st down. Sew in zipper. Turn up hems at lower edge of legs and sl st down. Sew pocket to right side of seat. Press seams.

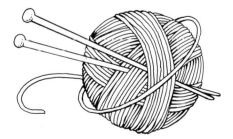

Loop Stitch Coat

Just the coat for taking Bear for a stroll on a chilly day. It is made of soft bouclé yarn, in loop stitch, with matching or contrasting edging. The adjustable hood will be very popular.

Sizes

The pattern is given in two sizes : 0 – 3 months and 1 year, or chest sizes 18in and 20in respectively.
length from shoulder, 16[18]in

sleeve seam, 7½[8½]in

Materials

16[17] 1 7/10oz balls of Unger Rhumba
2[2] 1oz balls of Unger Nanette
1 pair each of sizes 4 and 8 needles
4 buttons

Gauge

13 sts and 20 rows to 4in over loop st on size 8 needles

Back

Using size 4 needles and Nanette, cast on 93[101] sts.
1st row K1, *P1, K1, rep from * to end.
2nd row P1, *K1, P1, rep from * to end.
Rep these 2 rows for 10in, ending with a 2nd row. Cut off Nanette. Change to size 8 needles. Join in Rhumba.
Next row K1, (K2 tog) to end. **. 47[51] sts.
Commence loop st pat.
1st row (WS) K to end.
2nd row K1, *K next st without letting it drop off needle, yif pass yarn over left thumb to make a loop (about in long), yib and K st rem on LH needle, return 2 sts just made to LH needle and K them tog tbl – called loop 1 (L1) – K1, rep from * to end.
3rd row K to end.
4th row K2, *L1, K1, rep from * to last st, K1.
These 4 rows form pat. Rep them throughout. Cont in pat, dec one st at each end of 9th[11th] and every foll 8th [10th] row until 37[41] sts rem. Cont without shaping until work measures 16[18]in from beg, or length required, ending with a WS row.

Shape shoulders

Bind off 6[7] sts loosely at beg of next 2 rows and 7 sts at beg of foll 2 rows.
Bind off rem 11[13] sts.

Left front

Using size 4 needles and Nanette, cast on 45[49] sts. Work as given for back to **. 23[25] sts. Cont in pat as given for back, dec one st at end of 9th[11th] and every foll 8th[10th] row until 18[20] sts rem. Cont without shaping until work is 5[7] rows less than back to shoulders, ending at front edge.

Shape neck
Bind off 3 sts at beg of next row. Dec one st at beg of 2[3] foll alt rows, ending at side edge.

Shape shoulder
Bind off 6[7] sts at beg of next row. Work 1 row. Bind off rem 7 sts.

Right front
Work to match left front, reversing shaping.

Sleeves
Using size 4 needles and Nanette, cast on 41[45] sts. Work as given for back to **. 21[23] sts. Cont in pat as given for back, inc one st at each end of 5th and every foll 6th row until there are 29[31] sts. Cont without shaping until sleeve measures $7\frac{1}{2}[8\frac{1}{2}]$in from beg, ending with a RS row. Bind off loosely.

Hood
Using size 4 needles and Nanette, cast on 97[105] sts. Work as given for back to **. 49[53] sts. Cont in pat as given for back until work measures $7\frac{1}{2}[8\frac{1}{4}]$in from beg, ending with a RS row.

Shape back
Next row K24[26], turn and leave rem sts on a holder.
Dec one st at beg of next and foll 2 alt rows, then at same edge on foll 2[4] rows. Bind off rem 19 sts.
Return to sts that were left. With WS of work facing, rejoin yarn to next st, K2 tog, K to end. Complete to match first side.

Right front band
Using size 4 needles and Nanette, cast on 93[101] sts. Work 5 rows rib as given for back.
Next row (buttonhole row) Rib 3, * bind off 2, rib 15[17], rep from * twice more, bind off 2, rib 37[39].
Next row Rib to end, casting on 2 sts over those bound off in previous row.
Rib 5 more rows. Bind off in rib.

Left front band
Work to match right front band, omitting buttonholes.

Finishing
Do not press.
Join shoulder seams.
Sew in sleeves, matching center of bound-off edge to shoulder seams.
Join side and sleeve seams.
Sew on front bands.
Join back seam of hood. Sew on hood, beg and ending in center of front bands.
Sew on buttons.

Striped Jumpsuit

For playtime comfort nothing beats a knitted jumpsuit. Bold multicolored stripes give this one that extra style.

Sizes

The pattern is given in two sizes: 1 year and 3 years, or chest sizes 20in and 22in respectively.
length from shoulder, 23[28]in
inside leg seam, 9½[12]in
sleeve seam, 6¼[8¼]in

Materials

3 2oz balls of Brunswick Fore-'n-Aft Sport in main color A
2 balls of yarn in contrast color B
1 ball each of contrast colors C and D
1 pair each of sizes 4 and 5 needles
a 12[14]in zipper

Gauge

24 sts and 32 rows to 4in over st st on size 5 needles

Left half

Using size 4 needles and A, cast on 56[60] sts. Beg with a K row, work 8 rows st st, ending with a P row.
Next row P to end to mark hemline. Change to size 5 needles. Beg with a P row work 9 rows st st **. Join in B. Cont in st st and stripe sequence throughout of 6 rows B, 2 rows C, 14 rows B, 6 rows D, 14 rows A, 2 rows each of B, A, C, A, D, A, B, 14 rows A, 14 rows B and 6 rows A, work 20[30] rows. Inc one st at each end of next and 2[3] foll 10th rows, then at each end of every foll 4th row until there are 72[78] sts. P 1 row.

Shape crotch

Cast on 3 sts at beg of next 2 rows. Work 2 rows st st, ending at center back edge. Dec one st at center back edge on next and foll 6th row, *at the same time* dec one st at center front edge on next and foll 5 alt rows. 70[76] sts. Cont to dec at back edge only on every 6th row until 64[70] sts rem. Work 20[34] rows, ending with a K row.

Divide for armholes

Next row P29[32] sts and leave these sts on holder, bind off 6 sts for armhole, P to end ***.
Cont on last 29[32] sts for left half back.

Shape raglan

1st row K to last 3 sts, K2 tog, K1.
2nd row K1, P to end.
Rep last 2 rows 19[21] times more. Bind off.
With RS of work facing, rejoin yarn to left half front sts.
1st row K1, sl 1, K1, psso, K to end.
2nd row P to last st, K1.
Rep last 2 rows 13[15] times more, then work 1st row again. 14[15] sts.

Shape neck

Next row Bind off 3[4] sts, P to last st, K1.
Next row K1, sl 1, K1, psso, K to last 2 sts, K2 tog.
Next row P to last st, K1.
Rep last 2 rows 3 times more.
Next row K1, sl 1, K1, psso.
Next row P1, K1.
K2 tog. Fasten off.

Right half

Work as given for left half to ***. Cont on last 29[32] sts for right half front.

Shape raglan

1st row K to last 3 sts, K2 tog, K1.
2nd row K1, P to end.
Rep last 2 rows 13[15] times more. 15[16] sts.

Shape neck

Next row Bind off 3[4] sts, K to last 3 sts, K2 tog, K1.
Next row K1, P to end.
Next row K2 tog, K to last 3 sts, K2 tog, K1.
Next row K1, P to end.
Rep last 2 rows 3 times more.
Next row K2 tog, K1.
Next row K1, P1.
K2 tog. Fasten off.
With RS of work facing, rejoin yarn to right half back sts.
1st row K1, sl 1, K1, psso, K to end.
2nd row P to last st, K1.
Rep last 2 rows 19[21] times more. Bind off rem 9[10] sts.

Sleeves

Using size 4 needles and A, cast on 30[36] sts. Work as given for left half to **. Join in B. Work 6 rows st st, inc one st at each end of first row. Break off B. Join in C. Work 2 rows st st, inc one st at each end of first row. Break off C. Cont in A only, inc one st at each end of 5th and every foll 4th[6th] row until there are 50[54] sts. Work 5 rows st st, ending with a P row. Place marker at each end of last row. Work 4 more rows st st.

Shape raglan

1st row K1, sl 1, K1, psso, K to last 3 sts, K2 tog, K1.
2nd row K1, P to last st, K1.
Rep last 2 rows 19[21] times more. Bind off rem 10 sts.

Finishing

Press under a damp cloth with a warm iron. Join inside leg seams, center back seam and shaped section of front seam. Set in sleeves, sewing row ends above markers to bound-off sts at underarm. Join sleeve seams.
Neckband Using size 4 needles, A and with RS of work facing, K up 15[16] sts up right front neck, 9 sts across right sleeve, 13[15] sts from back neck, 9 sts across left sleeve and 15[16] sts down left front neck. 61[65] sts.
Next row P1, *K1, P1, rep from * to end.
Next row K1, *P1, K1, rep from * to end.
Rep last 2 rows once more, then first of them again. Bind off in rib.
Sew in zipper. Turn hems around legs and sleeves to WS at hemline and sl st in place. Press seams.

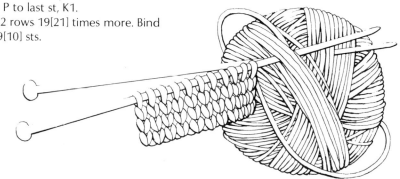

Two-tone Helmet

Knit a toddler a snug little hat with pompom and ear flaps to protect him from cold winter winds.

Size
The cap measures 16in around the brim.

Materials
1 50g ball of Bernat Saluki in main color A
1 ball of contrast color B
one pair each of sizes 2 and 4 needles
1 small button

Gauge
24 sts and 40 rows to 4in over g st on size 4 needles

Right ear flap
**Using size 2 needles and A, cast on 8 sts. K 3 rows g st.

Next row (buttonhole row) K3, bind off 2 sts, K to end.
Next row K3, cast on 2 sts, K to end.
Cont in g st for a further 14 rows.
Next row K2, pick up loop lying before next st and K tbl – called inc 1 –, K4, inc 1, K2.
Next row K to end.
Next row K2, inc 1, K6, inc 1, K2.
Next row K to end.
Cont inc in this way on next and every alt row until there are 22 sts, ending with an inc row **. K 8 rows without shaping in g st.
Next row Cast on 12 sts, K to end. 34 sts.
K 8 rows g st. Break off yarn and leave these sts on holder.

Left ear flap
Work as given for right ear flap from ** to ** omitting buttonhole rows. K 9 rows g st.
Next row Cast on 12 sts, K to end. 34 sts. K 7 rows g st.
Next row K to end of left ear flap, cast on 30 sts, K across sts of right ear flap. 98 sts. K 5 rows g st. Change to size 4 needles. Commence pat. Join in B.
1st row Using B, *K2, sl 2 P-wise, rep from * to last 2 sts, K2.
2nd row P2, *sl 2 P-wise, P2, rep from * to end.
Rep last 2 rows once more.
5th row Using A, K to end.
6th row Using A, K to end.
7th row Using A, P to end.
8th row Using A, K to end.
Rep these 8 rows 4 times more, then rep 1st–4th rows once more. Break off B.
Next row K6, K2 tog, (K10, K2 tog) 7 times, K6.
Next row K to end.
Shape crown
1st row *K7, K2 tog, rep from * to end.
2nd and every alt row K to end.
3rd row *K6, K2 tog, rep from * to end.
Cont dec in this way until 10 sts rem. Break off yarn, thread through rem sts, draw up and fasten off.

Finishing
Do not press. Join back seam. Sew button to left ear flap. Make pompom using both colors and sew to top of helmet.

Striped Robe

Colorful stripes, which are simple and fun to work, add style to this attractive little robe. For a modern look, choose brightly contrasting colors, use pastels for a more traditional effect.

Size
The pattern is sized to fit a baby up to 1 year old – or chest size 18–20in.

Materials
a total of 8oz of knitting worsted weight crepe yarn such as Bernat Saluki. However, for stripes you will need 2 1¾oz balls in each of colors A – pink and B – ivory and 1 ball in each of four other colors : C – blue, D – green, E – red and F – yellow
one pair each of sizes 2 and 4 needles
⅝yd of ⅜in wide ribbon for binding
1⅛yd of ¼in wide ribbon for ties

Gauge
24 sts and 32 rows to 4in over st st worked on size 4 needles

Horizontal stripe sequence
This consists of four rows each in colors F, C, B, E, D and A ; repeat this sequence as directed in the pattern. Cut off yarn after finishing each color ; the distance between stripes of the same color is too great to permit carrying the yarn up the side of the work.

Skirt back
Using size 2 needles and A, cast on 92 sts. Work 4 rows g st.
Change to size 4 needles. Beg with a K row, cont in st st and horizontal stripe sequence.
Dec one st at each end of 25th and every foll 8th row until 68 sts rem.
Work a total of 116 rows in stripes, finishing after last row of D in the 5th rep. Change to size 2 needles. Using A, work 4 rows g st. Bind off.

Skirt front
Work as given for skirt back.

Sleeves
Using size 2 needles and A, cast on 28 sts. Work 4 rows g st.
Change to size 4 needles. Beg with a K

row, cont in st st and stripe sequence. Inc one st at each end of 5th and every foll 4th row until there are 48 sts. Work a total of 44 rows in stripes, finishing after last row of D in the 2nd rep. Change to size 2 needles. Using A, work 4 rows g st. Bind off.

Yoke back
Using size 4 needles and B, cast on 57 sts. Beg vertical stripe pattern. Using B, K3 sts, using A, K3 sts ; alt K3 sts using B and A to end of row.
Cont in st st and vertical stripes as above until work measures 4in ending with a P

31

row.
Bind off 4 sts at beg of each of next 8 rows to shape shoulders.
Bind off remaining 35 sts.

Yoke left front
Using size 4 needles and B, cast on 29 sts.
Beg vertical stripe pattern. Using B, K3 sts, using A, K3 sts ; alt K3 sts using B and A to last 5 sts ; using B, K3 sts, using A, K2 sts.
Cont in vertical stripes until there are 11 rows less than back before shoulder shaping, ending at front edge.
Shape neck by binding off at beg of next and every alt row (i.e. same edge at start of P rows) 6 sts once, 2 sts twice, one st 3 times. The last row is a P row and 16 sts rem.
Bind off at beg of next and every alt row (i.e. same edge at start of K rows) 4 sts 4 times to shape shoulders.

Yoke right front
Using size 4 needles and B, cast on 29 sts.
Beg vertical stripe pattern. Using A, K2 sts, using B, K3 sts, using A, K3 sts ; alt K3 sts using B and A to end of row, finishing with 3 sts in B.
Cont in vertical stripes until there are 10 rows less than back before shoulder shaping, ending at front edge.
Cont as given for left front yoke, reversing position of neck shaping by binding off at beg of K rows. Reverse shoulder shaping by binding off at beg of P rows.

Finishing
Press lightly with a cool iron over a dry cloth.
Using a backstitch seam throughout, join shoulder seams.
Mark center of sleeve top and match to shoulder seam. Sew sleeve tops in position along sides of yoke.
Sew yoke to top of skirt, easing skirt slightly to fit yoke.
Join side and sleeve seams. Press finished seams.
Bind neck and front opening with ribbon. Sew on ribbon to tie at top of front opening.

Overalls and Pullover

A shaggy bear motif, worked in crochet, will make these overalls a favorite with the little one. A pullover in a contrasting color completes the outfit.

Sizes
The pattern is given for two sizes : 1 year and 2 to 3 years.
pullover
.chest, 20[22]in
length from shoulder, 11[12]in
sleeve seam, 7[8½]in
overalls
chest, 53[58]cm/21[23]in
length down center back to crotch, 12½[14½]in
inside leg seam, 8[9]in

Materials
Overalls
5[7] 50g balls of Bernat Saluki in main color A
1 pair each of sizes 2 and 4 needles
a steel size 1 crochet hook
4 small buttons
a 12[14]in zipper

Polar bear motif (optional)
1 ball of contrast color B and short lengths of yarn for features
a size C crochet hook
a piece of stiff cardboard 5 by ⅝in

Pullover
3[4] balls of contrast color C
1 pair each of sizes 3 and 5 needles
set of 4 size 2 needles pointed at both ends

Gauge
24 sts and 32 rows to 4in over st st worked on size 4 needles

Overalls
Right leg
Using size 2 needles and A, cast on 70[76] sts. Beg with a K row work 9 rows st st, ending with a K row.
Next row K to form hemline.
Change to size 4 needles. Beg with a K

row work 8 rows st st.
Next row *K one st from needle tog with one st from cast-on edge, rep from * to end to form hem.
Shape leg
Beg with a P row cont in st st, dec one st at each end of 2nd and every foll 6th row until 58[64] sts rem. Cont without shaping until leg measures 8[9]in from hemline, ending with a P row.
Shape crotch
Cast on 2[3] sts at beg of next 2 rows. 62[70] sts. Break off yarn and leave rem sts on holder.

Left leg
Work as given for right leg, but do not break off yarn.

Body
Next row K across left leg sts, then across right leg sts from holder. 124[140] sts.
Next row K2, P to last 2 sts, K2.
Keeping g st border of 2 sts correct at each end of every row, cont in st st until work measures 6[7]in from crotch, ending with a P row.
Shape neck
**Next row K27[30] sts, turn.
Next row Sl 1 P-wise, P to last 2 sts, K2.
Next row K21[24] sts, turn.
Next row Sl 1 P-wise, P to last 2 sts, K2.
Cont to work 6 sts less in this way on next and foll alt rows until the row K9 [12] sts, turn has been worked.
Next row Sl 1 P-wise, P to last 2 sts, K2.
Next row K to end across all sts.**
Rep from ** to **, reading K for P and P for K.
Change to size 2 needles. Keeping g st borders correct, work 7 rows K1, P1 rib.
Change to size 4 needles. Beg with a P row cont in st st until work measures 10[11½]in from crotch, ending with a P row.
Divide for armholes
Next row K27[30] sts, turn and leave rem sts on holder.
Complete left back first. P 1 row. Dec one st at armhole edge on next and foll alt

rows until 22[24] sts rem. Cont without shaping until armhole measures 2[2½]in from beg, ending at center back edge.

Shape back neck

Bind off 6[7] sts at beg of next row. Dec one st at neck edge on next and every row until 10[11] sts rem. Cont without

shaping until armhole measures 4½[5]in from beg, ending with a P row. Bind off. With RS of work facing, rejoin yarn to rem sts on holder, bind off first 8[10] sts for first underarm, K until there are 54[60] sts on right-hand needle for front, turn and leave rem sts on holder.

P 1 row. Dec one st at each end of next and foll alt rows until 44[48] sts rem. Cont without shaping until armholes measure same as back to neck shaping, ending with a P row.

Shape front neck

Next row K16[17] sts, turn and leave rem

sts on holder.

Dec one st at neck edge on next and every row until 10[11] sts rem. Cont without shaping until armhole measures 4[4½]in from beg, ending with a P row.

Next row (buttonhole row) K1, K2 tog, yo, K4[5], yo, K2 tog, K1.

Beg with a P row cont in st st until front measures same as back to shoulder, ending with a P row. Bind off.

With RS of work facing, rejoin yarn to rem sts on holder at front neck, bind off first 12[14] sts for front neck, K to end. Complete to match first side, reversing shapings.

With RS of work facing, rejoin yarn to rem sts on holder, bind off first 8[10] sts for underarm, K to end for right back. Complete as given for left back, reversing shapings.

Edging

Using size 1 hook, A, and with RS of work facing, rejoin yarn to neck at left back and work 1 row sc all around neck, shoulders and armholes to right back. Do not turn work, but work another row of sc to left back, working from left to right instead of right to left. Fasten off.

Polar bear motif

Using size C hook and B, make 21ch.

1st row Hold card at back of work with top edge level with working edge of crochet, insert hook into 2nd ch from hook, pass yarn under card from back to front, yo and draw through a loop, yo and draw through both loops on hook – called fur st –, work a fur st into each ch to end, 1ch. Turn. Withdraw card from loops.

2nd row Ss into first ch, ss into each of next 20 sts, 4ch. Turn.

3rd row Miss first ch, 1sc into each of next 3ch, work a fur st into each of next 21 sts, 1ch. Turn.

4th row Ss into first ch, ss into each of next 24 sts, 4ch. Turn.

5th row Miss first ch, 1sc into each of next 3ch, 1sc into each of next 3 sts, work a fur st into each of next 21 sts, 1ch. Turn.

6th row Ss into first ch, ss into each of next 25 sts, 1ch, turn.

7th row 1sc into each of next 7 sts, work a fur st into each of next 21 sts, 1ch. Turn.

8th row Ss into first ch, ss into each of next 27 sts, 1ch, turn.

9th row 1sc into each of next 7 sts, work a fur st into each of next 20 sts, 1ch, turn.

10th row Ss into first ch, ss into each of next 19 sts, 1ch, turn.

11th row Work a fur st into each of next 20 sts, 1ch. Turn.

12th row As 10th.

13th row Work a fur st into each of next 19 sts, 1ch, turn.

14th row Ss into first ch, ss into each of next 18 sts, 1ch, turn.

15th row Work a fur st into each of next 18 sts, 1ch, turn.

Shape first back leg

*Next row** Ss into each of next 4 sts, 1ch, turn.

Next row Work a fur st into each of next 4 sts, 1ch. Turn.

Rep last 2 rows once more.

Next row 1sc into each of next 3 sts, 2sc into last st. Fasten off.

Shape second back leg

Return to 15th row, rejoin yarn to last ss of 1st row of leg.

Next row Ss into each of next 3 sts, 1ch, turn.

Next row Work a fur st into each of next 3 sts, 1ch. Turn.

Rep last 2 rows once more.

Next row 1sc into each of next 2 sts, 2sc into next st. Fasten off.*

Shape front legs

Return to 15th row, miss 4 sts in center, rejoin yarn to next st and rep from * to * as given for back leg shaping.

Finishing

Press garment under a damp cloth with a cool iron. Join leg seams as far as crotch. Sew in zipper. Sew on buttons to correspond with buttonholes at shoulders. Press seams. Sew motif to front bib, then with short lengths of yarn embroider nose, ear, eye and claws.

Pullover
Back

Using size 3 needles and C, cast on 62[68] sts. Work 12 rows K1, P1 rib.

Change to size 5 needles. Cont in rib until back measures 7[7½]in from beg.

Shape armholes

Bind off 5 sts at beg of next 2 rows. Dec one st at each end of next and foll alt row until 40[46] sts rem. Cont without shaping until armholes measure 3[3½]in from beg.

Shape neck

Next row Rib 14[16] sts, turn and leave rem sts on holder.

Cont in rib, dec one st at neck edge on next 4 rows. Work 1 row.

Shape shoulder

Bind off at beg of next and foll alt row 5[6] sts twice.

With RS of work facing, sl first 12[14] sts on holder for center back neck, rejoin yarn to rem sts and rib to end. Complete to match first side, reversing shaping.

Front

Work as given for back until armholes measure 2[2½]in from beg.

Shape neck

Next row Rib 16[18] sts, turn and leave rem sts on holder.

Cont in rib, dec one st at neck edge on next and every row until 10[12] sts rem. Cont without shaping until armhole measures same as back to shoulder, ending at armhole edge.

Shape shoulder

Work as given for back shoulder shaping. With RS of work facing, sl first 8[10] sts on holder for center front neck, rejoin yarn to rem sts and rib to end. Complete to match first side, reversing shaping.

Sleeves

Using size 3 needles and C, cast on 36[38] sts. Work 12 rows K1, P1 rib. Change to size 5 needles. Cont in rib, inc one st at each end of 3rd and every foll 6th row, working extra sts into pat, until there are 48[52] sts. Cont without shaping until sleeve measures 7[8½]in from beg.

Shape top

Bind off 5 sts at beg of next 2 rows. Dec one st at each end of next and foll alt rows until 28 sts rem. Dec one st at each end of next and every row until 14 sts rem. Bind off in rib.

Turtleneck collar

Join shoulder seams. Using set of 4 size 2 needles, C, and with RS of work facing, K up 72[76] sts evenly around neck. Work 3[3½]in in rounds of K1, P1 rib. Bind off in rib.

Finishing

Set in sleeves. Join side and sleeve seams. Fold collar in half to RS of work. Press seams lightly.

Beach Outfit

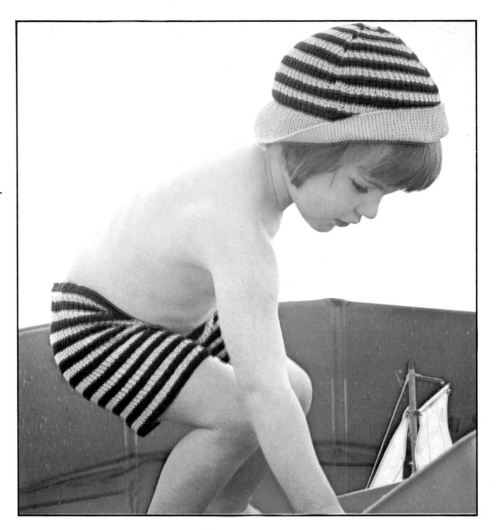

Shorts with a matching sun hat in colorful stripes are perfect for beach or backyard.

Sizes
The pattern is given in three sizes: 6 months, 2 years and 4 years, or chest sizes 19in, 21in and 23in respectively.
inside leg seam, 8½[9½:11]in

Materials
Pingouin Fil d'Ecosse No.5 in the amounts specified for the individual garments
1 pair each of sizes 2 and 3 needles

Shorts
1[1:2] 50g balls of yarn in main color A
1[1:1] ball of contrast color B
waist length of elastic

Hat
1[1:1] ball each of A and B

Gauge
32 sts and 38 rows to 4in over rib pat on size 3 needles

Shorts
Right leg
Using size 2 needles and A, cast on 93[99:105] sts. Beg with a K row work 9 rows st st. Join in B. Using B, P 3 rows. Change to size 3 needles. Commence rib.
Next row Using B, *K1, P1, rep from * to last st, K1.
Next row Using B, *P1, K1, rep from * to last st, P1.
Commence stripe pat.
1st row (RS) Using A, K to end.
2nd to 4th rows Using A, rib to end.
5th row Using B, K to end.
6th to 8th rows Using B, rib to end.
These 8 rows form striped rib pat and are rep throughout; *at the same time* when work measures 1¾[1¾:2¼]in from beg, inc one st at each end of next and every alt row until there are 105[111:117] sts. Work 2 rows without shaping. Dec one st at each end of next and every foll alt row 5 times in all, then at each end of every foll 6th[6th:8th] row 4 times in all. 87[93:99]

sts. Cont without shaping until work measures 9½[10½:12]in from beg, ending with 7th row of rib pat. Change to size 2 needles. Using B, P 3 rows. Using A and beg with a K row, work 6 rows st st. Bind off.

Left leg
Work as given for right leg.

Finishing
Press under a damp cloth with a warm iron. Join back and front seams. Fold hems to WS at lower edge of legs and at waist along P row and sl st into position. Thread elastic through waistband and secure. Press seams.

Hat
Crown
1st panel
Using size 3 needles and B, cast on 37 sts. Commence pat.
1st row Using B, K to end.
2nd to 4th rows Using B, work in rib as given for shorts.
5th row Using A, K to end.
7th to 8th rows Using A, work in rib as given for shorts.
These 8 rows form pat and are rep

throughout. Work a further 20 rows.
Shape top
Dec one st at each end of next and every foll alt row until 11 sts rem.
Next row K2 tog, pat to last 2 sts, K2 tog.
Next row Bind off working 2 tog along row to last st, bind off this st.
Work 3 more panels in same way.

Brim
Using size 3 needles and A, cast on 16 sts.
K 3 rows.
**Next row K to last 2 sts, turn.
Next row K to end.
Working across all sts, K 6 rows. **. Cont working in this way from ** to ** until work measures 18in from beg, along shorter edge. Bind off.

Finishing
Press crown pieces under a damp cloth with a warm iron. Join 4 crown pieces. Join cast-on and bound-off edges of brim tog. Overcast shorter edge of brim in place around crown. Press seams.

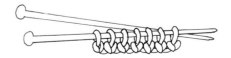

CROCHET

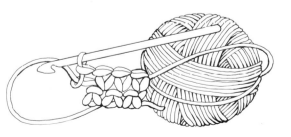

Striped Sleeping Bag

A simple pattern worked in contrasting colors makes a sleeping bag that is attractive as well as comfortable.

Size
total width around chest, 26in
length from shoulder, 22in
sleeve seam, 5½in

Materials
4 50g balls of Pingouin Confortable in main color A
2 balls of yarn in contrast color B
2 balls of yarn in contrast color C
a size F crochet hook
an 18in open-ended zipper
4 buttons

Gauge
18 sts and 10 rows to 4in over dc on a size F hook

Yoke and sleeves
Using size F hook and C, make 100ch and beg at back lower edge.
1st row Into 4th ch from hook work 1dc, 1dc into each ch to end. Turn. 98dc.
2nd row 3ch to count as first dc, miss first dc, 1dc into each dc to end, 1dc into turning ch. Turn. Join in A. Working in stripe sequence of 2 rows each of A, B, A and C throughout work 7 more rows in dc.

Shape neck
Next row Using C, work across first 42 sts, turn.
Complete this side first.
Next row Work to end.
Next row Using A, work to end, join in B and make 9ch for front neck. Turn.
Next row Using B, into 4th ch from hook work 1dc, 1dc into each ch and dc to end, 1dc into turning ch. Turn. 49dc. Work 5 more rows. Fasten off.
Return to sts that were left, miss 14 sts in center for back neck, rejoin C to rem sts, 3ch, 1dc into each dc to end. 42 sts. Complete to match first side, reversing shaping and making 7ch with separate length of yarn so that neck shaping is reversed.

Body section
Using size F hook and C, make 87ch. Work in one piece, beg at front edge.
1st row Into 4th ch from hook work 1dc, 1dc into each ch to end. Turn. 85dc. Work 17 more rows in stripe sequence as given for yoke and sleeves.

Shape flap
Next row Using A, work to end, do not turn, make 19ch, turn.
Next row Using A, into 4th ch from hook work 1dc into each ch and dc to end, 1dc into turning ch. 102dc.
Keeping stripe sequence correct, work 35 more rows. Fasten off. Turn.
Next row Keeping stripe sequence correct, miss first 17 sts, rejoin yarn to rem sts, 3ch, 1dc into each dc to end, 1dc into turning ch. 85dc. Complete to match first side, ending with one row in C. Fasten off.

Finishing
Join sleeve seams for 5in from lower edge. Join front and back bodice to yoke section all around chest.
Edging Using size F hook and C, work one row sc all around neck, front, lower edges and flap, make four 3ch loops evenly across flap edge for buttonholes. Sew zipper to front edges. Turn up flap and sew on buttons to correspond with loops.
Cuffs Using size F hook and A, work 1sc into each row end all around lower edge of sleeve. Work 3 more rounds sc. Fasten off.

Motif-trimmed Playsuit

Colorful rabbits enliven the front and back of these overalls. The matching socks have a notched stripe motif.

Sizes
The pattern is given in two sizes : 0–3

months and 1 year, or chest sizes 18in and 20in respectively.

overalls
length from top of bib to crotch,
13[14½]in

socks
foot seam, 3½[4]in
bottom of heel to top of sock, 7[7½]in

Materials
4 1¾oz balls of Bucilla Perlette in main

color A
1 ball each of two contrasting colors B
    and C
a steel size 1 crochet hook
a size C crochet hook
a size E crochet hook
2 buttons

Gauge
21 sts and 14 rows to 4in over hdc on size
E hook

Overalls
Front
Using size E hook and A, make 24[28]ch
for top of bib.
Base row 1hdc into 3rd ch from hook,
1hdc into each ch to end. Turn. 23[27] sts.
Pat row 2ch to count as first hdc, 1hdc
into each hdc to end, 1hdc into top of
turning ch. Turn.
Rep the pat row 6 times more.
Inc row 2ch, 1hdc into first hdc, 2hdc into
next hdc, 1hdc into each hdc to within
last 2hdc, 2hdc into next hdc, 2hdc into
last hdc.
Turn. (4hdc increased in row.) 27[31]hdc.
Pat 1 row.
Rep the last 2 rows once more. 31[35]hdc.
Fasten off.
Waistline
Next row Make 7ch, work 1hdc into each
hdc across lower edge of bib section,
make 8ch. Turn.
Next row 1hdc into 3rd ch from hook,
1hdc into each of next 5ch, 1hdc into
each of the 31[35]hdc on bib, then 1hdc
into each of rem 7ch. 45[49] sts.
Cont in pat until work measures 13¼[14¼]in
from top of bib.
***Divide for legs
1st leg Work across first 23[25]hdc, turn.
Next row Make 5ch, work 1hdc into 3rd
ch from hook, 1hdc into each of next
23[25]hdc.
Turn. 27[29]hdc.
** Work 2 rows without shaping.
Inc row 2ch, 1hdc into first hdc, 1hdc into
each hdc, 2hdc into turning ch. Turn.
29[31]hdc. Pat 6 rows.
Work inc row again, then cont without
shaping until work measures 5[5¼]in.
Fasten off.
2nd leg Make 4ch, then work 1hdc into
the 23rd[25th]hdc of 1st leg – i.e. into the
same hdc as last st on first row of 1st leg –
now work 1hdc into each hdc to end.
Turn. 23[25]hdc.
Next row Pat to last 4ch, then work 1hdc
into each of the 4ch. Turn. 27[29] sts.
Complete to match first leg from ** to
end.

Back
Work as given for front to within 2 rows

of division for legs.
Next row Pat to last 6 sts, 1sc into next st,
turn.
Next row 1ch, miss sc, 1sc into first hdc,
1hdc into each hdc to within last 6 sts,
1sc into next st, turn.
Rep last row 4 times more.
Next row Work to end.
Next row Work to end.
Now complete as for front from *** to
end.

Finishing
Join side seams and inside leg seams to
within 6 rows of lower edge of leg. Turn to
right side and sew remainder of seam.
Using size C hook and A, work 1sc into
each st all around lower edge of leg, do
not turn but work a row of crab st – sc
worked from left to right – ss into first st.
Fasten off. Finish lower edge of other leg
to match.
Left strap
Using size C hook and A, make 18[20]ch,
then with RS of work facing work 1sc into
the first row end of the left side of back
bib, working along armhole edge work
(2sc into next row end, 1sc into next row
end) 9 times, 1sc into each of 6
foundation ch at underarm, now work
(1sc into next row end, 2sc into next row
end) 9 times, 1sc into last row end at top
of bib, make 19[21] ch, turn.
Next row 1sc into 2nd ch from hook, 1sc
into each ch, 1sc into each sc around
armhole, then 1sc into each of the
18[20]ch.
Buttonhole row 1ch, 1sc into each sc to
within last 4sc, 2ch, miss next 2sc, 1sc
into each of last 2sc. Turn.
Next row 1ch, 1sc into each of first 2sc,
2sc into ch sp, then work 1sc into each sc
to end. Turn.
Next row 1ch, 1sc into each sc to end.
Turn.
Rep last row once more. Fasten off.
Using size 1 hook and A, work a row of
crab st.
Fasten off.
Right strap
Work as for left strap but start working
into the row ends of front bib first and
make buttonhole at beg of row thus : 1ch,
1sc into each of first 2sc, 2ch, miss next
2sc, 1sc into each sc to end.
Turn.
Neck edging (back and front alike) Using
size C hook, A and with RS facing work
1sc into each foundation ch on strap, 1sc
into each st across bib, then 1sc into each
foundation ch on other strap. Do not
turn. Change to size 1 hook and work a
row of crab st. Fasten off.
Sew buttons on back straps to
correspond with buttonholes.

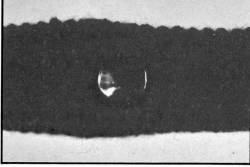

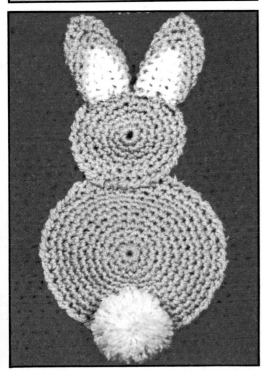

Press very lightly with a warm iron and a dry cloth.

Rabbit motif
Body
Using size C hook and B, make 3ch, ss into first ch to form a circle.
1st round Work 8sc into circle.
2nd round 2sc into each sc all around.
3rd and every foll alt round 1sc into each sc all around.
4th round (1sc into next sc, 2sc into next sc) 8 times, 24sc.
6th round (2sc into next sc, 1sc into each of next 2sc) 8 times, 32sc.
8th round (1sc into each of next 3sc, 2sc into next sc) 8 times, 40sc.
10th round (2sc into next sc, 1sc into each of next 4sc) 8 times, 48sc.
11th round 1sc into each sc all around.
12th round Working from left to right work a row of crab st, ss into first st. Fasten off.

Head
Work as for body up to and including the 7th round, then work the crab st edging. Fasten off.

Ears (make 2)
Using size C hook and C, make 6ch.
Base row 1sc into 2nd ch from hook, 1sc into each of next 3ch, 3sc into last ch, then working along other side of ch work 1sc into each of next 4ch. Turn.
Next row 1ch, 1sc into each sc to center sc of 3sc of previous row, 3sc into this sc, then work 1sc into each sc to end. Turn. Cut off B, join in A.
Rep last row twice more, then work a row of crab st.
Fasten off.
On flat edge of ear fold outer edges to center and sew together.

Finishing
For front view of rabbit, sew ears to back of head. Sew motif to bib, lapping head over body slightly. Embroider eyes and whiskers on head.
For back view of rabbit, sew ears to front of head. Sew motif to bib, lapping body over head slightly.
Using C, make a small pompom as foll: cut two cardboard circles of the required diameter and cut small circles in the center; wind yarn evenly over both circles and through holes until holes are nearly filled, then cont, using tapestry needle, until holes are completely filled. Cut through yarn around edge, between circles.
Tie a length of yarn around strands at center and cut away cardboard circles.
Sew pompom to body of rabbit.

Socks
Using size C hook and A, make 28ch, taking care not to twist the ch, ss into first ch to form a circle.
1st round 2ch, 1hdc into each ch to end, ss into top of first 2ch. Turn.
2nd round 2ch, miss first hdc, 1hdc into each hdc to end, ss into top of first 2ch. Turn.
Repeating round 2, work 1 round B, 1 round A, 1 round C and 1 round A.
Now working in A only, work 15[17] more rounds. Fasten off.
Shape instep
Cont in A only, miss first 9 sts, rejoin yarn to next st, work 1hdc into this st, then 1 hdc into each of the next 9 sts, turn. Work 4[6] rows.
Dec row 2ch, miss first hdc, (yo, insert hook into next st, yo and draw a loop through) twice, yo and draw through all loops on hook (1hdc decreased), 1hdc into each hdc to within last 3 sts, dec 1hdc, 1hdc into last st. Turn.
Rep last row once more.
Next row 2ch, (dec 1hdc) twice, 1hdc into last st. 4 sts. Fasten off.
Rejoin yarn to fasten-off place at heel, 2ch, then work 1hdc into each of next 8 sts, working up side of foot, work (2hdc into next row end, 1hdc into next row end, 2hdc into next row end) down other side of foot, then work 1hdc into each of the rem 9hdc, ss into top of first 2ch. Turn. 46[52] sts.
Shape toe
Next row 2ch, miss next hdc, 1hdc into each of next 20[23]hdc, (dec 1hdc) twice, 1hdc into each of rem 21[24] sts, ss into top of first 2ch. Turn.
Next row 2ch, miss 1hdc, 1hdc into each of next 19[22] sts (dec 1hdc) twice, 1hdc into each of rem 20[23]hdc, ss into top of 2ch. Turn.
Next row 2ch, miss next hdc, 1hdc into each of next 18[21] sts, (dec 1hdc) twice, 1hdc into each of rem 19[22] sts, ss into top of 2ch. Fasten off.

Finishing
Join foot seam. Press very lightly with a warm iron and dry cloth.

Textured Stitch Layette

A lattice pattern and bobble trim give a pleasing three-dimensional look to this layette, which comprises a blanket, jacket, cardigan, dress, pullover, overalls, bonnet, bootees and mittens. A little boy would look good in the overalls and cardigan (see page 47).

Size
The patterns are sized to fit a baby 0–3 months old, or chest size 18in.
length from shoulder – cardigan, 8in
sleeve seam – cardigan, 5in

Materials
For the entire layette, 24 50g balls of Phildar Sagittaire, 13 50g balls of Phildar Pronostic in main color A and 2 balls of Pronostic in contrast color B – amounts are also specified for the individual garments.
a size B crochet hook
a size C crochet hook
a size E crochet hook
a size F crochet hook

Blanket
19 50g balls of Phildar Sagittaire

Jacket
6 50g balls of Phildar Sagittaire
3 buttons

Cardigan
2 50g balls of Phildar Pronostic in main color A
a small amount of contrast color B
6 buttons

Dress
5 50g balls of Phildar Pronostic in main color A
a small amount of contrast color B
4 small buttons

Pullover
2 50g balls of Phildar Pronostic in main color A
a small amount of contrast color B

Overalls
2 50g balls of Phildar Pronostic in main color A
a small amount of contrast color B
2 small buttons

Bonnet
1 50g ball of Phildar Pronostic in main color A
a small amount of contrast color B

Bootees and mittens
1 50g ball of Phildar Pronostic in main color A

Gauge
For Sagittaire : 20 sts and 12 rows to 4in over pat on size F hook
For Pronostic : 20 sts and 11 rows to 4in over dc on size E hook

Blanket
Using size F hook make 151ch.
Base row 1dc into 4th ch from hook, 1dc into each ch to end. Turn. 149 sts. Commence pat.
1st row 3ch to count as first dc, *work around next dc by working yo, insert hook from front to back between next 2dc, around dc at left and through work from back to front, draw yarn through and complete dc in usual way called "1 double around front," or dc around ft, 1dc into next dc in the usual way, rep from * to end, ending with 1dc into top of ch. Turn.
2nd row 3ch, *1dc into top of next dc in the usual way, 1dc around ft, rep from * to last 2 sts, 1dc into each of last 2dc. Turn. Cont in pat until a total of 88 rows has been worked. Fasten off.
Edging
Using size C hook rejoin yarn to first of foundation ch, working along foundation ch work 1 sc into each ch to corner, 3sc into corner, working along row ends work (2sc into next row end, 1sc into next row end) to corner, 3sc into corner, 1sc into each tr, 3sc into corner, (2sc into next row end, 1sc into next row end) to corner, 2sc into corner, ss into first sc. Fasten off.
Fringe
Using three 6in lengths of yarn together knot fringe into every 3rd sc all around outer edge.

Jacket
Back
Using size F hook make 50ch and work base row and 2 pat rows as given for blanket. 49 sts.

Cont in pat until 18 rows have been worked from beg.
Shape armholes
Next row Ss over first 4 sts, 3ch, pat to within last 3 sts, turn.
Cont in pat until 27 rows have been worked from beg.
Shape shoulders
Next row Ss over first 4 sts, 3ch, pat to within last 3 sts, turn.
Rep last row once more.
Next row Ss over first 6 sts, 3ch, pat to within last 5 sts. Fasten off.

Right front
Using size F hook make 27ch and work base row and 2 pat rows as given for blanket. 25 sts.
Cont in pat until 18 rows have been worked from beg.
Shape armhole
Next row Ss over first 4 sts, 3ch, pat to end. Turn. Pat 6 rows.
Shape neck
Next row Ss over first 12 sts, 3ch, pat to end. Turn. Pat 1 row.
Shape shoulder
Next row Pat to within last 3 sts, turn.
Next row Ss over first 4 sts, 3ch, pat to end. Fasten off.

Left front
Work as given for right front, reversing shaping.

Sleeves
Using size F hook make 31ch and work base row and 2 pat rows as given for blanket, inc one st at each end of 2nd pat row. 29 sts.
Cont in pat, inc one st at each end of every 3rd row until there are 35 sts.
Cont without shaping until 16 rows have been worked from beg.
Shape top
Next row Ss over first 4 sts, 3ch, pat to within last 3 sts, turn.
Rep last row twice more. Fasten off.

Hood
Using size F hook make 61ch and work base row and 2 pat rows as given for blanket. Cont in pat until 14 rows have been worked from beg.
Fasten off.

Shape back

Miss first 20 sts, rejoin yarn to next st with a ss, 3ch, pat across next 18 sts, turn.
Pat 1 row.
Dec one st at each end of next row. Work 2 rows without shaping.
Rep last 3 rows once more. Fasten off. Join back seams.

Edging

Using size C hook join on yarn and work (1sc into next row end, 2sc into next row end) to seam, then work 7sc along center back neck, (1sc into next row end, 2sc into next row end) to face edge. Fasten off.

Finishing

Join shoulder seams. Set in sleeves, then join side and sleeve seams. Using size C hook join yarn to lower edge at center back and working along foundation ch work 1sc into each ch to right front edge, 3sc into corner, up right front work (1sc into next row end, 2sc into next row end) to neck, 3sc into corner, 1sc into each st along neck edge, (1sc into next row end, 2sc into next row end, 1sc into next row end) up side neck, 1sc into each st across back neck, (1sc into next row end, 2sc into next row end, 1sc into next row end) down side neck, 1sc into each st along front neck, (1sc into next row end, 2sc into next row end) along left front edge, 3sc into corner, 1sc into each ch along lower edge to center back, ss into first sc. Fasten off.

With RS together join hood to neck edge, leaving 4sc free at each front edge. Using size C hook work a row of sc evenly around face edge of hood and lower edge of sleeves.
Make 3 button loops on one side of front edge and sew buttons to other front edge to correspond with button loops.

Cardigan
Back
Using size B hook and A, make 47ch.
Base row 1sc into 2nd ch from hook, 1sc into each ch to end. Turn. 46sc.
Next row 1ch to count as first sc, 1sc into each sc to end. Turn.
Rep last row 4 times more.
Bobble row 1ch, 1sc into each of first 3sc, *omitting the last stage of last sc, drop A and draw through B, using B, work 5dc into next sc, remove hook from loop, insert hook from front to back into first of the 5dc, then draw dropped loop through – bobble made or MB –, now draw A through loop on hook and using A work 1sc into each of next 3sc, rep from * to last 2sc, 1sc into each of last 2sc. Turn. Cut off B.
Change to size E hook.
Next row 3ch, 1dc into each st to end, 1dc into top of 3ch. Turn.
Next row 3ch, 1dc into each dc to end. Turn.

Rep last row 9 times more.
Shape armholes
Next row Ss over first 4 sts, 3ch, 1dc into each dc to within last 3 sts, turn.
Cont without shaping until 8 rows have been worked from beg of armhole shaping.
Fasten off.

Left front
Using size B hook and A, make 24ch and work base row and up to beg of armhole shaping as given for back. 23 sts.
Shape armhole
Next row Ss over first 4 sts, 3ch, work to end. Turn.
Work 4 rows without shaping.
Shape neck
Next row Ss over first 11 sts, 3ch, work to end. Turn.
Work 2 rows. Fasten off.

Right front
Work as given for left front, reversing shaping.

Sleeves
Using size B hook and A, make 28ch and work base row as given for back.
27 sts.
Next row 1ch to count as first sc, 1sc into each sc to end. Turn.
Rep last row 4 times more.

Change to size E hook and work 1 row dc. 27 sts.
Cont in dc, inc one st at each end of every 3rd row until there are 35 sts, ending with an inc row.
Shape top
Next row Ss over first 4 sts, 3ch, 1dc into each dc to within last 3dc, turn.
Rep last row twice more.
Fasten off.

Finishing
Join shoulder seams. Set in sleeves, then join side and sleeve seams.
Neck edging
With RS facing, using size B hook and A, rejoin yarn to first st of right front neck and work 1sc into each st along neck edge, 1sc into next row end, 2sc into next row end, 1sc into next row end, 1sc into each st along back neck, 1sc into next row end, 2sc into next row end, 1sc into next row end, 1sc into each st along left front neck, turn.
Next row 1ch, 1sc into each st to end. Turn.
Rep last row once more. Fasten off.

Left front band
With RS facing, using size B hook join on yarn and work 1sc into each of the row ends of neck edging, then (1sc into next row end, 2sc into next row end) along front edge, turn.
Next row 1ch, 1sc into each sc to end. Turn.
Rep last row once more. Fasten off.

Right front band
With RS facing, using size B hook join on yarn and work (1sc into next row end, 2sc into next row end) along front edge, turn.
Buttonhole row 1ch, 1sc into first sc, *1ch, miss next sc, 1sc into each of next 5sc, rep from * 5 times more, ending with 1sc into each of last 2sc. Turn. 6 buttonholes.
Next row 1ch, 1sc into each sc and 1sc into each sp to end. Fasten off.
Sew on buttons. Press very lightly with a warm iron over a dry cloth.

Dress
Front yoke
Using size E hook and A, make 47ch.
Base row 1 sc into 3rd ch from hook, 1sc into each ch to end. Turn. 46 sts.
Bobble row 2ch to count as first sc, 1sc into each of next 2sc, *omitting the last stage of last sc, drop A and draw through B. Using B, work 5dc into next sc, remove hook from loop, insert hook from front to back into first of the 5dc, then draw dropped loop through – bobble made or MB – now draw A through loop on hook and using A work 1sc into each of next 3

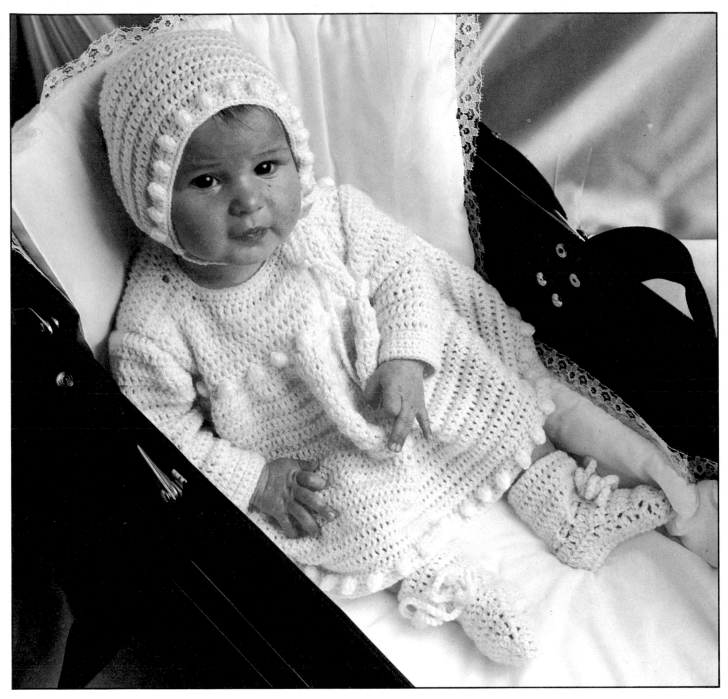

sc, rep from * to end, finishing with 1 sc into each of last 2sc. Turn.
Cut off B.
Next row 2ch to count as first sc, miss first sc, 1 sc into each st to end. Turn.
Shape armholes
Next row Ss over first 4 sts, 3ch, 1dc into each sc to within last 3 sts, turn. 40 sts.
Next row 3ch to count as first dc, 1dc into each dc to end. Turn.
Rep last row 3 times more.
Shape neck
Next row Work across first 10 sts, turn. Work 2 rows dc on these 10 sts. Fasten off. Miss center 20dc, rejoin yarn to next dc, 3ch, 1dc into each dc to end. Turn. Work 2 rows dc on these 10 sts. Fasten off.

Right back yoke
Using size E hook and A, make 23ch and work base row and bobble row as given for front yoke. 22 sts.
Next row 1ch, 1sc into each st to end. Turn.
Shape armhole
Next row Ss over first 4 sts, 3ch, 1dc into each sc to end. Turn. 19 sts.
Work 7 rows dc.
Fasten off.

Left back yoke
Using size E hook and A, make 23ch and work base row and bobble row as given for front yoke.
Next row 1ch, 1sc into each st to end. Turn.

Shape armhole
Next row 3ch to count as first dc, 1dc into each dc to within last 3 sts, turn. 19 sts. Work 7 rows dc. Fasten off.

Skirt
Join side seams of yoke sections. With RS of work facing and using size E hook, join yarn to right back yoke with a ss, 3ch, now work 2dc into each of the foundation ch to within last ch, 1dc into last ch. Turn. 178 sts.
Next row 3ch, miss first dc, 1dc into each dc to end. Turn.
Rep last row until skirt measures 8in, ending with a RS row.
Next row 1ch, 1sc into each dc to end. Turn.

Bobble row Work as given for bobble row of front yoke.
Next row 1ch, 1sc into each st to end. Turn.
Rep last row once more. Fasten off.

Sleeves
Using size B hook and A, make 28ch and work base row as given for back yoke. 27 sts.
Next row 2ch to count as first sc, miss first sc, 1sc into each sc to end. Turn.
Rep last row 4 times more.
Change to size E hook and work 1 row dc. 27dc.
Cont in dc, inc one st at each end of every 3rd row until there are 35 sts, ending with an inc row.
Shape top
Next row Ss over first 4 sts, 3ch, 1dc into each dc to within last 3dc, turn.
Rep last row twice more. Fasten off.

Neck border
Join shoulder seams. With RS facing, using size B hook and A, work 1sc into each of the 9 sts on left back yoke, then (2sc into next row end, 1sc into next row end, 2sc into next row end) down side of neck, 1sc into each sc across front neck, (2sc into next row end, 1sc into next row end, 2sc into next row end) up side of neck, then 1sc into each of the 9 sts on right back yoke. Turn. 50sc.
Next row 1ch, 1sc into each sc to end. Turn.
Rep last row once more. Fasten off.

Button border
With RS of work facing join yarn to first row end of right back neck and work 1sc into this row end, then 1sc into each of next 2 row ends, (2sc into next row end, 1sc into next row) down dc row ends, 1sc into each of the sc row ends and (2sc into

next row end, 1sc into next row end) twice on the first 4 dc rows of skirt. Turn.
Next row 1ch, 1sc into each sc to end. Turn.
Rep last row once more. Fasten off.

Buttonhole border
Join yarn to 4th row end of dc on skirt, work 1sc into this row end, 2sc into next row end, 1sc into next row end, 2sc into next row end, 1sc into each of the sc row ends, then (1sc into next row end, 2sc into next row end) up dc row ends on yoke, then 1sc into each of the 3sc row ends of neck border. Turn.
Buttonhole row *2ch, miss next 2sc, 1sc into each of next 3sc, rep from * 3 times more, 1sc into each sc to end. Turn.
Next row 1ch, 1sc into each sc and 2sc into each ch sp to end. Fasten off.

Finishing
Join sleeve seams to within 2 rows of top shaping. Set in sleeves. Join center back skirt seam. Lap buttonhole border over button border and sew in place. Sew on buttons to correspond with buttonholes.

Pullover
Back
Using size B hook and A, make 47ch.
Base row 1sc into 3rd ch from hook, 1sc into each ch to end. Turn. 46 sts.
Next row 2ch, 1sc into each st to end. Turn. Rep last row 4 times more.
Bobble row 2ch to count as first sc, 1sc into each of next 2sc, *MB with B, 1sc into each of next 3sc with A, rep from * to end, finishing with 1sc into each of last 2sc. Turn. Cut off B.
Change to size E hook.
Next row 3ch to count as first dc, 1dc into each st to end, 1dc into top of 3ch. Turn.
Next row 3ch, 1dc into each dc to end. Turn.

Rep last row 9 times more.
Shape armholes
Next row Ss over first 4 sts, 3ch, 1dc into each dc to within last 3 sts, turn.
Cont without shaping until 8 rows have been worked from beg of armhole shaping.
Shape neck
Next row Work across first 13 sts, 1hdc into next st, 1sc into next st, ss into next st. Fasten off.
Next row Miss the ss, sc and hdc, ss into next st, 1sc into next sc, 1hdc into next st, 1dc into each of rem 10 sts. Fasten off.
Miss the center 8dc, ss into next st, 1sc into next st, 1hdc into next st, then work 1dc into each of the rem 13dc. Turn.
Next row Work across first 10dc, then work 1hdc into next st, 1sc into next st, ss into next st.
Fasten off.
Work a row of bobbles across all sts.
Next row 1ch, 1sc into each st to end. Fasten off.

Front
Work as given for back to completion of armhole shaping. Cont without shaping until 5 rows have been worked from beg of armhole shaping.
Shape neck
Next row Work across first 13 sts, 1hdc into next st, 1sc into next st, ss into next st. Fasten off.
Next row Miss the ss, sc and hdc, ss into next st, 1sc into next sc, 1hdc into next st, 1dc into each of rem 10 sts. Turn.
Next row Work across first 7dc, then work 1hdc into next st, 1sc into next st, ss into next st. Fasten off.
Miss center 8 sts, ss into next st, 1sc into next st, 1hdc into next st, then work 1dc into each of rem 13dc. Turn.
Next row Work across first 10dc, 1hdc into next st, 1sc into next st, ss into next st. Fasten off.
Next row Miss ss, sc and hdc, ss into next st, 1sc into next st, 1hdc into next st, then work 1dc into each of rem 7 sts. Fasten off.
Next row Working across all sts, work 1sc into each st to end. Turn.
Rep last row once more. Fasten off.

Sleeves
Work as given for sleeves of dress.

Finishing
Count up to the 8th row of armhole on back and mark with a pin. Match points of front to markers. Fold remainder of back armhole over front and sew down along armhole edge so that back overlaps front at shoulder on right side of work. Join side seams. Join sleeve seams to

within last 2 rows before shaping, then set in sleeves taking the double thickness at shoulder into the seam of sleeve inset.

Overalls

Front
Using size E hook and A, make 23ch for top edge of bib.
Base row 1sc into 3rd ch from hook, 1sc into each ch to end. Turn. 22 sts.
Next row 3ch to count as first dc, 1dc into each sc to end. Turn. 22dc.
Work 8 rows dc. Fasten off.

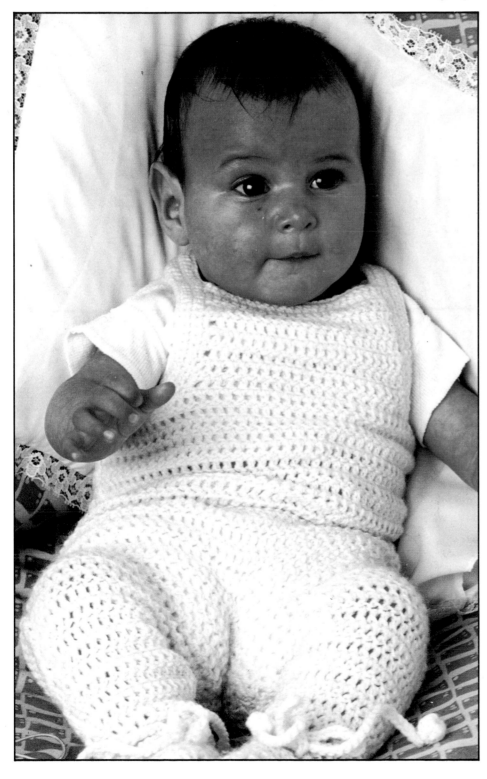

Next row Make 12ch, then work 1dc into each dc of bib, make 14ch, turn.
Next row 1dc into 4th ch from hook, 1dc into each of the 9ch, 1dc into each dc of bib, then 1dc into each of the 12ch. Turn. 46 sts. Work 17 rows dc.

Divide for legs
Next row Work across first 23 sts for 1st leg, make 5ch, turn.
Next row 1dc into 4th ch from hook, 1dc into next ch, then work 1dc into each dc to end. Turn. 26 sts.
****Cont in dc, dec one st at inside leg edge

on next 2 rows, then work 1 row without shaping. Rep last 3 rows until 14 sts rem, ending with 1 row worked straight.
Eyelet hole row 3ch, 1dc into next dc, *1ch, miss next dc, 1dc into next dc, rep from * to end. Turn.
Next row 3ch, *1dc into next sp, 1dc into next dc, rep from * to end, 1dc into top of 3ch. Turn. 14 sts.
Shape instep
Dec one st at inside edge of next and foll 2 alt rows, then dec one st at each end of next row. Fasten off.**
Next row Make 3ch, then work 1dc into each of the rem 23dc for 2nd leg. Turn.
Next row Work to end, then work 1dc into each of the 3ch. Turn. 26dc.
Now work as 1st leg from ** to **.

Back
Using size E hook and A, make 48ch.
Base row 1dc into 4th ch from hook, 1dc into each ch to end. Turn. 46 sts.
Shape back
Next row Work in dc to within last 7 sts, 1hdc into next st, 1sc into next st, turn.
Next row 1sc into first st, 1hdc into next st, work in dc to within last 7 sts, 1hdc into next st, 1sc into next st, turn.
Rep last row 4 times more.
Next row 1sc into next st, 1hdc into next st, 1dc into each dc, then 1dc into each st to end. Turn.
Next row 3ch, 1dc into each st to end. Turn. 46 sts.
Cont in dc without shaping until back measures same as front measured at side edges.
Now divide for legs and work legs as for front to completion of eyelet hole row.
Next row 3ch, *1dc into next sp, 1dc into next dc, rep from *to end, 1dc in top of 3ch. 14 sts. Fasten off.

Left leg
Rejoin yarn to first dec row end on front and work 3ch, 1dc into same row end as join, (1dc into next row end, 2dc into next row end) twice, 1dc into each of the 6 sts along toe edge, (2dc into next row end, 1dc into next row end) 3 times, then 1dc into each of the 14dc on back. Turn.
Work 2 rows straight on these dc. Fasten off.

Right leg
Join yarn to first of 14dc on back, 3ch, 1dc into each of next 13dc, (1dc into next row end, 2dc into next row end) 3 times, 1dc into each of the 6 sts along toe edge, (2dc into next row end, 1dc into next row end) twice, 2dc into next row end. Turn. Work 2 rows straight on these dc. Fasten off.
Join inner leg, side seams and foot seams.

Ties (make 2)
Using size E hook and A double, make a

ch approx 22in long. Fasten off. Thread ties through eyelet holes.

Bobbles (make 4)
Using size E hook and B, make 4ch, ss into first ch to form a ring.
Next round 3ch, 11dc into ring, ss into top of 3ch. Fasten off, leaving a long end. Thread end around top of dc, pull up tightly and secure. Attach one bobble to each end of ties.

Straps
Using size B hook and A, make 60ch, then working along left side edge of bib, with RS facing work (2sc into next row end, 1sc into next row end) along edge of bib, 1sc into each foundation ch along back, then (2sc into next row end, 1sc into next row end) along other side of bib, make 61ch. Turn.
Next row 1sc into 3rd ch from hook, 1sc into each ch, 1sc into each sc all around, then 1sc into each ch to end. Turn.
Buttonhole row 1ch, 1sc into each of first 2sc, *2ch, miss next 2sc, 1sc into each of next 3sc, rep from * twice more, then cont working 1sc into each sc to within last 14 sts, (2ch, miss next 2sc, 1sc into each of next 3sc) twice, 2ch, 1sc into each of last 2sc. Turn.
Next row 1ch, 1sc into each sc and 2sc into each sp all around. Fasten off.
With RS of work facing, rejoin yarn to first of foundation ch on left strap and work 1sc into each of the 60ch, then work 1sc into each of the foundation ch across top of bib, 1 sc into each of the foundation ch on other strap. Fasten off. Sew 2 buttons inside back waist.

Bonnet
Using size B hook and A, make 61ch.
Base row 1sc into 3rd ch from hook, 1sc into each ch to end. Turn. 60 sts.
Bobble row 2ch to count as first sc, 1sc into each of next 3sc, *MB with B, 1sc into each of next 3sc with A, rep from * to end. Turn. Cut off B.
Next row 2ch to count as first sc, 1 sc into each sc to end. Turn. Change to size E hook.
Next row 3ch to count as first dc, 1dc into each sc to end. Turn.
Cont in dc until 13dc rows have been worked. Fasten off.
Next row Miss first 20 sts, rejoin yarn to next st with a ss, 3ch, 1dc into each of next 19dc, turn.
Now work 10 rows in dc, dec one st at each end of every 3rd row.
Fasten off.

Finishing
Join side back head seams. Using size B

hook, A and with RS of work facing, work 1sc into each of the foundation ch all around face edge working 3sc into last ch, then work (1sc into next row end, 2sc into next row end) to seam, 1sc into each dc along back neck edge, then (1sc into next row end, 2sc into next row end) along to face edge, ss into first sc. Turn.
Eyelet hole row 4ch, miss first 2sc, *1hdc into next dc, 1ch, miss next sc, rep from * to end, finishing 1 sc into last sc. Fasten off.

Tie
Using size E hook and A double, make a ch approx 45in long. Fasten off.
Thread through eyelet holes.
Make 2 bobbles as given for overalls and sew one to each end of tie.

Bootees
1st bootee
Using size E hook and A, make 30ch.
Base row 1sc into 3rd ch from hook, 1sc into each ch to end. Turn. 29 sts.
Next row 3ch to count as first dc, 1dc into each sc to end. Turn.
Next row 3 ch, 1dc into each dc to end. Turn.
Rep last row 3 times more.
Eyelet hole row 4ch, miss first 2dc, 1dc into next dc, *1ch, miss next dc, 1dc into next dc, rep from * to end. Turn.
Next row 3ch, *1dc into next sp, 1dc into next dc, repeat from * to last sp, 1dc into sp. Turn. 28dc.
Next row 3ch, dec over next 2dc, 1dc into each of next 8dc, dec 1dc, 1dc into next dc, turn. Mark the point between the 7th and 8th dc of the rem 14dc for back heel.
**Next row 3ch, 1dc into each dc to end. Turn.
Now dec one st at each end of next and foll alt row, then dec one st at each end of next row. Fasten off.**
Rejoin yarn to first dec row end on edge

farthest away from the 14 unworked dc, 3ch, 1dc into same row end as join, (1dc into next row end, 2dc into next row end) twice, then 1dc into each of the 6 sts along toe, then (2dc into next row end, 1dc into next row end) 3 times, 1dc into each of the 14 unworked dc, turn.
Work 2 rows straight on these dc. Fasten off.

2nd bootee
Work as for 1st bootee until eyelet hole row and foll row have been completed. Fasten off.
Next row Miss first 14 sts, (mark the point between the 7th and 8th sts), rejoin yarn to next st, 3ch, dec over next 2dc, 1dc into each of next 8dc, dec 1dc, dc into top of the 3ch. Turn.
Now work as instep of 1st bootee from ** to **
Rejoin yarn to fasten-off point of the 14 unworked sts, 3ch, 1dc into each of next 13dc, (1dc into next row end, 2dc into next row end) 3 times, 1dc into each of the 6 sts along toe edge, (2dc into next row end, 1dc into next row end) twice, 2dc into next row end. Turn.
Work 2 rows straight on these dc. Fasten off.

Finishing
Join side leg seam. Fold each bootee in half taking the marked point between the 7th and 8th dc for back heel, then join foot seam.

Ties (make 2)
Using size E hook and A double, make a ch approx 22in long. Fasten off.
Thread through eyelet holes.
Make 4 bobbles as for overalls.
Sew to each end of ties.

Mittens
Work as given for bootees until the eyelet hole row has been completed.
Next row 3ch, *1dc into next sp, 1dc into next dc, rep from * to end, working last dc into 3rd of the 4ch. Turn. 29dc.
Work 4 rows dc.
Dec row 3ch, dec 1dc, 1dc into each of next 9dc, dec 1dc, 1dc into next dc, dec 1dc, 1dc into each of next 9dc, dec 1dc, 1dc into top of 3ch. Turn. Cont to dec in this way, on next two rows working 2dc less between dec on each row.
Fasten off.

Finishing
Fold mittens in half and join side seam. Make ties and bobbles as for bootees.

Shell Pattern Outfit

Yarn with a shiny thread running through it gives a lustrous look to this ensemble. The shell pattern is complemented by the ribbed fabric of the yoke.

Sizes

The pattern is given in two sizes : 0–3 months and 6 months, or chest sizes 18in and 19in respectively.
length from center-back neck, 11[12]in
sleeve seam, 4¾[5¼]in.

Materials

Brunswick Sparkletwist Baby in the amounts specified for the individual garments
a size E crochet hook
a size F crochet hook

Jacket

3 50g balls of yarn

3 buttons
1⅛yd of ⅜in wide ribbon

Bonnet

1 50g ball of yarn
1⅛yd of ⅝in wide ribbon

Gauge

22 sts to 4in and 22 rows to 5in over yoke pat on size F hook

Jacket

Back yoke

Using size E hook make 23[26]ch for left cuff.
Base row (WS) 1hdc into 3rd ch from hook, 1hdc into each ch to end. Turn. 22[25] sts.
Commence pat.
1st row 2ch to count as first sc ; working into *back* loops only, work 1sc into each st to end. Turn.
2nd row 2ch to count as first hdc, 1hdc into each st to end. Turn.
Rep the last 2 rows until work measures 4½[5]in from beg, ending with a 2nd pat row.
Next row Work 4ch for underarm, 1sc into 3rd ch from hook, 1sc into next ch, pat to end. Turn. 25[28] sts.
Cont in pat until work measures 14[15]in from beg, ending with a 1st pat row.
Next row Pat to last 3 sts, turn and leave last 3 sts for underarm. 22[25] sts.
Cont in pat until work measures 18½[20]in from beg, ending with a 1st pat row. Fasten off.

Left front yoke

Work as given for back yoke until front measures 1 row less than back yoke to

first underarm, so ending with a 1st pat row. Fasten off.

Shape underarm

Next row Work 3ch, then pat across sts of sleeve. Turn.

Next row Pat across 22[25] sts, 1sc into each of next 3ch. Turn. 25[28] sts.

Cont in pat over all sts until front measures 3[3½]in from underarm, ending with a 1st pat row.

Shape neck

Next row Pat to last 5[6] sts, turn.

Dec one st at neck edge on next 3 rows. 17[19] sts. Work 4 rows without shaping. Fasten off.

Right front yoke

Using size E hook make 18[20]ch. Work base row as given for back yoke. 17[19] sts.

Next row (buttonhole row) 2ch, pat 1[2] sts, (2ch, miss 2 sts, pat 3 sts) 3 times, pat 0[1].

Work 2 rows in pat, then inc one st at neck edge on next 3 rows, so ending with a 2nd pat row.

Fasten off.

Shape neck

Next row Work 5[6]ch, pat across sts of front. Turn.

Next row Pat to last 5[6]ch, 1hdc into each of next 5[6]ch. Turn. 25[28] sts.

Cont in pat until front measures 3[3½]in from end of neck shaping, ending with a 1st pat row. Fasten off.

Next row Miss first 3 sts for underarm, rejoin yarn to next st, 2ch, pat to end. Turn. 22[25] sts.

Cont in pat until front measures 4½[5]in from underarm, ending with a 1st pat row.

Fasten off.

Back skirt

Using size E hook and with RS of work facing, work 50[56]sc across lower edge of back yoke. Turn.

**Next row (eyelet-hole row) 2ch, 1hdc into next st, *1ch, miss next st, 1hdc into each of next 2 sts, rep from * to end. Turn.

Next row 2ch, 1sc into each hdc and ch of previous row. Turn. 50[56]sc. Change to size F hook. Commence pat.**

1st size only

Base row 2ch, 1sc into next st, *3ch, miss next st, 1sc into each of next 3 sts, rep from * to last 4 sts, 3ch, 1sc into each of last 2 sts. Turn.

2nd size only

Base row 2ch, 1sc into first st, *3ch, miss next st, 1sc into each of next 3 sts, rep from * to last 3 sts, 3ch, miss next st, 1sc into each of last 2 sts. Turn.

Both sizes

***1st row 2ch, 1sc into next st, *5dc into 3ch sp, 1sc into center sc of 3sc, rep from * to end, finishing with 1sc into last st. Turn.

2nd row 2ch, *3ch, 1sc into each of center 3dc of group, rep from * to end, finishing with 2ch, 1dc into last st. Turn.

3rd row 3ch, 2dc into 2ch sp, *1sc into center sc of 3dc, 5dc into 3ch sp, rep from * to end, finishing with 2dc into 3ch sp, 1dc into last st. Turn.

4th row 2ch, 1sc into next dc, *3ch, 1sc into each of center 3dc of group, rep from * to end, finishing with 3ch, 1sc into each of last 2sts. Turn.

The last 4 rows form the pat. Rep them 4 times more.

1st size only

Rep 1st row once more. Fasten off.

2nd size only

Rep 1st-3rd rows inclusive once more. Fasten off.

Right front skirt

Using size E hook and with RS of work facing, work 26[29]sc across lower edge of right front yoke. Work as given for back skirt from ** to **.

1st size only

Base row Work as given for back.

2nd size only

Base row 2ch, 1sc into next st, *3ch, miss next st, 1sc into each of next 3 sts, rep from * to last 3 sts, 3ch, miss next st, 1sc into each of last 2 sts. Turn.

Both sizes

Work as given for back skirt from *** to end.

Left front skirt

Work as given for right front skirt.

Finishing

Press lightly on WS using a cool iron over dry cloth. Join shoulder and upper sleeve seams, then skirt and underarm seams.

Front and neck edging Using size E hook and with RS of work facing, work 1 row of sc up right front, around neck edge and down left front, working 3sc into each corner. Fasten off.

Using size E hook and with RS of work facing, rejoin yarn to top of right front and work around neck edge as foll : 1ch, *1sc into each of next 2 sts, 3ch, ss into first ch — picot formed, 1sc into next st, rep from * to top of left front. Fasten off.

Cuff edging Using size E hook and with RS of work facing, work 36[42]sc around cuff edge. Join with a ss into first sc.

2nd round Work in sc, dec 6 sts evenly.

3rd round Work picots as given for neck edging. Fasten off.

Sew on buttons to correspond with buttonholes. Thread ribbon through eyelet holes to tie at front.

Bonnet

Using size E hook make 68[74]ch. Work base row and pat 3 rows as given for jacket back yoke. 67[73] sts. Commence pat.

Base row 2ch, 1sc into next st, *3ch, miss 3 sts, 1sc into each of next 3 sts, rep from * to last 5 sts, 3ch, miss 3 sts, 1sc into each of last 2 sts. Turn.

Cont in pat as given for back skirt until bonnet measures 4[4½]in from beg, ending with a 2nd or 4th pat row.

Next row 1ch, 1sc into each sc and ch of previous row. Turn.

Work 3 more rows in sc.

Shape crown

1st row 2ch, 1sc into each of next 0[3] sts, (1sc into each of next 15 sts, work 2sc tog) 3 times, 1 sc into each of next 15[18] sts. Turn. 64[70] sts.

2nd and every alt row 1ch, 1sc into each st of previous row. Turn.

3rd row 2ch, 1sc into each of next 0[3] sts, (1sc into each of next 7 sts, work 2sc tog) 7 times, 1sc into each of next 0[3] sts. Turn. 57[63] sts.

5th row 2ch, 1sc into each of next 0[3] sts, (1sc into each of next 6 sts, work 2sc tog) 7 times, 1sc into each of next 0[3] sts. Turn. 50[56] sts.

7th row 2ch, 1sc into each of next 0[3] sts, (1sc into each of next 5 sts, work 2sc tog) 7 times, 1sc into each of next 0[3] sts. Turn. 43[49] sts.

Cont to dec in this way on every alt row until 8[14] sts rem.

2nd size only

Next row Work (2sc tog) 7 times.

Both sizes

Cut yarn, thread through rem 8[7] sts, draw up and fasten off securely.

Finishing

Press as given for jacket. Join seam as far as start of crown shaping.

Edging Using size E hook and with RS of work facing, work one round of sc around front and neck edges. Fasten off.

Cut ribbon in half ; make a rosette at one end of each length and sew to bonnet as shown.

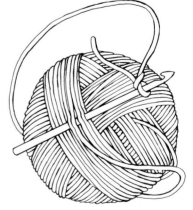

Openwork Top

An openwork pattern, ties at the wrists and sewn-on motifs are featured on this appealing top.

Sizes
The pattern is given in two sizes : 0–3 months and 1 year, or chest sizes 18in and 20in respectively.
length from center-back neck,
10½[11½]in
sleeve seam, 5½[6]in

Materials
3[4] 1¾oz balls of Bucilla Perlette
a size C crochet hook
a size E crochet hook
7 small buttons
2 motifs (optional)

Gauge
24 sts and 24 rows to 4in over sc worked on size E crochet hook

Using size E hook make 117[125]ch and work in one piece to underarm.
Base row Into 5th ch from hook work 4 dc leaving last loop of each st on hook, yo and draw through all loops, – called "1 cluster," or 1 cl, *1ch, miss 1ch, 1cl into next ch, rep from * to last 2ch, 1ch, miss 1ch, 1dc into last ch. Turn. 56[60] cl plus 1dc at each end.
1st row (RS) 4ch, miss first cl, *1dc into next ch sp between cl, 1ch, rep from * to end, 1dc into 3rd of first 4ch. Turn.
2nd row 4ch, 1cl into first ch sp, 1ch, 1cl into next ch sp, 1ch, rep from * ending * 1ch, 1cl into last ch sp, 1ch, 1dc into 3rd of first 4ch. Turn.
The last 2 rows form pat. Rep these 2 rows 8[9] times more, then first of them again.
Shape waist
Next row 2ch, *(1sc into next ch sp, 1sc into next dc) twice, insert hook into next ch sp, yo and draw loop through, insert hook into next dc, yo and draw loop through, yo and draw through all loops on hook, – called dec 1sc – , rep from * to last 2ch, sp and dc, 1sc into ch sp, 1sc into dc, 1sc into last ch sp, 1sc into 3rd of first 4ch. Turn.
Work 4[6] rows sc.
Divide for armholes
Next row 2ch, 1sc into each of next 21[22]

sc, turn.
Complete left back on these 22[23] sts.
Next row 2ch, dec 1sc, work in sc to end. Turn.
Next row 2ch, work in sc to end. Turn.
Rep last 2 rows until 12 sts rem. Fasten off.
With RS of work facing, miss first 4[5] sc for underarm, rejoin yarn to next sc, 2ch, 1sc into each of next 43[45] sc, turn.
Complete front on these 44[46] sts.
Next row 2ch, dec 1sc, work in sc to last 3sc, dec 1sc, 1sc into turning ch. Turn.
Next row 2ch, work in sc to end. Turn.
Rep last 2 rows until 30 sts rem, ending with a WS row.
Shape neck
Next row 2ch, 1sc into each of next 8sc, turn.
Dec 1sc at neck edge on every row, *at same time* dec 1sc at raglan edge as before until all sts are worked off. Fasten off.
With RS of work facing, miss first 12sc for center neck, rejoin to next sc, 2ch, 1sc into each sc to end. Complete to match first side, reversing shaping. Fasten off.
With RS of work facing, miss first 4[5] sc for underarm, rejoin yarn to next sc, 2ch, 1sc into each sc to end. Turn.
Complete to match left back, reversing shaping.

Sleeves
Using size E hook make 27[31] ch. Work base row as given for skirt.

Next row (RS) 2ch, miss first ch sp, *1sc into next cl, 1sc into next ch sp, rep from * ending with 1sc into 3rd of first 4ch. Turn. 24[28] sc.
Cont in sc, inc 1sc at each end of every 8th row until there are 30[34] sc. Cont without shaping until sleeve measures 5½[6]in from beg, ending with a WS row.
Shape top
Next row Ss over 2[3] sc, work in sc to last 2[3] sc, turn.
Dec 1sc at each end of next and every alt row until 4 sts rem. Fasten off.

Neckband
Join raglan seams. Using size C hook and with RS of work facing, work 61[65] sc around neck edge. Turn.
Next row 4ch, *1cl into next sc, 1ch, miss 1sc, rep from * to end, ending with 1dc in last sc. Fasten off.

Borders
Using size C hook and with RS of work facing, work 1 row sc along left back edge, working 2sc into end of each cl row, 2sc into each 1st pat row and 1sc into each sc row. Turn.
Next row (buttonhole row) 2ch, 1sc into each of next 2sc, 2ch, miss 2sc, * 1sc into each of next 6sc, 2ch, miss 2sc, rep from * 5 times more, work in sc to end. Turn.
Next row Work in sc to end, working 2sc into each 2ch buttonhole. Turn.
Work 2 rows sc. Fasten off.
Work button border in same way along right back edge, omitting buttonholes.

Finishing
Press sc sections only under a dry cloth with a cool iron. Join sleeve seams. Press seams. Sew on buttons. Sew on motifs to center front, if required. Using size E hook and 2 ends of yarn, make a crochet ch 24in long. Thread through neck to tie at back. Make ch 16in long in same way for each sleeve.

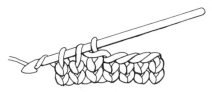

Flower-trimmed Shawl

A delicate border of blossoms and lace trims this lovely shawl, made in a random pastel yarn. The main part of the shawl is given a catherine-wheel effect with swirling lines of open-work.

Size
The shawl measures approximately 48in in diameter when pressed.

Materials
10 40g balls of Brunswick Bambini Ombre
a size C crochet hook

Gauge
26dc to 4¼in on size C hook

Main section
Work 4ch and ss into first ch to form a circle.
1st round (5ch, 1sc into circle) 8 times, ss into center of first loop. 8 loops.
2nd round 1sc into first loop, (4ch, 1sc into next loop) 7 times, 4ch, 1dc into first sc.
3rd round 2dc into first loop, (3ch, 1dc into next sc, 2dc into next loop) 7 times.
4th round (3ch, miss next dc, 1dc into each of next 2 sts, 2dc into next loop) 8 times.
5th round (3ch, miss next dc, 1dc into each of next 3 sts, 2dc into next loop) 8 times.
6th round (3ch, miss next dc, 1dc into each of next 4 sts, 2dc into next loop) 8 times.
7th round (3ch, miss next dc, 1dc into each of next 5 sts, 2dc into next loop) 8 times.
8th round (3ch, miss next dc, 1dc into each of next 6 sts, 2dc into next loop) 8 times.
Work 3 more rounds working 1 more dc between the 2dc worked into each loop, 11dc in each panel.
12th round (3ch, miss next dc, 1dc into each of next 5 sts, 3ch, miss next 2 sts, 1dc into each of next 3 sts, 2dc into next loop) 8 times.
13th round (3ch, miss next dc, 1dc into each of next 4 sts, 2dc into next loop) 16 times.
14th round (3ch, miss next dc, 1dc into each of next 5 sts, 2dc into next loop) 16 times.

15th round (3ch, miss next dc, 1dc into each of next 6 sts, 2dc into next loop) 16 times.
Work 5 rounds, working 1 more dc between the 2dc worked into each loop. 13dc in each panel.
21st round (3ch, miss next dc, leaving last loop of each on hook work 1dc into each of next 2dc, yo and draw a loop through all 3 loops on hook – 1dc decreased, 1dc into each of next 10dc, 2dc into next loop) 16 times.
22nd round (3ch, 1dc into each of next 12dc, 2dc into next loop) 16 times.
23rd round (3ch, 1dc into each of next 13dc, 3dc into next loop) 16 times.
24th round (3ch, 1dc into each of next 14dc, 2dc into next loop) 16 times.
Dec in this way on next and foll 4th round and then work 3 rounds without shaping. 32 rounds worked, 22dc in each panel.
Cont in pat, dec 1dc at beg of every panel on next and every 3rd round until 55 rounds from beg have been worked, ending with 3ch, ss into first st of next panel. 37dc in each panel.
56th round 3ch, 1dc into each of next 36 sts, 3dc into next loop (1dc into each of next 37 sts, 3dc into next loop) 15 times, ss into top of the 3ch.

Border
Start flower insertion :
57th round 11ch, 1tr into same place as ss, *4ch, miss next 4 sts, 1sc into next st, 4ch, miss next 4 sts, now work 1tr, 4ch, yo 4 times, insert hook in next st, yo and draw loop through, (yo and draw through 2 loops on hook) 5 times – called 1 triple treble, or 1 tr tr, 4ch, and 1tr all into next st, rep from * to last 9 sts, 4ch, miss next 4 sts, 1sc into next st, 4ch, miss next 4 sts, 1tr into base of 11ch, 4ch, ss into 7th of the 11ch.
58th round *4ch, leaving last loop of each on hook work 4dtr all into next tr so having 5 loops on hook, yo and draw through 4 loops on hook – petal formed ; work a petal into next sc and a petal into next tr ; now leaving last loop of each on hook work 3dtr all into next tr tr, yo and draw through first 3 loops on hook – half petal formed ; yo and draw through all 5 loops on hook, 5ch, ss into top of same tr tr that half petal was worked into, rep

from * to end, finishing ss into base of 4ch at beg of round.
59th round *Work a half petal into center of next petal group but draw through 4 loops on hook, (4ch, 1 petal into center of same group but draw through 5 loops on hook) 3 times, 4ch, ss into next ss of previous round, rep from * to end.
60th round 7ch, 1tr into top of next petal, *6ch, 1sc into top of next petal, 6ch, leaving last loop of each on hook work 1tr into next petal, 1tr tr into next ss, 1tr into top of next petal, yo and draw through all 4 loops on hook, rep from * to end, finishing with a tr into top of last petal, ss into top of 7ch.
61st round 3ch, 5dc into next 6-ch sp, *1dc into next sc, 5dc into next 6-ch sp, rep from * to end, finishing with 5dc all into last 6-ch sp, ss into top of the 3ch.
62nd round 3ch, *1dc into next st, (1ch, miss next st, 1dc into next st) twice, 1dc into next st, rep from * to last 4 sts, 1dc into next st, (1ch, miss next st, 1dc into next st) twice, ss into top of the 3ch.
63rd round 3ch, *1dc into next sp, 2dc into next dc, 1dc into next sp, 1dc into each of next 3dc, rep from * to last 5 sts, 1dc into next sp, 2dc into next dc, 1dc into next sp,
1dc into last 2dc, ss into top of the 3ch.
64th round 5ch, (1tr into same place as ss, 1ch) 4 times, 1tr into same st, *miss next 2 sts, 1sc into next st, 4ch, miss next 3 sts, 1tr into next st, 4ch, miss next 3 sts, 1sc into next st, miss next 2 sts, 1tr into next st, (1ch, 1tr into same st) 5 times, rep from * to last 11 sts, miss next 2 sts, 1sc into next st, 4ch, miss next 3 sts, 1tr into next st, 4ch, miss next 3 sts, 1sc into next st, ss into 4th of the 5ch.
65th round Ss to center of first 6-tr group, *4ch, 1tr into next single tr, (1ch and 1tr) 5 times into same single tr, 4ch, 1sc between 3rd and 4th tr of next 6-tr group, rep from * to end, ss into ss at beg of round.
66th round * (5ch, leaving last loop of each on hook work 1tr into each of next 2 sts, yo and draw through all 3 loops on hook – V formed) 3 times, 5ch, 1sc into next sc, rep from * to end, ss into base of 5ch at beg of round.
67th round Ss to top of first V, 9ch, *1tr into same st, work 1tr, 5ch, 1tr, 5ch and

1tr all into next V, 1dtr, 5ch and
1tr all into next V, rep from * to within last
2 Vs, 1tr, 5ch, 1tr, 5ch and 1tr all into next
V, 1tr, 5ch and 1tr into next V, ss into 4th
ch at beg of round.
68th round *3ch, 1sc into same st, 7ch,
miss next tr, 1sc into next tr, 3ch, 1sc into

same st, 7ch, 1sc into next tr, 3ch, 1sc
into same st, 7ch, miss next tr, 1sc into
next tr, 3ch, 1sc into same st, 7ch, 1sc
into next tr, rep from * to end, ss into base
of the 3ch.
Fasten off.

Finishing
Press shawl lightly on the wrong side,
using a cool iron over a dry cloth.

Lacy Coat

This charming little coat, featuring the ever-popular shell pattern combined with a vertical motif, is ideal for a special outing. Make it all in one color or striped.

Sizes
The pattern is given in two sizes : 0–3 months and 1 year, or chest sizes 18in and 20in respectively.
length from center back neck, 10in sleeve seam, 6in.

Materials
Phildar Pronostic in the amounts specified for the two different versions
a size E crochet hook
3 small buttons

Plain version
3 50g balls of yarn

Two-color version
2 50g balls of yarn in main color A
1 ball of contrast color B

Gauge
20 sts and 12 rows to 4in over dc on size E hook
For two-color version work as for plain version in colors as foll : yoke and sleeves in A. Skirt in stripe sequence of 2 rows B and 2 rows A throughout. Edgings in B.
Yoke (worked in one piece) Using size E hook make 62ch for neckline.

1st row Into 4th ch from hook work 1dc, 1dc into each ch to end. Turn. 60dc.

2nd row (RS) 3ch to count as first dc, 1dc into each of next 10dc, 5dc into next dc, 1dc into each of next 8dc, 5dc into next dc, 1dc into each of next 18dc, 5dc into next dc, 1dc into each of next 8dc, 5dc into next dc, 1dc into each of next 10dc, 1dc into 3rd of the 3ch. Turn.

3rd row 3ch to count as first dc, (work one pair of crossed dc by missing next dc, 1dc into next dc, 1dc into missed dc – called cr dc) 6 times, 5dc into next dc – i.e., center dc of 5dc gr in previous row – 6cr dc into next 12dc, 5dc into next dc, 11cr dc into next 22dc, 5dc into next dc, 6cr dc into next 12dc, 5dc into next dc, 6cr dc into next 12dc, 1dc into 3rd of the 3ch. Turn.

4th row 3ch to count as first dc, 1dc into each of next 14 sts, 5dc into next dc, 1dc into each of next 16 sts, 5dc into next dc, 1dc into each of next 26 sts, 5dc into next dc, 1dc into each of next 16 sts, 5dc into next dc, 1dc into each of next 14 sts, 1dc into 3rd of the 3ch. Turn.

5th row 3ch to count as first dc, 8cr dc into next 16dc, 5dc into next dc, 10cr dc into next 20dc, 5dc into next dc, 15cr dc into next 30dc, 5dc into next dc, 10 cr dc into next 20dc, 5dc into next dc, 8cr dc into next 16dc, 1dc into 3rd of the 3ch. Turn.

6th row 3ch to count as first dc, 1dc into each of next 18 sts, 5dc into next dc, 1dc into each of next 24 sts, 5dc into next dc, 1dc into each of next 34 sts, 5dc into next dc, 1dc into each of next 24 sts, 5dc into next, dc, 1dc into each of next 18 sts, 1dc into 3rd of the 3ch. Turn.

7th row 3ch to count as first dc, 10cr dc into next 20dc, 5dc into next dc, 14cr dc into next 28dc, 5dc into next dc, 19cr dc into next 38dc, 5dc into next dc, 14cr dc into next 28dc, 5dc into next dc, 10cr dc into next 20dc, 1dc into 3rd of the 3ch. Turn.

8th row 3ch to count as first dc, 1dc into each of next 23 sts, 3ch, miss next 32dc for first armhole, 1dc into each of next 44 sts, 3ch, miss next 32dc for 2nd armhole, 1dc into each of next 23 sts, 1dc into 3rd of the 3ch. Turn.

Skirt
Next row 4ch to count as first tr, 2tr into first st, *1ch, miss 2 sts, (yo, insert hook in next st, draw through a loop extending it for ⅝in) 3 times, yo and draw through all 7 loops on hook, 1ch to secure st – called rope st–, 1ch, miss 2 sts, 5tr into next st, rep from * 14 times counting each ch at underarms as one st, 1ch, miss 2 sts, 1 rope st into next st, 1ch, miss 2 sts, 3tr into 3rd of the 3ch. Turn.

Next row 4ch to count as first tr, 2tr into first st, *1ch, 1 rope st into rope st of previous row inserting hook through center of all loops, 1ch, 5tr into center st of 5tr gr below, rep from * 14 times, 1ch, 1 rope st into next rope st, 1ch, 3tr into 4th of the 4ch. Turn.
Rep last row twice more.

Next row 4ch to count as first tr, 2tr into first st, 1tr into next st, *1ch, 1 rope st into next rope st, 1ch, miss first st of 5tr gr below, 1tr into next st, 5tr into center st, 1tr into next st, rep from * 14 times, 1ch, 1 rope st into next rope st, 1ch, miss first st of last 3tr gr, 1tr into next st, 3tr into 4th of the 4ch. Turn.

Next row 4ch to count as first tr, 2tr into first st, 1tr into next st, *1ch, 1 rope st into next rope st, 1ch, 1tr into 3rd st of 7tr gr below, 5tr into center st, 1tr into next st, rep from * 14 times, 1ch, 1 rope st into next rope st, 1ch, 1tr into 3rd st of last 4tr gr, 3tr into 4th of the 4ch. Turn.
Rep last row twice more.

Next row 4ch to count as first tr, 2tr into first st, 1tr into each of next 2 sts, *1ch, 1 rope st into next rope st, 1ch, 1tr into 2nd st of 7tr gr below, 1tr into next st, 5tr into center st, 1tr into each of next 2 sts, rep from * 14 times, 1ch, 1 rope st into next rope st, 1ch, 1tr into 2nd st of 4tr gr below, 1tr into next st, 3tr into 4th of the 4ch. Turn.

Next row 4ch to count as first tr, 2tr into first st, 1tr into each of next 2 sts, *1ch, 1 rope st into next rope st, 1ch, 1tr into 3rd st of 9tr gr below, 1tr into next st, 5tr into center st, 1tr into each of next 2 sts, rep from * 14 times, 1ch, 1 rope st into next rope st, 1ch, 1tr into 3rd st of last 5tr gr, 1tr into next st, 3tr into 4th of the 4ch. Turn.
Rep last row twice more. Fasten off.

Sleeves
Using size E hook and with RS of work facing, rejoin yarn to first ch below armhole.

1st round 3ch to count as first dc, 41dc evenly around armhole. Join with a ss into 3rd of the 3ch.

2nd round 3ch to count as first dc of cr dc, work in cr dc to end. Join with a ss into 3rd of the 3ch.

3rd round 3ch to count as first dc, dec over next 2dc thus : (yo insert into next st and draw through a loop) twice, yo and draw through all 5 loops on hook, work in dc to last 2 sts, dec over next 2 sts. Join with a ss into 3rd of the 3ch.
Rep 2nd and 3rd rounds 6 times more.
Edging
Next round 4ch, miss next sp between dc, *1dc into next sp, 3ch, miss next sp, rep from * to end. Join with a ss into 2nd of the 4ch.
Fasten off.

Finishing

Do not press.

Edging Using size E hook and with RS of work facing, rejoin yarn to lower edge of right front skirt, work 36sc up right front edge to yoke, 2sc into end of 8th row of yoke, 2ch to form a button loop, miss 7th row, 4sc into end of 5th and 6th rows,

2ch, miss 4th row, 4sc into 3rd and 2nd rows, 2ch, miss first row, 1sc into ch at corner of neck, 3ch, 1sc into sp between 2nd and 3rd dc of first row of yoke, *3ch, miss next sp, 1sc into next sp, rep from * around neck, ending with 1sc into ch at corner of neck, 17sc along left front edge of yoke and 36sc down left front edge of

skirt, cont along lower edge of coat thus : (3ch, 1sc into next sp) 5 times, *1sc into next sp, (3ch, 1sc into next sp) 9 times, rep from *14 times, 1sc into next sp, (3ch, 1sc into next sp) 4 times, 3ch. Join with a ss into first ch. Fasten off.

Sew on buttons to correspond with button loops.

Two-piece Suit

Here is an outfit that is as stylish as it is practical – a pullover and matching trousers featuring boldly contrasting stripes.

Sizes

The pattern is given in three sizes : 0–3 months, 1 year and 3 years, or chest sizes 18in, 20in and 22in respectively.

sweater
length from shoulder, 11[11½:13]in
sleeve seam, 5[6:6½]in
trousers
waist to crotch, 7[8:9]in
inside leg seam, 8[9½:11½]in

Materials

5 50g balls of Bernat Saluki in main color A
2 balls of yarn in contrast color B
a size E crochet hook
a size G crochet hook
a length of in wide elastic equal to waist measurement

Gauge

18 sts and 21 rows to 4in over sc worked on size F hook

Sweater
Back

Using size F hook and B, make 47[51:55]ch.
Base row 1sc into 2nd ch from hook, 1sc into each ch to end. Turn.
Next row 1ch, 1sc into each sc to end. Turn.
Rep last row until work measures 2in from beg. Change to A and work 4 rows. Change to B and work 4 rows. Cut off B. Cont with A until work measures 5[6:6]in from beg.
Shape sleeves

Inc row 1ch, 1sc into first sc, 2sc into next sc, 1sc into each sc to within last 2sc, 2sc into next sc, 1sc into last sc. Turn.
Rep last row 9[10:11] times more.
Next row Fasten off. Make 9[12:14]ch, then work 1sc into each sc across back, make 10[13:15]ch, turn.
Next row 1sc into 2nd ch from hook, 1sc into each ch, then 1sc into each sc across back and 1sc into each ch to end. Turn. 84[96:106]sc.
Work 16[18:20] rows without shaping.

Fasten off.

Front

Work as given for back until 7[8:9] rows have been completed on sleeves.
Shape neck

Next row Work across first 31[36:41] sts, turn.
Cont on these sts until front measures same as back. Fasten off.
Miss center 22[24:26] sts for front neck, rejoin yarn to next st and work to end of row. Complete to match first side.

Neck edging

Join shoulder and upper sleeve seams. Using size C hook join A to center back neck and work 1sc into each st across back neck, 1sc into each row end down neck edge, 1sc into each sc along front neck, 1sc into each row end up side neck, then 1sc into each sc along back neck to center, turn.
Next row 1ch, 1sc into each sc all around. Turn.
Change to B, with B rep last row 4 times more.
Fasten off.
Join seams.

Cuffs (alike)

Using size E hook join A to lower edge of sleeve and work 1sc into each row end along this edge. Turn.
Next row 1ch, 1sc into each sc to end. Turn.
Change to B. Cont in sc, work 2 rows B, 2 rows A and 6 rows B.
Fasten off.
Join side and underarm seams.

Trousers
First side

Using size F hook and A, make 47[51:55]ch for waist edge.
Base row 1sc into 2nd ch from hook, 1sc into each ch to end. Turn.
Work 5 rows sc.
Shape back

Next row Ss across first 4 sts, 1ch, 1sc into each st to end.
Turn. 42[46:50] sts.
Next row Work to within last 4 sts, turn. 38[42:46] sts.
Rep last 2 rows twice more, then the first

of these 2 rows again.
Next row Work to end across all sts. Turn. 46[50:54] sts.
** Cont without shaping until work measures 7[8:9]in measured at side edge (shortest edge).
Shape crotch

Next row Fasten off. Make 5ch, work 1sc into each sc across work, make 6ch, turn.
Next row 1sc into 2nd ch from hook, 1sc into each of next 4ch, 1sc into each sc to end. 1sc into each of next 5ch.
Turn. 56[60:64]sc.
Cont in sc until leg measures 4[5½:7½]in.
Now work 4 rows B, 4 rows A and 12 rows B.
Fasten off. **

Second side

Work as given for first side to back shaping.
Next row Work to within last 4 sts, turn.
Next row Ss across first 4 sts, 1ch, work to end. Turn.
Rep last 2 rows twice more.
Next row Work to end across all sts. Now work as given for first side from ** to **.

Finishing

Join waist to crotch seam, then join inside leg seams. Work herringbone casing over elastic on WS of waist.

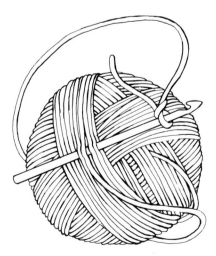

Three little Smocks

Three pretty variations on the smock theme: one with sleeves and two – striped and plain – without, all made in a fine, soft yarn.

Size
The patterns are sized to fit a baby 0–6 months old, or chest size up to 19in.
length from shoulder, sleeved smock, 11¼in, excluding contrast edging
sleeve seam, 6in
length from shoulder, sleeveless smocks, 10¾in, excluding edging

Materials
Pingouin Confortable Fin 4 ply in the amounts specified for the individual garments
a steel size 5 crochet hook
a steel size 1 crochet hook

Sleeved smock
2 50g balls of yarn

a small amount of yarn in a contrasting color for edging and ties

Sleeveless smocks
1 50g ball of yarn in color A
1 50g ball of yarn in color B

Gauge
24 sts and 12 rows to 4in over dc on a steel size 5 hook

Smock with sleeves
Note: to make the smock striped, work every two rows in a contrasting color.

Front
Using size 5 hook make 58ch. Work 1dc into 4th ch from hook, 1dc into each ch to end, 56 sts.
Work 20 rows dc inc one st at each end of every row. 96 sts.
Skirt should measure approximately 7in. Fasten off.

Bodice
Ret to ch at beg of skirt. Miss first 7ch for armhole. With RS facing, using size 5 hook, rejoin yarn to 8th ch and work a row of sc, leaving last 7ch for second armhole. 44 sts. Cont in sc for 3in.

Shape neck
Work across first 16sc on next row, then turn and work on these sts only.
Dec 1 st at beg of next row for neck edge, then cont in sc to end of row. Turn. Cont to dec 1 st at beg of every alt row in the same way until 11 sts remain. Fasten off.
Ret to sts at center of bodice.
With RS of front facing, miss first 12 sts and rejoin yarn to next sc.
Complete other side of neck to match first, dec 1 st at neck edge on every alt row, until 11 sts rem. Fasten off.

Right back
Using size 5 hook make 29ch. Work 1st row as given for front. 27 sts. Inc 1 st at

beg of next row. Inc 1 st at same edge on every row, keeping other edge straight for center back opening, until skirt measures the same as front skirt. 47 sts. Fasten off.

Bodice
Ret to ch at beg of skirt. With RS facing and using size 1 hook, rejoin yarn to 8th chain from shaped edge, leaving first 7 ch for armhole. Work in sc to end of row. 22 sts.
Cont without shaping until bodice measures $3\frac{1}{8}$in from beg, ending at armhole edge.

Shape neck
Work across first 13 sc on next row, turn and leave rem sts for back neck. Dec 1 st at beg of next and every foll row until 11 sts rem and work measures same as front to shoulder. Fasten off.

Left back
Work in the same way as right back, reversing shaping.

Sleeves
Join shoulder seams using backstitch. Using size 5 hook and with RS of front facing, rejoin yarn to inside armhole at shaped side edge. Work 1 row of sc up one side of yoke to inside edge of armhole. 58 sts. Turn. Work 2 rows in dc on these sts.
Cont in dc dec 1 st at beg of every row until sleeve measures $7\frac{1}{2}$in from beg. Fasten off. Work 2nd sleeve in same way on other side of yoke.

Finishing
Darn in all loose ends of yarn on WS. Press lightly.
With WS facing, join top edges of sleeves to armholes at top of skirt, using a flat seam.
Join side and sleeve seams using backstitch.

Edging
Using main color and size 5 hook and with RS of left back facing, join yarn to corner and work a row of sc all around, up right back, around neck and down left back to corner, working 3 sc into each corner and missing 1 st at each corner of inside neck. Fasten off.

Contrast edging and ties
With RS facing join contrast color yarn to same corner as before.
Work 1 row sc all around hem and up back edge to point where skirt is joined to bodice, work 65ch, then work 1 ss into each ch just worked, back to edge again, to form first tie.
Cont in sc to first neck edge corner, then

work another tie in the same way. Cont in sc around neck without missing 1 st at inside neck edges, to next back edge corner. Work another tie in same way at this corner. Complete edging working another tie in same way where yoke joins skirt. Fasten off. Darn in all ends on WS.

Sleeveless smocks
Note: to make the striped version, work two rows in each color down skirt, ending by working one row in the first color used. Work the yoke all in one color.

Front skirt
Using size 5 hook and A, make 58ch. Work 1dc into 4th ch from hook, 1dc into each ch to end. Turn. 56dc. Work 20 more rows in dc, inc 1 st at beg of every row; 76 sts. Draw yarn through last loop and fasten off.

Front yoke
Ret to ch at beg of skirt.
With RS facing, using B and size 1 hook, rejoin yarn to 8th ch from side edge, leaving first 7ch for armhole. Work 1ch, then 1 sc into each ch, working last sc into 8th ch from end, leaving last 7ch for second armhole.
Cont in sc on these sts for $2\frac{1}{2}$in.
Work across first 13 sc, turn and work on these sts only for $1\frac{3}{4}$in.

Shape neck
Fasten off. Ret to sts at neck edge. Miss first 18 sts for center neck. Rejoin yarn to next sts and complete to match first side. Draw yarn through and fasten off.

Back skirt
Work as for front skirt.

Back yoke
Work as for front, but work for 3in before shaping neck and work for $1\frac{1}{4}$in only for neck.

Finishing
Darn loose ends into WS of work. Press pieces lightly.
Join side seams using a flat seam.

Edging and shoulder ties
Using size 5 hook, B and with RS facing, join yarn to underarm at side seam. Work a row of sc around armhole to shoulder. Work 65ch at corner of shoulder, turn and ss into each ch just worked, back to shoulder to make the first tie. Work in sc to next corner and work another tie in same way. Cont to work around neck in sc, missing 1 st at inside neck corners, then work across shoulder and make a tie at each of the corners as before. Work down armhole and around back in the same way, making 1 tie at each corner on shoulders as before. Join last sc to the first sc worked with a ss. Draw yarn through and fasten off. Darn in any loose ends on the WS of work.

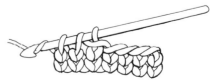

Two Bonnets

Two bewitching bonnets to make a little girl feel extra-special, both with trimming in contrasting colors.

Size

The patterns are sized to fit a child 1 to 2 years old.

Materials

Bonnet with flower trim

1 50g ball of Brunswick Wil o' Wisp in main color A
1 ball each of contrast colors B and C
a size E crochet hook

Bonnet with scalloped edging

1 50g ball of Phildar Sagittaire in main color A
1 ball each of contrast colors B and C
a size F crochet hook

Gauge

For Brunswick Wil o' Wisp: 20 sts and 10 rows to 4in over dc on size E hook.
For Phildar Sagittaire: 10 groups to 3in and 9 rows to 4in over pat on size F hook.

Bonnet with flower trim

Using size E hook and A, make 4ch. Join with a ss to first ch to form circle.
1st round 3ch to count as first dc, 13dc into circle. Join with a ss to 3rd of first 3ch. 14 sts.
2nd round 3ch, 1dc into same place, 2dc into each dc to end. Join with a ss to 3rd of first 3ch. 28 sts.
3rd round 3ch, 1dc into same place, 1dc into next dc, *2dc into next dc, 1dc into next dc, rep from * to end. Join with a ss to 3rd of first 3ch. 42 sts.
4th round 3ch, 1dc into same place, 1dc into each of next 2dc, *2dc into next dc, 1dc into each of next 2dc, rep from * to end. Join with a ss to 3rd of first 3ch. 56 sts.
5th round 3ch, 1dc into same place, 1dc into each of next 3dc,*2dc into next dc, 1dc into each of next 3dc, rep from * to end. Join with a ss to 3rd of first 3ch. 70 sts.
6th round 3ch, 1dc into same place, 1dc into each of next 9dc, *2dc into next dc, 1dc into each of next 9dc, rep from * to end. Join with a ss to 3rd of first 3ch. 77 sts.

Cont to inc 7 sts in each round twice more. 91 sts. Work 1 round without shaping.
10th round 3ch, 1dc into same place, 1dc into each dc to end. 92 sts.
Work 4 rounds without shaping. Break off yarn.

Ear shaping

Next row Miss first 20dc, rejoin yarn into next dc, 1ch, 1hdc into each of next 2dc, 1dc into each of next 5dc, 1hdc into each of next 2dc, 1sc into next dc. Break off yarn.
Next row With RS of work facing, rejoin yarn to 2nd st before beg of last row, 1ch, 1sc into next st, 1hdc into each of next 2 sts, 1dc into each of next 7 sts, 1hdc into each of next 2 sts, 1sc into each of next 2 sts. Break off yarn.
Next row With RS of work facing, rejoin yarn to first st before beg of last row, 1ch, work 2sc, 2hdc, 3dc, 2dc into next st, 3dc, 2hdc, 3sc. Break off yarn.
With RS of work facing, rejoin yarn to 31st st before end of round and work second ear shaping in same way.
With RS of work facing, rejoin yarn to beg of round, 3ch, work 1dc into each dc all around, inc one dc in center of each ear shaping. Join with a ss to 3rd of first 3ch.
Rep last round once more. Break off yarn.
With RS of work facing, miss first 6 sts, rejoin yarn to next st, 3ch, 1dc into each dc to last 6 sts. Fasten off.
Rejoin yarn to beg of round, 1ch, 1sc into each st all around. Join with a ss to first ch. Fasten off.

Ties (make 2)

Using size E hook and A, make a length of ch 14in long and work 1 row sc along ch. Fasten off.
Sew to center of each ear piece.

Flower

Inner part

Using size E hook and A, make 4ch. Join with a ss to first ch to form circle.
1st round 1ch, 14sc into circle. Join with a ss to first ch. 15 sts.
2nd round *5ch, miss 2sc, 1sc into next sc, rep from * 4 times more. Join with a ss to first of 5ch.
3rd round Into each 5ch loop, work 1sc, 1hdc, 2dc, 1hdc, 1sc, ending with a ss into

first sc. Fasten off.

Outer part

Using size E hook and A, make 6ch. Join with a ss to first ch to form circle.
1st round 3ch, 23dc into circle. Join with a ss to 3rd of first 3ch. 24sts.
2nd round *3ch, miss 2dc, 1sc into next dc, rep from * 6 times more, 3ch, miss 2dc, Join with a ss to first of first 3ch. 8 loops.
3rd round Into each loop work 1sc, 1ch, 3dc, 1ch, 1sc. Join with a ss to ss at end of last round.
4th round *5ch, 1sc into back of sc on 2nd round, rep from * 7 times more, omitting last sc. Join with a ss to first 5ch. Break off A. Join in B to a 5ch loop.
5th round Using B, work 1sc, 1ch, 6dc, 1ch, 1sc into each loop. Join with a ss to ss at end of last round.
6th round *6ch, 1sc into back of sc on 4th round, rep from * 7 times more, omitting last sc. Join with a ss to first of first 6ch. Break off B. Join in C to a 6ch loop.
7th round Using C, work 1sc, 1ch, 8dc, 1ch, 1sc into each 8ch loop. Join with a ss to ss at end of last round. Fasten off.
Sew both parts of flower at one side of bonnet over ear.

Bonnet with scalloped edging

Small flower motif

Using size F hook and A, make 4ch. Join with a ss to first ch to form circle.
1st round 1ch, 14sc into circle. Join with a ss to first ch. 15 sts.
2nd round *5ch, miss 2sc, ss into next sc, rep from * 4 times more, working last ss into ss at end of last round.
3rd round Into each 5ch loop work 1sc, 1hdc, 2dc, 1hdc, 1sc. Join with a ss to first sc.
Fasten off.

Large flower motif

Using size F hook and A, make 6ch. Join with a ss to first ch to form circle.
1st round 3ch, 23dc into circle. Join with a ss to 3rd of first 3ch. 24 sts.
2nd round *3ch, miss 2dc, 1sc into next dc, rep from * 6 times more, 3ch, miss 2dc. Join with a ss to ss at end of last round.
3rd round Into each 3ch loop work 1sc, 1ch, 3dc, 1ch, 1sc. Join with a ss to ss at

end of last round.

4th round *5ch, 1sc into back of sc on 2nd round, rep from * all around. Join with a ss to ss at end of last round. Break off A. Join in B to 5ch loop.

5th round Using B, into each 5ch loop work 1sc, 1ch, 4dc, 1ch, 1sc. Join with a ss to first sc.

6th round *6ch, 1sc into back of sc on 4th round, rep from * to end. Join with a ss to ss at end of last round.

7th round Into each 6ch loop work 1sc, 1ch, 6dc, 1ch, 1sc. Join with a ss to ss at end of last round.

8th round *7ch, 1sc into back of sc on 6th round, rep from * to end. Join with a ss to ss at end of last round. Break off B. Join in C to 7ch loop.

9th round Using C, into each 7ch loop work 1sc, 1ch, 3dc, 2tr, 3dc, 1ch, 1sc. Join with a ss to ss at end of last round.

10th round As 8th round, working into back of sc on 8th round.

11th round Into each 7ch loop work 1sc, 1ch, 3dc, 3tr, 3dc, 1ch, 1sc. Join with a ss to ss to end of last round. Fasten off. Sew small flower into center of large flower.

Bonnet

Using size F hook, A and with RS of work facing, rejoin yarn to sc between 2 petals, 1ch, *into lower edge of each petal work 4ss, 1sc, 4ss, 1sc into join between petals, rep from * all around flower, ending with a ss into first 1ch. 80 sts.

Next round 1sc into each ss all around, omitting sc. Join with a ss to first sc. 64 sts.

Next row Ss over first 5 sts and into 6th st, 3ch, yo, insert hook into next st and draw up a loop, yo, insert hook into next st and draw up a loop, yo and draw through 4 loops, yo and draw through rem 2 loops, *yo, insert hook into same st as before and draw up a loop, yo, insert hook into next st and draw up a loop, yo and draw through 4 loops, yo and draw through rem 2 loops, rep from * 50 times more, 1dc into next st, turn.

Next row 3ch, yo, insert hook between dc and first group and draw up a loop, yo, insert hook between first and second groups and draw up a loop, yo and draw through 4 loops, yo and draw through rem 2 loops, *yo, insert hook into same place and draw up a loop, yo, insert hook between next 2 groups, yo and complete as previous group, rep from * to end, 1dc into 3rd of first 3ch. Rep last row 7 times more.
Turn.

Next row Ss into first 3 sts, 1 sc into each of next 2 sts, 1hdc into next st, pat to last 6 sts, 1hdc into next st, 1sc into each of next 2 sts, 3 ss into last 3 sts. Fasten off.

Finishing

Bonnet edging Using size F hook, C and with RS of work facing, rejoin yarn to front corner, miss one sp between groups, 9dc into next sp, *miss 3 sps, 9dc into next sp, rep from * to end, miss last sp, ss into corner. Break off C. Join in B to 4th sp from corner, noting that you should press first row of shells down toward you so that you are working behind them and that row in B will be under row in C when bonnet is worn, work 9dc into middle sp between each shell of previous row, ending with ss into 4th sp from end.

Neck edging Using size F hook, A and with RS of work facing, rejoin yarn to front corner, work 1sc into each sp around neck edge, turn.

Next row *3ch, 1dc into base of these 3ch, miss 1sc, 1sc into next sc, rep from * to end. Fasten off.

Make a twisted cord and thread through holes around neck to tie at front.

Border-trim Robe

Just right for story time or for saying goodnight to her favorite doll – a warm robe with a decorative border.

Sizes

The pattern is given in three sizes : 0–3 months, 2 years and 5 years, or chest sizes 18in, 21in and 24in respectively. *length from shoulder,* 18[21 :24]in *sleeve seam,* 6[7 :8¼]in

Materials

4[5 :5] 50g balls of Bernat Saluki in main color A
1 [1 :2] balls of yarn in contrast color B
1 [1 :1] ball each of contrast colors C and D
a size E crochet hook
a size F crochet hook
5 buttons

Gauge

18 sts and 10 rows to 4in over dc worked on size F hook

Back and fronts

Using size F hook and A, make 120[139 :158]ch. Beg at lower edge and work in one piece to underarm.
1st row Into 4th ch from hook work 1dc, 1dc into each ch to end. Turn. 118[137 :156]dc.
2nd row 3ch to count as first dc, miss first dc, 1dc into each dc to end. Turn. Rep 2nd row 4[6 :8] times more.
Shape skirt
Next row 3ch, work 9[11 :12]dc, *work 2dc tog, 22[26 :30]dc, rep from * 3 times more, work 2dc tog, 10[11 :13]dc. Turn. 113[132 :151]sts.
Work 3 rows without shaping.
Next row 3ch, work 9[10 :12]dc, *work 2dc tog, 21[25 :29]dc, rep from * 3 times more, work 2dc tog, 9[11 :12]dc. Turn. 108[127 :146]sts.
Work 3 rows without shaping.
Next row 3ch, work 8[10 :11]dc, *work 2dc tog, 20[24 :28]dc, rep from * 3 times more, work 2dc tog, 9[10 :12]dc. Turn. 103[122 :141] sts.
Work 3 rows without shaping. Cont dec in this way on next and every foll 4th row until 88[102 :116] sts rem. Cont without shaping until work measures 11¾[14¼ :16½]in from beg.

Divide for armholes

Next row 3ch, work 18[21 :24]dc, turn. Complete this front first. Dec one st at beg of next row and at same edge on next 2[3 :4] rows. 16[18 :20] sts. Cont without shaping until armhole measures 2[2¼ :2¾]in from beg, ending at armhole edge.
Shape neck
Next row Pat to last 2[3 :4] sts, turn.
Next row Ss over first 2 sts, pat to end. Turn.
Dec one st at neck edge on next 4 rows, then cont without shaping if necessary until armhole measures 4¼[5 :5½]in from beg. Fasten off.
Return to where work was left, miss first 4[5 :6] sts for underarm, rejoin yarn to next st, 3ch, work 41[47 :53]dc, turn. Complete back. Dec one st at each end of next 3[4 :5] rows. 36[40 :44] sts. Cont without shaping until back measures same as front to shoulder. Fasten off.
Return to where work was left, miss first 4[5 :6] sts for underarm, rejoin yarn to next st, 3ch, pat to end. Complete to match first front, reversing shaping.

Sleeves

Using size F hook and A, make 31[34 :37] ch. Work first 2 rows as given for back and fronts. 29[32 :35]dc. Cont in dc, inc one st at each end of next and every foll 3rd row until there are 35[40 :45]dc. Work 1 row.

Shape top

Next row Ss over first 2[3 :3] sts, pat to last 2[3 :3] sts, turn.
Dec one st at each end of next 4[5 :5] rows, then 2 sts at each end of next 3[3 :4] rows. 11[12 :13] sts. Fasten off.

Pockets (make 2)

Using size E hook and A, make 18ch.
1st row Into 3rd ch from hook work 1sc, 1sc into each ch to end. Break off A. 17sc.
2nd row With RS facing, join in B, 4ch, miss 1sc, keeping last loop of each st on hook work 3dc into next sc, yo and draw through all 4 loops on hook – called 1 cl–, 1ch, rep from * 6 times more, miss 1sc, 1dc into last sc. Break off B.
3rd row With RS facing, join in C, 3ch, 1cl into first 1ch sp, *1ch, miss 1sc, 1cl into

next sc, rep from *6 times more, 1dc into top of dc of last row. Break off C.
4th row With RS facing, join in D, 4ch, miss first 1cl, *1cl into next 1ch sp, 1ch, rep from * 6 times more, 1dc into top of dc of last row. Break off D.
Rep 3rd, 4th and 3rd rows once more, working in B, C and D. With RS of work facing, join in B, 1ch, work 1sc into each sc to end, then work a row of crab st (sc worked from left to right). Fasten off.

Finishing

Press lightly under a dry cloth with a cool iron. Join shoulder and sleeve seams. Set in sleeves.
Edging Using size E hook, A and with RS of work facing, rejoin yarn at center back of lower edge and work in sc all around edges, working 1sc into each st along lower edge and approx 3sc into every 2 rows up front edge. Join with a ss to first sc. Break off A.
Next round With RS facing, join in B to ss, 4ch, miss 1sc, *1cl into next sc, 1ch, miss 1sc, rep from * all around, inc at each corner at bottom and top of front edges by working (1cl, 1ch, 1cl) into sc at corners. Join with a ss to 3rd of first 4ch. Break off B.
Next round Join in C to ss at end of last round, 3ch, 1cl into first 1ch sp, *1ch, 1cl into next 1ch sp, rep from * all around, inc at corners as before. Break off C.
Next round Join in D to ss at end of last round, 4ch, 1cl into next 1ch sp, noting that this is after the first 1cl in C, *1ch, 1cl into next 1ch sp, rep from * all around, inc at corners as before. Break off D.
Next round Join in B to ss at end of last round, 1ch, *1sc into 1ch sp, 1sc into 1cl, rep from * all around, still inc at corners. Join with a ss to first 1ch.
Do not turn but work a row of crab st all around, as given for pockets. Fasten off. Work around sleeve edges in same way. Sew on pockets. Sew on buttons ; use holes in border for buttonholes.

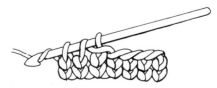

Dress and Hat

A delicate shell pattern forms the skirt of this charming little dress and the brim of the matching hat. Make it either in solid colors or in the random yarn shown here (available by mail order from England; see page 184).

Sizes
The pattern is given in three sizes: 0–3 months, 1 year and 3 years, or chest sizes 18, 20 and 22in respectively.
length from shoulder (adjustable), 15[15:16]in

Materials
2[2:3] 1¾oz balls of Bucilla Perlette – solid colors only – or 3[3:4] 25g balls of Twilley's Random Lyscordet – in main color A
1[1:2] ball each of contrasting colors B and C in Perlette, or 1[1:2] balls each of B and C in the Lyscordet (Lyscordet colors shown are: A – R69, B – 22 and C – 27)
a size C crochet hook
a size E crochet hook
an 8[10:10]in zipper
2yd of narrow ribbon

Gauge
20 sts and 14 rows to 4in over dc worked on size C hook

Dress
Bodice
Using size C hook and A, make 108[116:124]ch. Work in one piece to underarm.
1st row (RS) Into 4th ch from hook work 1dc, 1dc into each ch to end. Turn. 106[114:122]dc.
Cont in dc until work measures 2[3:4]in from beg, ending with a WS row.
Divide for armholes
Next row 3ch, 1dc into each of next 22[24:26]dc, turn.
Complete left back first. Dec one dc at armhole edge on every row 5 times in all. 18[20:22]dc. Cont without shaping until armhole measures 3[3:4]in from beg, ending at armhole edge.
Shape shoulder
Next row Pat over first 9[10:11]dc. Fasten off.
With RS of work facing, miss first 7dc for underarm, rejoin yarn to next st, 3ch, 1dc into each of next 45[49:53]dc, turn. Dec one st at each end of next 5 rows. 36[40:44]dc. Cont without shaping until armholes measure 3 rows less than back to shoulder ending with a WS row.
Shape neck
Next row Pat over first 9[10:11]dc, turn. Work 2 rows dc. Fasten off.
With RS of work facing, miss 18[20:22]dc for center front neck, rejoin yarn to next dc, pat to end. Complete to match first side.
With RS of work facing miss next 7dc for underarm, rejoin yarn to next st, 3ch, 1dc into each dc to end. Turn. Complete to match left back, reversing shaping.

Skirt
Using size E hook and A, rejoin yarn to commencing ch of bodice.
1st row (eyelet hole) 4ch to count as first dc and 1ch sp, miss 1dc, 1dc into next dc, *miss 1dc, 1ch, 1dc into next dc, rep from * to end. Turn. Do not break off A. Join in B.
2nd row Using B, 3ch to count as first dc, * into next ch sp work (2dc, 2ch, 2dc) rep from * to end, 1dc into 3rd of first 3ch. Turn. Do not break off B. Join in C.

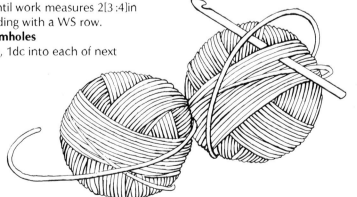

3rd row Using C, 3ch to count as first dc, * into next 2ch sp work (2dc, 2ch, 2dc) rep from * to end, 1dc into 3rd of first 3ch. Turn.
The 3rd row forms pat. Rep 3rd row 16 times more or to required length, working in stripes of 1 row A, 1 row B and 1 row C throughout.

Finishing
Join shoulder seams. Do not press.
Edging Using size C hook, A and with RS of work facing, work 2 rows sc around neck and armholes. Fasten off. Join back seam, leaving opening for zipper. Sew in zipper. Thread ribbon through eyelet holes at waist to tie at front.

Hat
Using size C hook and A, make 6ch. Join with a ss to first ch to form circle.
1st round 3ch to count as first dc, 11dc into circle. Join with a ss to 3rd of first 3ch.
2nd round 3ch, 1dc into first dc, 2dc into each dc to end. Join with a ss to 3rd of first 3ch. 24dc.
3rd round 3ch, 1dc into first dc, 1dc into each of next dc, * 2dc into next dc, 1dc into next dc, rep from * to end. Join with a ss to 3rd of first 3ch. 36dc.
4th round 3ch, 1dc into first dc, 1dc into each of next 2dc, * 2dc into next dc, 1dc into each of next 2dc, rep from * to end. Join with a ss to 3rd of first 3ch. 48dc.
Cont inc 12 sts in this way on every round until there are 84dc. Work 9 more rounds in dc without shaping. Change to size E hook.
Next round (eyelet hole) 4ch to count as first dc and 1ch sp, miss 1dc, *1dc into next dc, 1ch, miss 1dc, rep from * to end. Join with a ss to 3rd of first 4ch. Do not break off A. Join in B.
Next round Using B, 3ch (1dc, 2ch, 2dc) into first ch sp, * (2dc, 2ch, 2dc) into next ch sp, rep from * to end. Join with a ss to 3rd of first 3ch, then ss across to center of first 2ch sp. Break off B. Join in C. Rep last round using C and A. Fasten off.

Finishing
Block or press according to yarn used. Thread ribbon through eyelet holes to tie at center back.

Dress and Headscarf

Simple lines combine with a feminine lacy pattern in this smart little dress with its matching headscarf.

Sizes
The pattern is given in two sizes : 1 year and 3 years, or chest sizes 20in and 22in respectively.
length from shoulder, 15¾[17]in

Materials
2 50g balls of Pingouin Perlé Fin in main color A
2 balls of yarn in contrast color B
a size C crochet hook
one button

Gauge
4 pats and 14 rows to 4in on size C hook

Dress
Front
Using size C hook and A, make 86[92]ch.
1st row Into 3rd ch from hook work 1sc, 1sc into each ch to end. Turn. 85[91] sts.
2nd row (RS) 4ch, miss 3sc, *yo, insert hook into next sc and draw through a loop, yo and draw through first 2 loops on hook (yo, insert hook into same sc and draw through a loop, yo and draw through first 2 loops on hook) twice, yo and draw through all 4 loops on hook – called "group" or gr – 3ch, miss 2sc, 1sc into next sc, 3ch, miss 2sc, rep from * to end omitting 3ch, miss 2sc at end of last rep. Turn.
3rd row Working 3ch to count as first st work 1gr into first sc, *3ch, 1sc into next gr, 3ch, 1gr into next sc, rep from * ending with last gr into 2nd of 4ch. Turn.
4th row Join in B. 4ch, *1gr into next sc, 3ch, 1sc into next gr, 3ch, rep from * omitting 3ch at end of last rep. Turn.
5th row With B as 3rd.
The last 2 rows form the pat. Cont in stripe sequence of 2 rows A and 2 rows B, rep them until 9[11] rows have been worked from beg.
Next row 4ch, 1gr into next sc, (3ch, 1sc into next gr, 3ch, 1gr into next sc) 3 times, *1ch, 1sc into next gr, 1ch, 1gr into next sc,* (3ch, 1sc into next gr, 3ch, 1gr into next sc) 5[6] times, rep from * to * once more, pat to end.
Turn.

Next row Working 3ch to count as first st work 1gr into first sc, (3ch, 1sc into next gr, 3ch, 1gr into next sc) 3 times, 3ch, 1sc into next gr, *1gr into next sc, 3ch, 1sc into next gr* (3ch, 1gr into next sc, 3ch, 1sc into next gr) 5[6] times, rep from * to * once more, pat to end. Turn.
Next row 4ch, (1gr into next sc, 3ch, 1sc into next gr, 3ch) 3 times, 1gr into gr at center of dec, (3ch, 1sc into next gr, 3ch, 1gr into next sc) 4[5] times, 3ch, 1sc into next gr, 3ch, 1gr into gr at center of dec, 3ch, 1sc into next gr, pat to end. Turn.
Next row Pat to end. Turn. 12[13] pats. Pat 14 more rows, then rep the 4 dec rows, keeping the decs in line above previous ones. 10[11] pats. Cont without shaping until work measures 11¾[12½]in from beg, ending with a WS row.
Shape armholes
Next row Miss first gr, sc and next gr, rejoin yarn to next sc, working 3ch to count as first st work 1gr into same sc, pat to within 2nd sc from last, ending with 1gr into this sc. Turn. 7[8] pats. Cont without shaping until armholes measure 3[3¼]in from beg, ending with a WS row.

Shape neck
Next row Working 3ch to count as first st work 1gr into first sc, 3ch, 1sc into next gr, 3ch, 1gr into next sc, 3ch, 1sc into next gr, turn.
Cont on these sts until armhole measures 4[4¼]in from beg, ending at armhole edge.
Shape shoulder
Next row Ss into first gr, 3ch, 1sc into next sc, 3ch, 1hdc into next gr. Fasten off. With RS of work facing, miss 3[4]gr in center for front neck, rejoin yarn to next gr, 4ch, pat to end. Turn.
Complete to match first side, reversing shaping.

Back
Work as given for front until armhole shaping has been completed. Cont without shaping until armholes measure ¾[1⅛]in from beg, ending with a WS row. Mark center st of work with a colored thread.

Divide for opening
Next row Pat to marker, turn.
Cont on these sts until armhole measures

same as front to shoulder, ending at armhole edge.
Shape shoulder
Next row Ss over first sc and gr, 3ch, 1sc into next sc, 3ch, 1sc into next gr, 3ch, 1gr into next sc. Fasten off.
With RS of work facing, rejoin yarn to center st, pat to end. Turn.
Complete to match first side, reversing shaping.

Finishing
Do not press. Join shoulder and side seams.
Neck edging Using size C hook, A and with RS of work facing, work a row of sc around neck edge. Complete with a row in pat at 2nd row of front.
Complete armholes in the same way.
Sew button to top of back opening and make a loop on other side to correspond.

Headscarf
Using size C hook and A, make 99ch.
1st row Join in B. Into 6th ch from hook work 1gr, 3ch, miss 2ch, 1sc into next ch, *3ch, miss 2ch, 1gr into next ch, 3ch, miss 2ch, 1sc into next ch, rep from * to end. Turn. 16 pats.
2nd row As 3rd row of dress front.
3rd row With A as 4th row of dress front.
4th row Ss to first gr, 4ch, 1gr into next sc, pat to end, finishing with 1sc into last gr, turn.
Cont in pat and stripe sequence of 2 rows B and 2 rows A throughout, dec ½ pat at each end of every foll alt row until 1 pat rem. Fasten off.
Front edging
Using size C hook, A and with RS of work facing, work 1 row of pat along front edge.

Finishing
Do not press. Cut rem yarn into lengths of approx 5½in and knot a fringe along both shaped edges. Trim fringe.

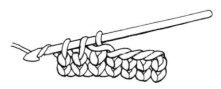

SEWING

Quilted Portable Bed

This sturdy portable bed, made with a firm base and soft padding, is perfect for transporting a small baby with a minimum of fuss. For best effect make the lining and outsides in contrasting colors.

Size
The finished bed measures 29in long and 12in wide.

Materials
a piece of ¼in thick particle board, 29 by 12in
a coping saw
sandpaper in various grades
a piece of ⅜in foam, 29 by 12in
2¼yd of 48in wide reversible printed, quilted fabric (Fabric A)
⅞yd of 48in wide color-coordinated printed fabric (Fabric B)
1⅛yd of 37in wide heavyweight polyester batting
18in metal, heavy-duty zipper
½yd of 2in wide white eyelet lace
⅝yd of 1in wide bias binding to match Fabric A
paper for making patterns

Making the portable bed
Round off the corners of the piece of particleboard as shown. First mark two points the distance indicated from each upper corner. Join each two points with a curved line (use a plate or other curved object as a guide). Using the coping saw, cut away the corners along the curved lines. Smooth the edges with sandpaper. Round the other corners very slightly with sandpaper.(Fig. 1)

Using the board as your pattern, draw, then cut the following pieces: one piece of foam, the same size as the board, for the mattress; two pieces of Fabric B, 1¼in larger than the board on the top and side edges and 4in longer at the base, for the mattress cover; one piece of Fabric A, 1¼in larger than the board on all sides, for the base; one piece of quilted fabric, ⅝in larger than the board on all sides, for the top cover. Mark the center points A and B on the base piece.

To make the pattern for the sides, measure the distance from A to B on the quilted base piece – going around the edge, not straight down the middle – and add 1¼in to this figure for seam allowances. From paper cut a strip to this length, 8in wide. Shape this pattern as shown, so that base and sides are 5in deep and the top slopes up to 8in. Check that the pattern fits around the side of the base from A to B, plus seam allowances. (Fig. 2)

Using this pattern cut four side pieces in Fabric A and two pieces in batting.

For the handles cut two strips of Fabric A, each 43 by 6in.

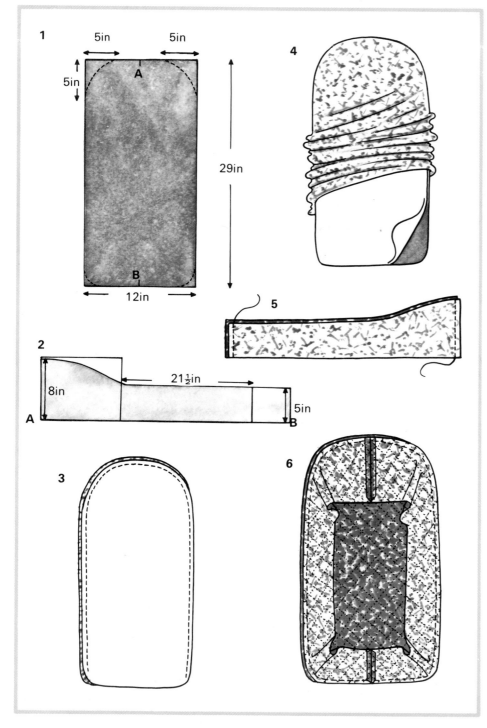

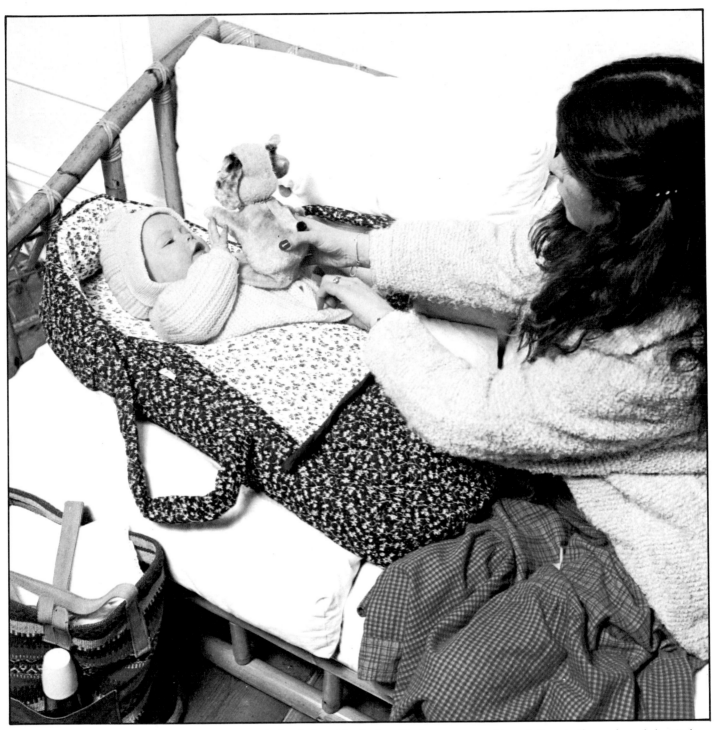

Place the two mattress cover pieces (Fabric B) together, right sides facing. Pin, baste and stitch along top and side edges, taking ⅝in seam allowance. Trim the seams. (Fig. 3)

Turn up a small double hem on the raw edges; pin, and topstitch the hem in place. Turn the cover right side out.

Place the piece of foam on one side of the board. Slip the mattress cover over board and foam. Tuck in the excess fabric at the lower end to envelop the board and hold the foam in place. Both the cover and the foam can easily be removed for washing. (Fig. 4)

Place two quilted side pieces together

with the darker sides facing. Pin, baste and stitch the ends together, taking ⅝in seam allowance. Press seams open. This makes the outer side of the bed. (Fig. 5)

Pin, baste and stitch this outer side to the quilted base, darker sides together, around the outer edge, matching the end seams to points A and B on the base. (Fig. 6)

Pin, baste and stitch the two handle strips together, darker sides facing, to form one long strip. (Fig. 7)

Fold the strip in half lengthwise (darker side inside). Pin, baste and stitch along the long side, ⅝in from the edge. (Fig. 8). Trim seam allowances and turn the strip right

side out. Turn in the ends and slipstitch them closed. Place one end on top of the other and zigzag stitch twice to form a strong join.

Pin and baste the handle in place on the base and sides (Fig. 9). When held by the handles the empty bed should slope gently downward at the foot, to compensate for the weight of the baby's head. If possible, carefully test the balance with the baby in the bed, and reposition the handles if necessary, so that the bed will be horizontal in use.

Stitch the handles in place securely at sides and on underside of base, using a double row of stitching at base and side positions as shown, to make the handles as strong as possible. Note : It is essential, for obvious reasons, that all work on the handles be done with great care.

The finished length of the top cover must be 21½in. Turn back 10½in along the upper edge of the cover. Insert the eyelet lace between the two layers with the right side of the edging facing upward and the raw edge well into the fold. Pin, baste and stitch, ¼in from the folded edge. Turn the folded-over piece back flat ; the eyelet lace will be held in this tuck. (fig. 10).

Fold under the upper edge 3in above the lace ; check that the cover measures 21½in in length, plus ⅝in seam allowance. Baste along the folded edge. Trim the hem allowance to 2in. Turn under ⅜in and hand-hem the folded edge in place.

Pin, baste and stitch the left-hand side of the zipper to the right-hand side of the

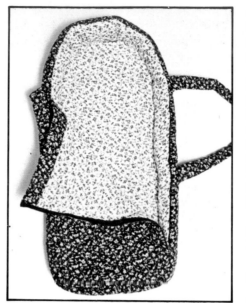

cover, so that the teeth are ⅛in from the top. Turn under the upper edge of the zipper tape and hand-sew it in place on the cover.(fig. 11).

Fold the bias binding in half lengthwise ; press. Slip the binding over the seam allowance and zipper tape and fold in the upper edge of the binding to neaten it. Hand sew the binding to the tape, next to the teeth, and to the underside of the cover along the other long edge and across the top. Cut off the excess binding at the lower end, leaving ¾in below the zipper.

Pin, baste and stitch the remaining two side pieces together at the ends, with lighter sides facing. Press seams open.

Pin, baste and stitch the batting side pieces together at the two ends.

Placing darker sides together, pin and baste the top cover to the outer side piece (already attached), matching edges and starting with the left-hand side of the cover (opposite the zipper) and working around to the base of the zipper. With the zipper closed, continue pinning and basting the zipper to the right-hand side.

Pin and baste the lighter sides to the top edge of the already-attached side pieces, with right sides together, matching raw edges. The seam allowance of the top cover will be sandwiched between the two side covers.

Finally, pin and baste the batting sides in place on top of the fabric sides, matching the top edges. (fig. 12).

Stitch all around, through all three layers of sides and top cover, catching in right-hand side of zipper.

Turn under the raw edge of bias binding at base of zipper and carefully hand sew it in place.

Turn the sides of the bed right side out so that the batting is now enclosed between the two fabric layers. Trim off seam allowance of batting along the inside edge. Turn under the raw edge of inner side piece and hand sew it in place.

Fit the mattress inside the bed with the foam side uppermost.

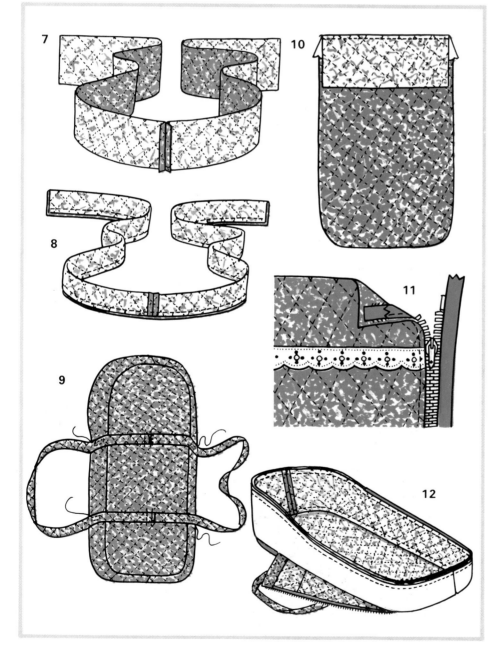

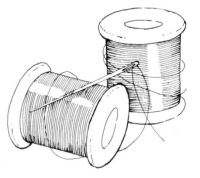

Nursery Accessories

These matching accessories, made in a pretty cotton print, will help to keep the nursery neat. They would make a very welcome present for an expectant mother.

Materials
Baby care basket
a basket, about 16 by 13 by 5in
1yd of 36in wide printed cotton
1½yd of ½in wide eyelet lace edging with one straight finished edge
3½yd of ¼in wide elastic
1½yd bias binding
a piece of quilted plastic in a harmonizing color and a piece of cardboard to fit base of basket

Laundry bag
1yd of 36in wide sailcloth
3yd of ½in wide eyelet lace edging
36 by 4in strip of cotton print fabric
1½yd thick piping cord

Diaper holder
1½yd of 36in wide cotton print
1¾yd of ½in wide eyelet lace edging
a plastic ring, about 5in in diameter
a piece of stiff cardboard, 12in square

Diaper bag
¼yd each of clear plastic, sailcloth and printed cotton, all 36in wide
2¾yd of bias binding

Cotton ball bag
⅝yd of 36in wide printed cotton
1½yd of ½in wide eyelet lace edging
1yd fine piping cord

Coat hanger
a baby coat hanger
a 13 by 3in strip of plastic foam
a 16 by 4in piece of printed cotton
bias binding
a short length of ribbon

Pincushion
2 pieces of printed cotton, each 8in square
¾yd of ½in wide eyelet lace edging
synthetic stuffing

Making the baby care basket
For the lining cut one or more strips –
widthwise across the fabric – measuring, in length, the distance around the inside of the basket plus 1¼in for each seam required and, in width, the depth of the basket plus 3in.

For the pockets cut two strips of fabric widthwise totalling 72in in length and as deep as the basket plus 1½in.

Join the ends of the lining strips to make a continuous strip. Hem one long edge of the strip to make a casing for the elastic, leaving a gap for inserting the elastic.

Stitch the eyelet lace edging over the casing by topstitching ½in from the edge. (Fig. 1)

Cut a length of elastic to fit tightly around the outer edge of the basket, allowing a little extra for overlapping the ends. Insert it in the casing and stitch the ends together.

Place the lining in the basket with the elastic gripping under the rim. Smooth it down the sides and onto the base, pleating the fabric at corners so that it lies smoothly. Pin the pleats in place, remove lining from basket and topstitch the pleats to secure them. Mark the inner
base line with basting stitches. (Fig. 2)

Join the short ends of the pocket strips. Turn under a ¾in hem for a casing and stitch it close to the raw edge, leaving a gap for inserting the elastic. Make another line of stitching ½in above the first line. Insert the elastic and pull it up so that the pocket section fits loosely inside the basket. Stitch the elastic ends together.

Turn under ½in along the lower edge of pocket strip; press. Pin wrong side of pocket section to right side of lining along the line of basting at the lower edge, pleating the pocket fabric at intervals to make it fit. Stitch it in place. (Fig. 3)

Stitch pocket to lining at each corner, from bottom to top and through the elastic. Similarly stitch the layers together at the center of each long side, to form two pocket sections.

Place the cardboard on the bottom of the basket. Bind the edges of the piece of quilting and drop it in place over the cardboard.

Making the laundry bag
Cut a rectangle of sailcloth measuring 34 by 29in with the longer side on

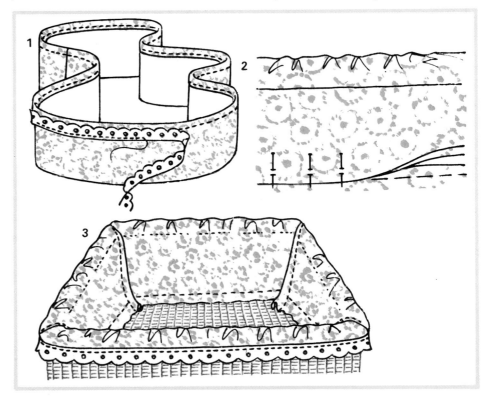

the selvage.

Starting at the selvage, with right side of fabric upward, turn back a ¼in hem on both short sides, for a distance of 8in. (Note that the hem is turned onto the right side.) Stitch in place.

Baste the edging to the selvage, right sides facing, so that the edging extends beyond the selvage. (Fig. 4)

Turn the trimmed edge over to the right side to make a hem 4in deep. Pin and baste it in place. Stitch along the basted edge, and then add another line of stitching 1½in above the first, to make a casing for the cord. (Fig. 5)

Turn under and press ¼in hems on both long edges of the cotton print strip. Baste eyelet lace edging just under both folded edges.

Position the strip on the right side of the sailcloth 3½in from the lower edge. Topstitch along both long edges. (Fig. 6)

Fold the sailcloth in half, right sides together, to join side edges. Pin and stitch the side seam, ¼in from raw edges, beginning just below the casing. Stitch along the lower edges. Add another line of stitching just outside the first as

reinforcement.

Turn the bag right side out. Thread cord through the casing and knot the ends to prevent unraveling.

Making the diaper holder

Cut three strips of fabric, each 24 by 13in, for sides and back. Cut two strips, each 24 by 5in, for fronts, one rectangle 26 by 13in for base and a strip 6½ by 4in to hold the ring in position.

Pin and stitch the side and back sections together along their long edges, taking ½in seams.

Turn under and stitch a narrow hem on the inner front edge of each front section. Topstitch lengths of edging over the stitching lines. (Fig. 7)

Join the front sections to the side sections along the unhemmed edges.

Fold the base section in half, wrong sides together, to make a square; press.

Place the lower edges of the front section, right sides downward, on the folded edge of the square, side seams at corners so as to leave a gap in the middle. Pin and stitch, taking ½in seams. Similarly join side sections to the adjacent sides of

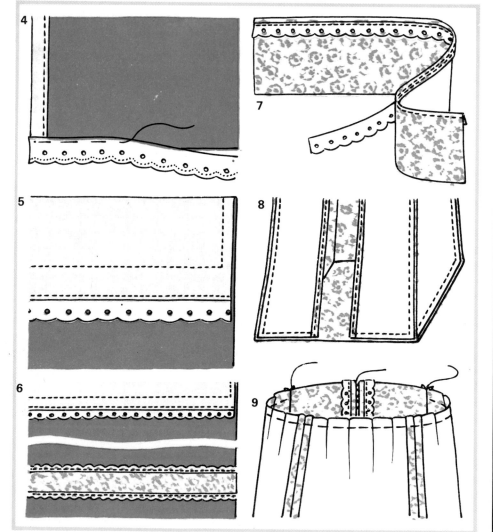

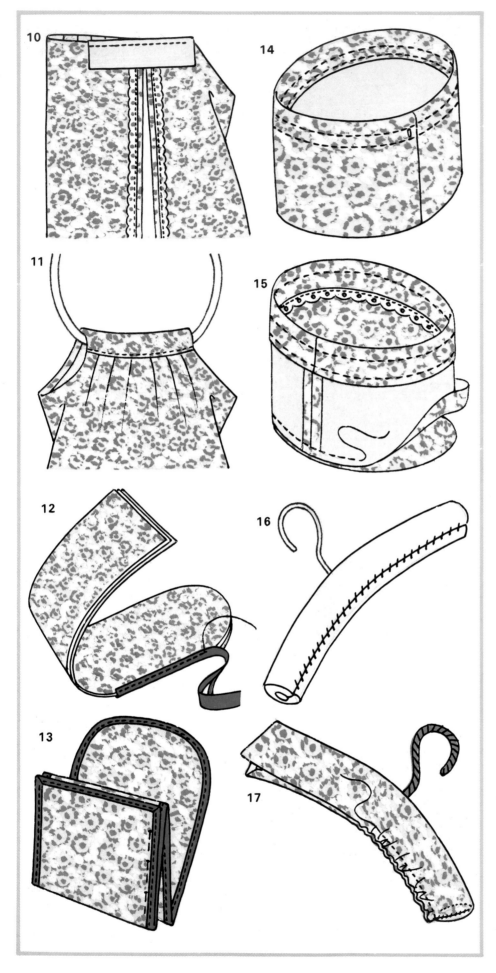

the square, stitching through all three layers. Finally, stitch the back section to the bottom layer only of the square, thus leaving an opening for the cardboard. (Fig. 8)

Fold the small strip in half lengthwise, right sides together. Stitch along the long edge and turn strip right side out. Fold in the ends and stitch across them.

Lay the diaper holder flat with upper front edges meeting at the center and upper edges level. Join the front edges temporarily with a few basting stitches.

Pleat the side and back sections so that combined they measure the same width as the front. Stitch across the pleats, close to the edge, to hold them in place. (Fig. 9)

On the front, fold down the outer corners so that the front measures the same as the length of the strip. Pin one long edge of the strip over the raw edge of the front and topstitch it in place. (Fig. 10)

Slip the ring under the strip and top-stitch the other long edge to the pleated edge, positioning the center pleats at the center point of the strip. (Fig. 11)

Cut 6in of edging; run a gathering thread through the straight edge, and draw it up to form a rosette. Sew rosette to meeting point of center-front edges.

Insert cardboard in base.

Making the diaper bag

Place the printed cotton right side downward, lay the sailcloth on top of it, and lay the clear plastic on top of the sailcloth. Machine stitch the layers together, close to the edges, rounding the corners at one end. Trim excess fabric.

Fold binding over the edges and machine stitch it in place, starting at the middle of one side. (Fig. 12)

Fold up the uncurved end $7\frac{1}{2}$in, printed fabric outside, to make one pocket. Pin it along the sides. Make another pocket by making a fold of the same depth in the remaining fabric. Stitch these two pockets together at the sides, close to the binding. (Fig. 13)

The curved end folds over to form a flap.

Making the cotton ball bag

Cut a strip of fabric 22 by 8in and a circle 8in in diameter.

Stitch together the short sides of the strip.

Turn under $\frac{1}{4}$in on one remaining edge; press. Turn down this folded edge $1\frac{1}{2}$in. Stitch near the first fold, then again $\frac{1}{2}$in above this to make a casing for the cord. Cut a small slit in the outer layer of the casing, near the side seam. Work around the slit in closed blanket stitch. (Fig. 14)

Cut two lengths of edging, each 22in long. Topstitch one length just below the casing and the other ¾in from the lower edge.

Turn under ¼in along the lower edge; press. Clip this hem allowance at short intervals. Turn strip wrong side out.

Pin, baste and stitch strip to circular base, right sides together. Turn bag right side out. (Fig. 15)

Thread cord through casing and tie a knot at each end to prevent unraveling.

Making the coat hanger

Fold the plastic over the hanger, snipping it at the center in order to get it over the hook. Sew the edges together. (fig.16).

Wrap bias binding around the hook to cover it and tie the ends together around the hanger.

Fold under approximately ⅜in on the raw edges of the printed cotton and press. Snip the fabric at the center and slip it over the hanger. Overcast the ends together. Work small running stitches along the base, joining the two edges, gathering the fabric slightly and back-stitching at intervals. (fig.17).

Overcast the raw edges around the hook. Decorate the hanger with a bow.

Making the pincushion

Lay one of the squares right side upward and pin the edging around all four sides, with the edges together and the lace pointing toward the center.

Lay the other square on top, right side downward. Pin and baste on three sides only. Stitch the three layers together on these three sides, the lace on the fourth side to the lower layer only.

Turn the pincushion right side out and fill it firmly with the stuffing. Close the opening with slipstitching.

Christening Gown and Bonnet

Lavishly trimmed with lace, this beautiful christening gown is one to be treasured for generations.

Materials

2½yd of 36in wide lawn
6yd of 1in wide cotton lace insertion
11½yd of ¼in wide lace
6yd of ½in wide lace
⅝yd narrow woven tape
10 pearl buttons
1yd of ¾in wide ribbon
graph paper marked in 1in squares
Note: a sewing machine with zigzag stitch is essential.

Making the pattern

Using the graph paper, enlarge the pattern pieces given on pages 82–83. Each square on the pattern represents 2 square inches on your paper. Add seam allowances to the pattern, adding ¾in to the sides and sleeves and ¼in on all other edges.

Cut out the pattern pieces and transfer all markings to them.

Cutting out

Iron the fabric flat and straighten it if necessary so that tucks will lie exactly on the grain. Pin the pattern to the fabric as shown on the cutting layout.

Cut out the pattern and transfer all markings to the pieces.

Cut a bias strip 10½ by ¾in for the neckline.

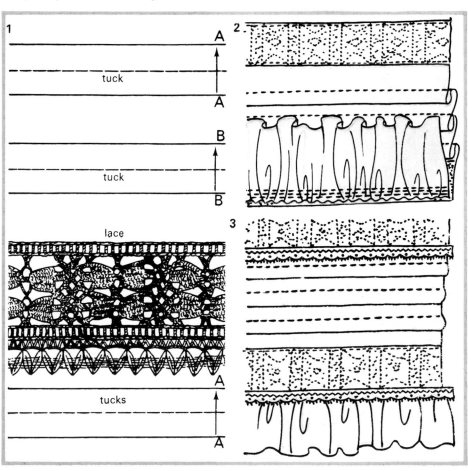

Making the gown

Fold, pin and stitch the tucks on the front panel, as shown in Fig. 1.

Cut six lengths of lace insertion to fit front panel. Pin each length in place on the right side; baste and stitch, using a small zigzag, close to the edges.

Make two rows of gathering stitches on the hem ruffle. Gather the ruffle to fit the front panel, distribute fullness evenly and pin, baste and stitch ruffle to lower edge of panel, placing right sides and raw edges together. Press seam allowances upward. (Fig. 2)

Trim away the fabric under the lace close to the stitching line. Stitch in wide lace to the lower edge of the lace insertion. (Fig. 3)

Make tucks on sleeves and yoke, and stitch on insertion and edging lace.

Turn under and stitch narrow hems on both long sides and one short side of each streamer.

Gather tops of sleeves, back panels and front panel to fit the corresponding edges of the yoke.

Placing right sides together, baste and stitch front of yoke to front panel. Cut the back of the yoke along the center-back line. (Fig. 4) Baste and stitch the yoke backs to the dress back sections.

Fold a pleat in the unstitched end of each streamer and baste streamers in place at the upper corners of the front panel so that they point toward the center front.

Placing right sides together, baste and stitch the front panel to the side fronts, taking in the streamers.

Baste the gathered upper sleeves under the lace insertion at the sides of the yoke and zigzag stitch in place. (Fig. 5)

Stitch narrow lace along sides and lower edge of front panel and wider lace, slightly gathered, around the yoke.

Turn under in twice on both center-back edges and hand-hem.

Placing right sides together and raw edges even, baste and stitch the neck binding to the neckline, in from the edges. Clip curves. Turn in short ends, fold binding to wrong side, turn under the free edge of the binding and slipstitch it in place on the stitching line. Topstitch, $\frac{1}{2}$in

wide lace to upper edge of binding.

Cut two eyelet holes in underside of binding in from center-back edge and work buttonhole stitch around them. Thread tape through eyelets, draw up neckline to fit neck comfortably and sew ends of binding securely in place. (Fig. 6)

Work 10 thread loops along right-hand edge of back, spacing them evenly from neckline down to about 4in from lower edge. Sew buttons to left-hand side.

Placing right sides together, baste and stitch side and sleeve seams. Press.

Turn under $\frac{3}{4}$in on lower edges of sleeves and stitch in place close to raw edges. Make eyelets in the hem, on the inside, as in neck binding, placing them in $\frac{3}{8}$in from the seamline.

Stitch $\frac{1}{2}$in wide lace to the lower edge of the sleeve hem, stitching very close to the edge. (Fig. 7)

Thread tape through each sleeve hem, draw up sleeve to fit arm comfortably and sew ends of tape securely in place under seam allowances.

Turn under $\frac{1}{4}$in, then a further 1in along the lower edge of gown. Baste in place

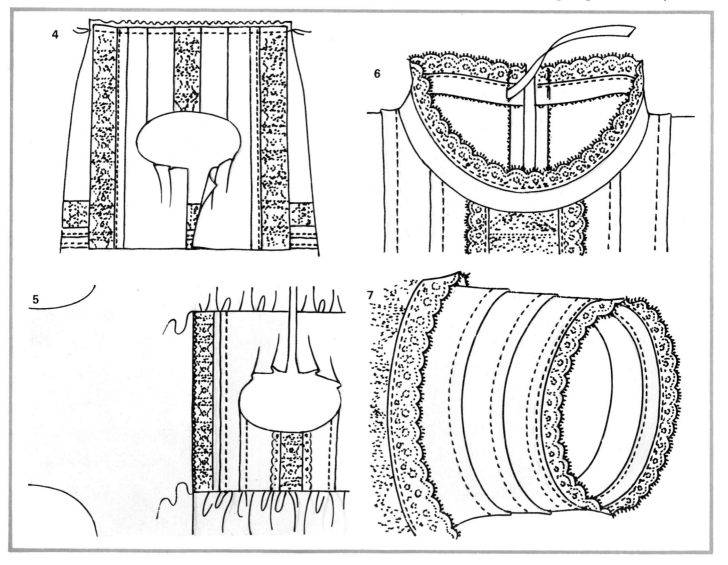

and hand-hem. Stitch ½in lace under edge.

Making the bonnet

Stitch the in wide lace to one long edge of the bonnet ruffle. Run a gathering thread along the other edge and gather up the ruffle to fit the brim.

Make tucks on brim as on front panel of gown. Stitch insertion lace to one edge, using zigzag stitch. Adjust gathers on ruffle and baste the free edge of the insertion lace over the gathering. Stitch, using zigzag. Trim ruffle seam allowance close to stitching and press toward brim.

Lay the ruffled edge of brim over side AA of main bonnet piece, with both right sides upward and zigzag stitching over the bonnet stitching line. Pin and baste in place. (Fig. 8)

Fold down the main bonnet piece, away from the ruffle, and slipstitch the folded edge along the zigzag stitching, using very small stitches.

Stitch back seam BC, right sides together. Turn under ¼in on edge of crown; press. Pin and baste a length of ½in lace just under folded edge, gathering slightly; topstitch.

Run a line of gathering stitches along edge CC and draw up gathers to fit edge of crown. Adjust gathers evenly and, placing right sides together, baste and stitch bonnet to crown. Press.

Turn under and stitch small double hems on long edge of brim and side edges of brim and bonnet, baste in place and stitch. Baste in wide lace just under the edges and stitch in place. Sew ribbon ties to sides of bonnet. (Fig. 9)

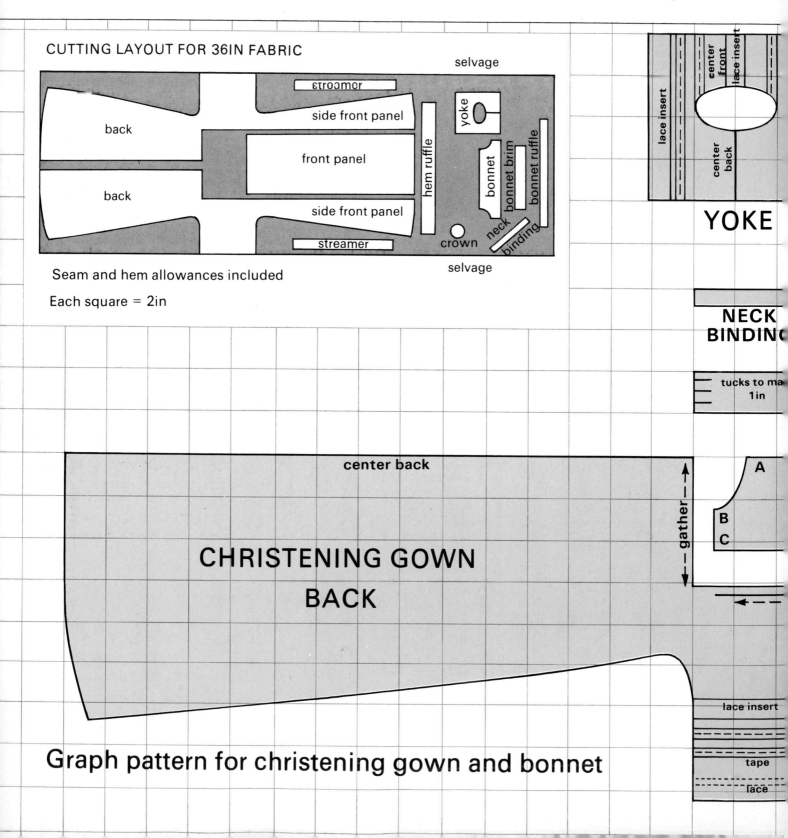

CUTTING LAYOUT FOR 36IN FABRIC

selvage

streamer

side front panel

back

front panel

yoke

hem ruffle

bonnet

bonnet brim

bonnet ruffle

back

side front panel

streamer

crown

neck binding

selvage

Seam and hem allowances included

Each square = 2in

YOKE

lace insert

center front

lace insert

center back

NECK BINDING

tucks to ma
1in

center back

gather

A

B
C

CHRISTENING GOWN

BACK

lace insert

tape

lace

Graph pattern for christening gown and bonnet

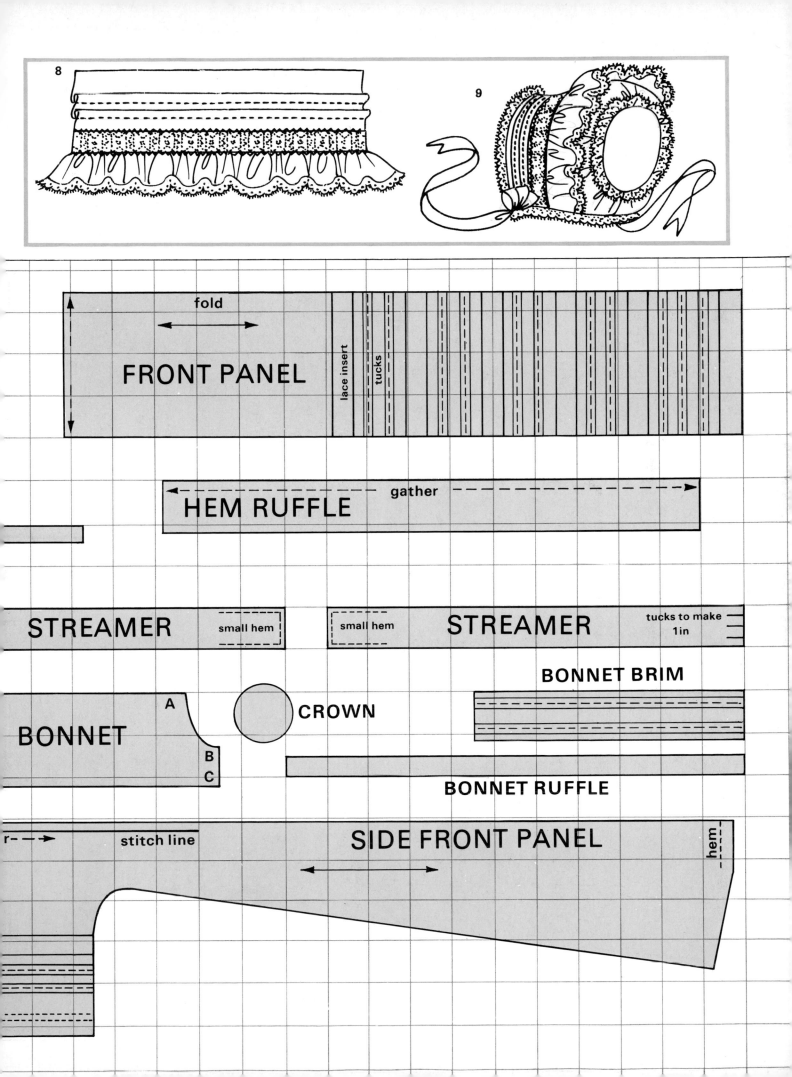

8

9

FRONT PANEL

fold

lace insert

tucks

HEM RUFFLE

gather

STREAMER

small hem

small hem

STREAMER

tucks to make
1in

BONNET BRIM

BONNET

A

B

C

CROWN

BONNET RUFFLE

r

stitch line

SIDE FRONT PANEL

hem

Embroidered Sheet and Pillowcase

Crisp, cheerful gingham always brightens a nursery, as this pretty crib set proves. Embroider in cross-stitch and lazy daisy with lace edging. Choose matching colors.

Size
The sheet – excluding ruffle – measures 60 by 40in, and the pillowslip – excluding ruffle – measures 15½ by 14in.

Materials
2⅛yd of 45in wide white cotton fabric
2⅛yd of 45in wide red and white checked gingham, with ⅛in checks; the checks on some ginghams are not exactly square, so make sure that the fabric you buy has square checks, in order that the embroidery can be worked successfully.
5yd of 1⅛in wide white eyelet lace edging
5 skeins of white stranded embroidery floss
a crewel needle, size 7
tracing paper
dressmaker's carbon paper
an embroidery hoop

Cutting out
For the sheet, cut a piece of white fabric 61 by 41in. For the embroidered border cut a piece of gingham 5½ by 41in.

For the pillowslip cut one piece of white fabric for the front, measuring 15 by 16½in, and two for the back, one measuring 15 by 14in and the other 15 by 5in. For the embroidered border, cut a piece of gingham 5½ by 16½in.

Working the embroidery
Fold the pieces of gingham in half in both directions, crease lightly and mark the creases with basting.

Leaving seven squares free on each side of the horizontal center line, work the cross stitch borders on the long sides of the gingham. Start at the center point (marked with an arrow in the diagram) and work outward in both directions. Use 3 strands of thread. Each stitch is worked on one square. (Fig. 1)

Trace the flower motifs onto the tracing paper and then transfer them, using the dressmaker's carbon, onto the gingham, positioning the central motif over the crossed lines of basting and spacing the others evenly along the horizontal center of the fabric. Again using 3 strands of thread, embroider the flowers, working section 1 in back stitch, section 2 in satin stitch and section 3 in detached chain stitch. Press the embroidery on the wrong side. (Fig. 2)

Making the sheet
Turn under and stitch double hems, ¼in deep, on all four edges of the white fabric.

Turn under ½in on all four sides of the gingham; baste this hem in place. Baste the trimming under the folded edge, with raw edges even. Gather the trimming to ease it around the corners. Overlap the short ends of the trimming so that the pattern matches; overcast the raw edges together and slipstitch the ends together on the right side to neaten them.

Place the gingham on the right side of the sheet at one short end so that the trimming extends over the edges at the top and sides. Baste and machine stitch in position.

Making the pillowslip
Turn under the lower long edge of the gingham for ½in and press. Baste a length of trimming just under this folded edge so that raw edges underneath are even.

Place the gingham on the right side of the front section of the pillowslip so that the top and side raw edges are even. Baste the gingham in place. Machine stitch along the trimmed edge.

Place the remaining trimming along the remaining three sides of the gingham so that the raw edges are even and the finished edge points inward. Baste in place, gathering the trimming at the corners.

Turn under and stitch double hems, ¼in deep, on one 15in edge of each back section. To form the overlap, place the larger back section on the front section with right sides facing and raw edges even. Place the smaller back section onto the opposite end of the front, again with right sides facing and outer raw edges even.

Baste and machine stitch around all four edges, leaving ½in seam allowance. Finish the raw edges with zigzagging or overcasting.

Turn the finished pillowslip right side out and press lightly.

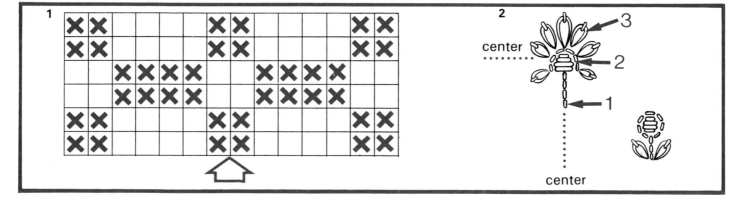

84

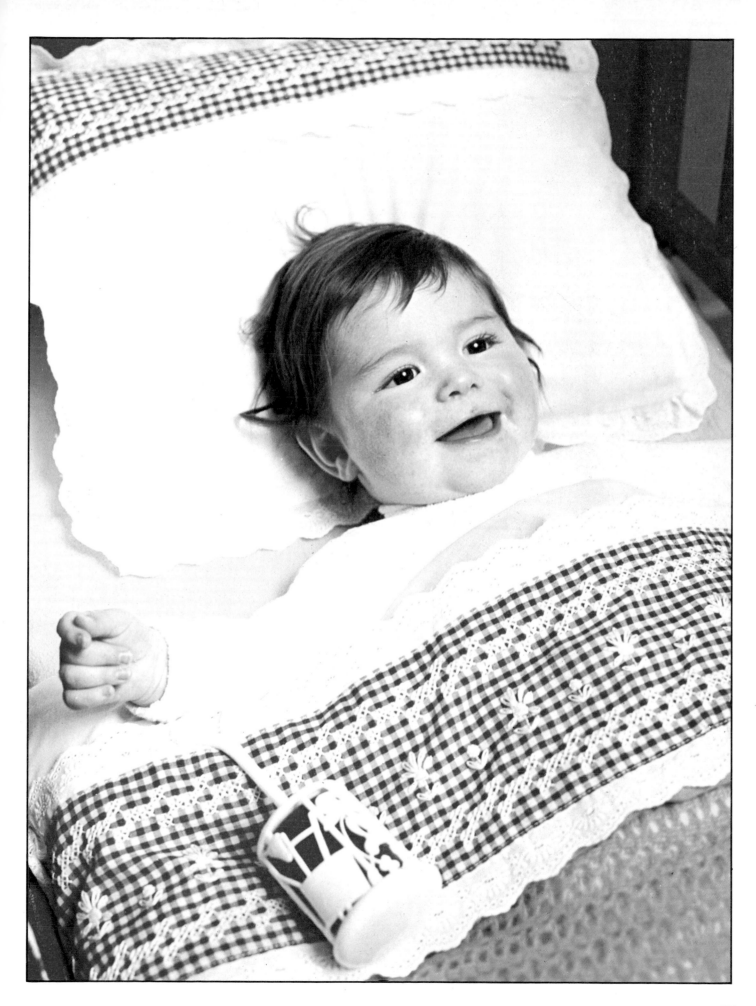

Baby-carrying Sling

Simple to make – safe for baby. This convenient sling allows you to carry your baby with you, in a position babies find reassuring, while leaving your hands free.

Size
The completed sling measures approximately 16in in length.

Materials
1⅛yd of strong, closely-woven fabric, such as heavy poplin; if fabric is 51in wide, or wider, you need only buy 1⅛yd
2 wooden rings 2¾in in diameter
a scrap of medium weight batting
tracing paper
a ruler

Making the sling
Trace the patterns given on pages 88–89.

Extend the main piece by 2¼in by continuing the long lines and joining them at the bottom. Cut out the traced patterns.

From the fabric cut two main pieces and two headrest pieces, positioning them on the straight grain as indicated on the patterns.

From the remaining fabric cut the straps. You will need three straps measuring 51 by 4in and two measuring 11¾ by 4in. If your fabric is less than 51in wide you will need to piece the longer straps, cutting two lengths 26 long and joining the ends with ⅜in seams.

Place the two main pieces together, right sides facing. Pin, baste and stitch the side edges together, taking ⅜in seams. (Fig. 1)

Turn the piece right side out. Baste down the side seams, close to the edges. Using a fairly long stitch, topstitch down both sides, close to the edges. Add a second line of topstitching about ¼in inside the first. (Fig. 2)

Place the headrest pieces together, right sides facing. Pin, baste and stitch along the curved edge, taking ⅜in seams. (Fig. 3) Clip the curves.

Open the headrest flat. Pin one long strap to one side edge of the headrest, right sides facing. Stitch, taking a ⅜in seam. Join another long strap to the other end of the headrest. Press seams open.

Place one straight edge of the headrest on the upper, curved edge of the main piece, right sides facing. Pin, baste and stitch the pieces together, through all three thicknesses. (Fig. 4)

Turn under and press ⅜in along the

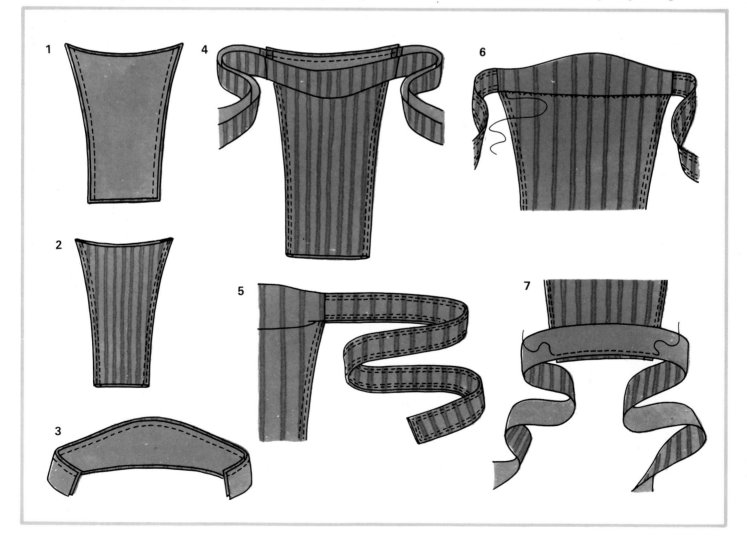

three remaining edges of each strap. Fold the strap in half lengthwise, wrong sides facing, and pin and baste the edges together. Topstitch along all three sides, close to the edge, then add a second line of topstitching about ¼in inside the first. (Fig. 5)

Trim ⅜in from all edges of the headrest pattern. Using this trimmed pattern, cut two pieces from batting. Place these two pieces together and baste around the edges.

Place the batting inside the headrest and pin it in place.

Turn under ⅜in along the remaining straight edge of the headrest. Pin, baste and stitch it in place along the existing stitching line. (Fig. 6)

Place the remaining long strap on the lower edge of the main piece, matching the center of the strap to the center of the main piece and with right sides facing. Pin baste and stitch through all three thicknesses (Fig. 7). Press the seam allowances toward the strap.

Turn under ⅜in on the remaining edges of the strap, fold it in half and finish it as you did the two other long straps. (Fig. 8)

Fold each of the shorter straps in half lengthwise, right sides together. Pin, baste

Trace pattern for baby-carrying sling

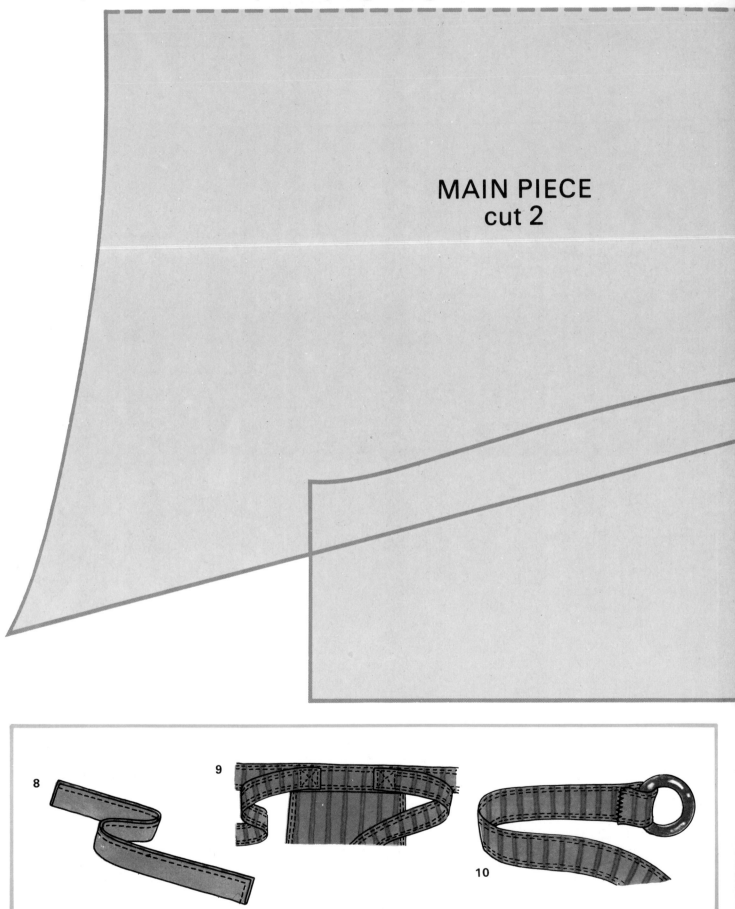

MAIN PIECE
cut 2

8

9

10

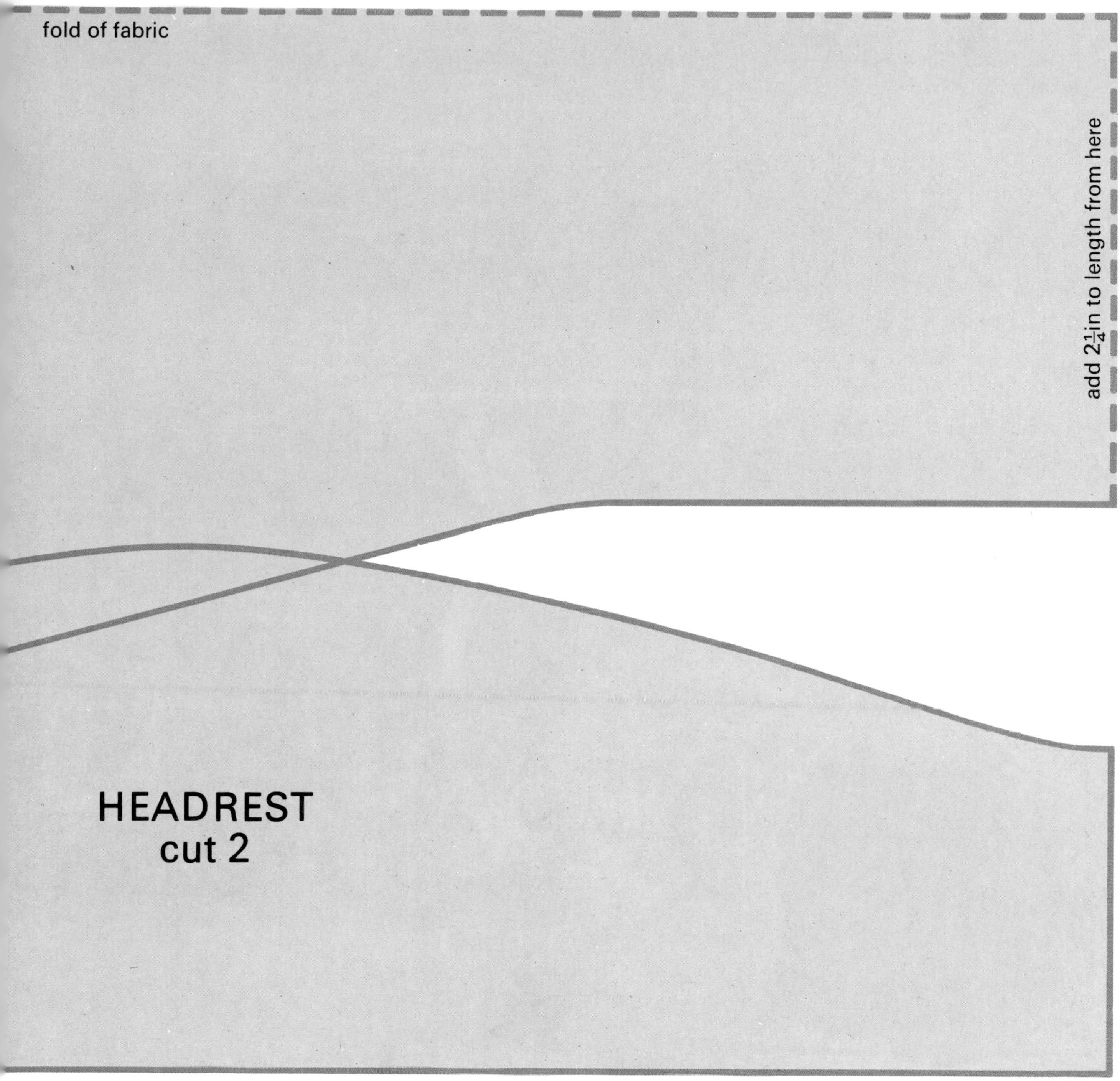

fold of fabric

add 2¼in to length from here

HEADREST
cut 2

and stitch the long side and one short side. Clip across the corner. Turn the strap right side out and baste close to the edges. Topstitch along both long sides and across one end, then add another line of topstitching inside the first.

Mark a point 1¼in from the center of the base strap. Place the closed end of one short strap at this mark. Pin, baste and stitch it in place, following the existing lines of stitching and reinforcing the stitching by working from corner to corner to form an ''x''. Join the remaining

short strap in the same way, 1¼in to the other side of the center point. (Fig. 9)

Thread the unstitched end of one short strap through a wooden ring and fold it back onto the underside. Pin it in place, then stitch over the end using a closed zigzag stitch. Complete the other short strap in the same way. (fig.10).

Using the sling
Place the sling on a flat surface, with the short straps underneath. Place the baby on the sling. Bring the lower edge of the

sling through the baby's legs. Bring the baby to a sitting position – or turn it over – and tie the ends of the long base strap in a firm knot at the back (see page 87 photograph). Position the baby against the front of your body. Put the long left-hand strap over your left shoulder and bring it across your back through the ring on the short right-hand strap. Similarly thread the right-hand long strap through the left-hand ring. Pull the straps together and tie them firmly in a knot at the back.

Trims for Stretch-suit

Smarten a baby's plain stretch suit by adding a collar, "shoes" and a bib.

Materials
a baby's terry cloth stretch suit
$\frac{3}{8}$yd of 36in wide printed fabric
$\frac{3}{8}$yd of 36in wide stretch terry cloth to match suit
$\frac{3}{8}$yd of 36in wide white cotton fabric
$\frac{3}{8}$yd of 37in wide lightweight polyester batting
2yd contrasting bias binding
$\frac{3}{4}$yd of $\frac{3}{8}$in wide lace edging
1 skein of stranded embroidery floss to match bias binding
a crewel needle, size 5 or 6
2 small buttons
tracing paper
dressmaker's carbon paper
embroidery hoop – optional

Making the pattern
Using the tracing paper trace and cut out the pattern for the bib, including the sailboat motif.

Trace the patterns for the collar and shoes. Check that they fit your suit and make any necessary adjustments to the patterns before cutting them out.

Cutting out
From the printed fabric, terry cloth, white cotton backing and batting cut out one 9in square of each.

Cut two collar sections from the printed fabric.

Cut two shoe sections from the printed fabric and two from the white cotton backing.

Making the bib
Transfer the boat design onto the right side of the square of printed fabric, using the dressmaker's carbon and a pencil, making sure that it is placed in the center.

Place the batting between the printed fabric and the white cotton, with the right sides of these fabrics facing outward. Carefully baste the layers together, working large stitches from the center of the square out to each side. This will prevent the layers from slipping out of place when you work the quilting embroidery. (Fig. 1)

Using all six strands of embroidery floss, work the boat design in chain stitch. You can work the embroidery in your hand or use an embroidery hoop to hold the fabric taut. Press the work lightly with a steam iron or a dry iron over a damp cloth.

Baste the square of terry cloth to the back of the quilted bib, working the basting stitches close to the embroidery as shown. (Fig. 2)

Pin the paper pattern for the bib over the quilting so that the traced design is aligned with the embroidery. Trim away the excess fabric outside the pattern pieces.

Baste and stitch the bias binding to the front of the bib along the sides and lower edge, aligning the raw edges and stitching on the fold line of the binding. Fold the binding to the wrong side and slipstitch it to the line of machine stitching. (Fig. 3)

Bind the neck edge in the same way,

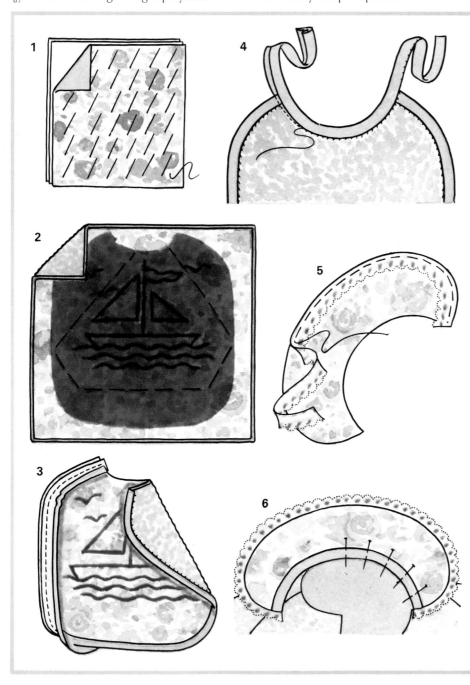

but leave 5in of binding at each end of the neck for ties. Fold the binding to the wrong side and fold each tie piece in half. Slipstitch from the end of one tie around the neck to the end of the other tie. (Fig. 4)

Making the collar

Baste the lace around the outer edge of one collar section on the right side of fabric, placing the lace with the finished edge inward and the raw edge $\frac{3}{8}$in from the edge of the collar. (Fig. 5)

Pin the two collar sections together with right sides facing. Baste and stitch the two pieces together, $\frac{1}{2}$in from the edge, catching in the lace, leaving the neck edge unstitched. Trim and clip the curved edges and turn the collar right side out. Baste around the stitched edge, press and remove basting thread.

Bind the neck edge in the same way as on the bib.

Matching the center of the collar to the center back of the suit, pin the collar to the inside of the neck, working from the center around to each front. Hand-sew the collar in place so that it can be removed and attached to another suit if necessary. (Fig. 6)

Making the shoes

Baste and stitch one printed fabric shoe section to one white shoe section, placing right sides together and taking $\frac{3}{8}$in seams. Leave the two ends unstitched. Trim seams, clip curves and turn the shoes right side out.

Bind the inner curved edge of the shoe in the same way as for the bib. (Fig. 7)

Cut a strip of binding to fit right across the shoe to form a bar, allowing a little extra on each end. Place the binding across the upper edges of the shoe as shown and baste in place. Fold the binding in half, tuck in the raw ends and press. Slipstitch the binding folds together in the middle and the remaining edges to the wrong side of the shoe. (Fig. 8)

Sew a small button on the outer side of the shoe. Pin and neatly slipstitch the shoe onto the foot of the suit along the outer edges. (Fig. 9)

Make the other shoe in the same way.

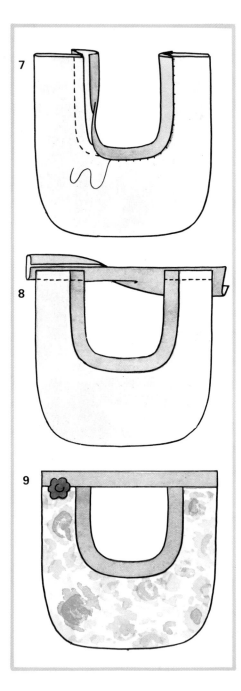

Trace pattern

cut around solid line when quilted embroidery is complete

sewing line   - - - - - -

BIB

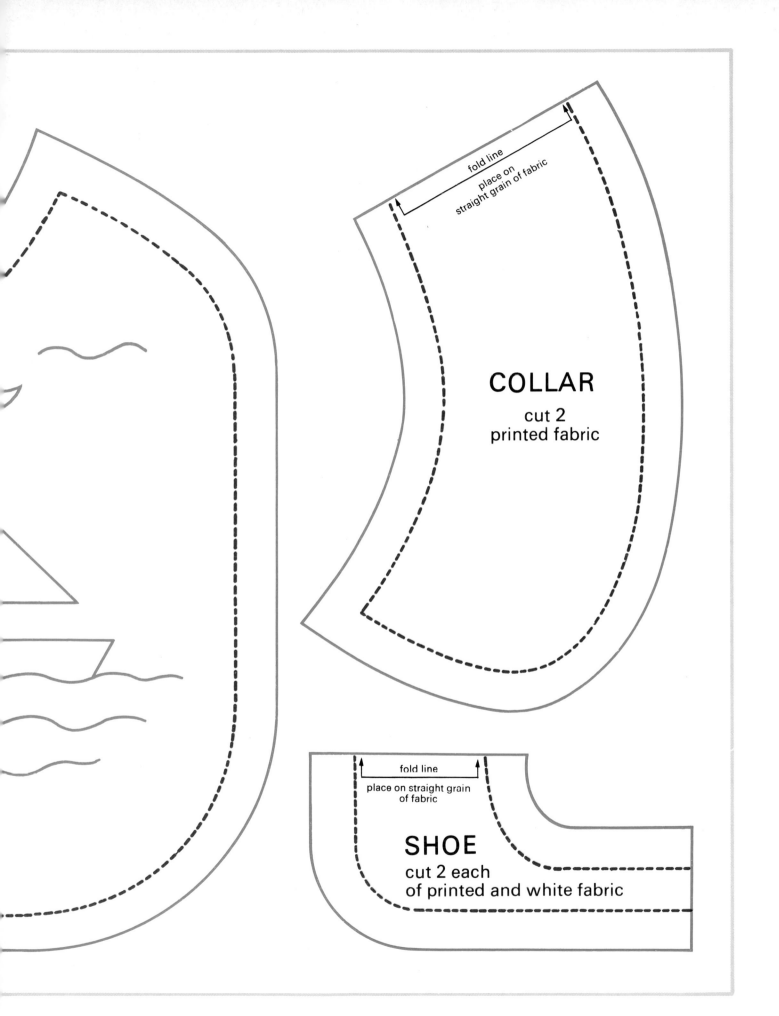

COLLAR

cut 2
printed fabric

fold line

place on
straight grain of fabric

SHOE

cut 2 each
of printed and white fabric

fold line

place on straight grain
of fabric

Appliquéd Bibs

These ample bibs, made of terry cloth and decorated with charming appliquéd characters, are just the thing for messy mealtimes.

Size
Each bib is 10in wide and 11in long.

Materials
¾yd of terry cloth; fabric 36in wide is adequate for three bibs
contrasting fabric for binding and ties – a piece 15in square for each bib
scraps of fabric for appliqué
contrasting, as well as matching, thread
embroidery thread
tracing paper
graph paper marked in 1in squares

Making the pattern
Using graph paper, enlarge the pattern pieces. One square on the page

represents 1 square in on your paper. A seam allowance of ½in is included.

Cut out the pattern pieces and transfer markings to them.

Cutting out

Fold the terry cloth lengthwise so that the double thickness is wide enough for the bib pieces. Place the pattern on the fabric with the center front edge on the fold; pin it in place and cut it out.

Fold the contrasting fabric in half on the bias. Position the three binding pieces as indicated by the grain lines and cut them out. Transfer the dots to the fabric pieces.

Making the bib

Placing right sides together, baste and stitch a side binding strip to each end of the lower edge strip, stitching as far as the dot and taking ½in seam allowances. Similarly baste and stitch the shoulder bindings to the side bindings. Trim all seams and press them open. (Fig. 1)

Placing right side of binding to wrong side of bib, baste and stitch the binding to the bib. Layer the seam allowances, tapering them narrowly at the corners. Turn the binding to the right side and baste along the stitched edge to hold it in position. (Fig. 2)

Turn under the raw edges of the binding so that it is ⅝in wide, and baste it in place. Using thread matching the terry cloth, topstitch all around the inner edge of the binding close to the fold. Remove all basting and press. (Fig. 3)

Placing right sides together, pin and stitch the two tie pieces together at the short, straight ends. Trim seam allowances and press them open. Fold the tie in half lengthwise, right sides together. Pin, baste and stitch across diagonal ends and long edges as far as the dots. Trim seams to ¼in and clip to the dots. Turn the tie right side out. Baste along stitched edges to push stitching to edge. Press and remove basting thread. (Fig. 4)

Placing right sides together and matching tie seam to center front, pin one edge of the tie to the neck edge of the bib. Stretch the tie so that the ends of the opening are at the bound edges of the bib. (Fig. 5) Baste and stitch. Trim the seam. Turn the free edge of the tie to the wrong side. Fold under the seam allowance and slipstitch it along the stitching line. (Fig. 6).

Working the appliqué
Caterpillar

Using tracing paper, trace the whole caterpillar, except the antennae, marking in the sectional lines. Cut along the lower edge of the hat to separate it from the caterpillar and also cut away the top of the hat.

Cut out the three pieces from three different fabrics. Baste them in place on the bib. Using a small, close zigzag stitch (or a closed blanket stitch) work all around the outside edges and along all the sectional lines.

Cut the eyes and bow tie from the paper pattern and cut these out in fabric. Stitch these in place on the caterpillar.

Using embroidery thread work small circles of satin stitch in the eyes to make the irises. Work the mouth in stem stitch. For the antennae use a long machine zigzag or a slanted satin stitch, finishing with French knots, using several strands of embroidery thread.

Remove all basting and press the work on the wrong side.

Clown

Using tracing paper, trace the whole shape, marking in sectional lines. Cut along the sectional lines to separate the feet, hands, ruffle, face, hair and hat.

Cut out these pieces in different fabrics. Position the main body piece on the bib and baste it in place. Then baste the other pieces in place. Using a small, close zigzag stitch (or a closed blanket stitch) work all around the outside shape and along the sectional lines.

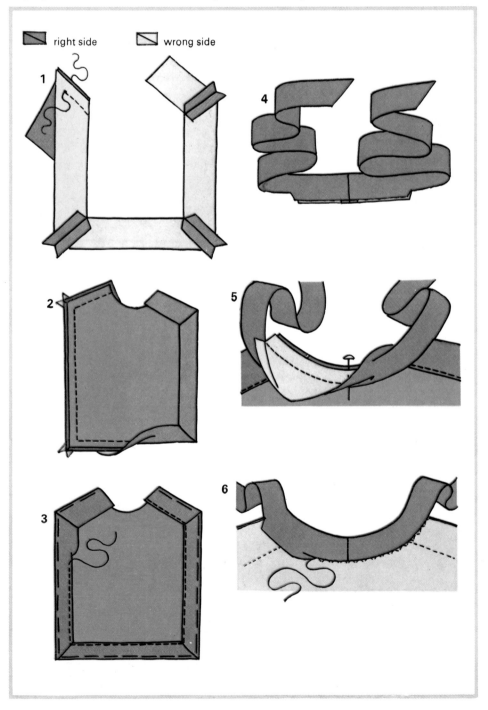

right side   wrong side

1   4   2   5   3   6

Cut the eyes, mouth and pompoms in fabric and stitch them in place; or work them in contrasting embroidery thread. Work a few stitches over the narrow parts of the sleeves and legs.

Remove all basting and press the work on the wrong side.

Mouse
Using tracing paper, trace the whole shape and mark in the sectional lines, eyes and ears. Cut away the head, ears, underbody and tail pieces. Cut out each piece from different fabrics, using the same fabric, however, for the ears and underbody.

Baste the pieces in place and stitch all around them using a small, close zigzag stitch (or a closed blanket stitch).

Cut the eye pieces from the pattern and cut these out in fabric. Baste and stitch these in place. Fill in the inner corners of the eye with satin stitch, using embroidery thread. Work the eyebrows and nostrils in stem stitch.

Remove all basting and press the work on the wrong side.

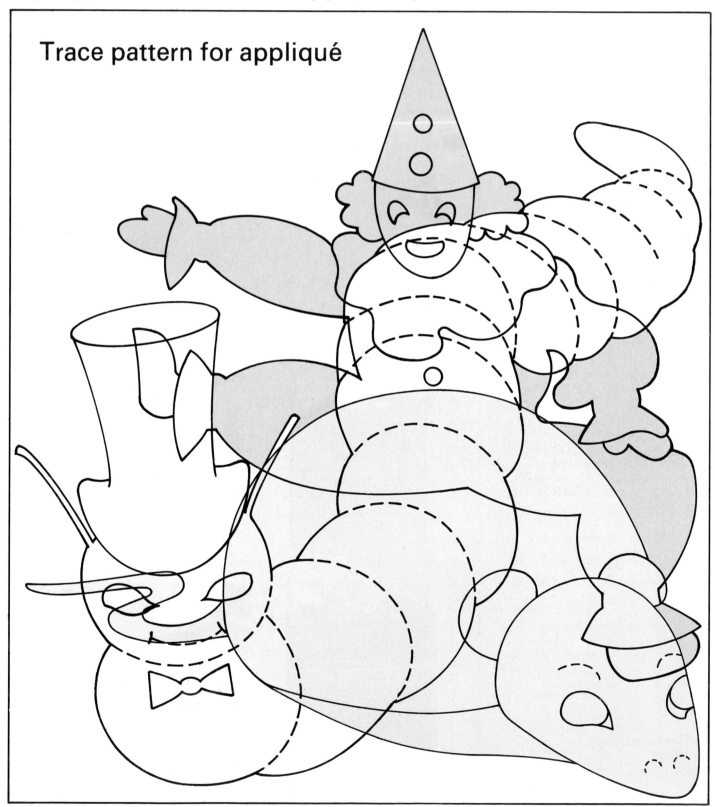

Trace pattern for appliqué

Graph pattern for baby's terry cloth bibs

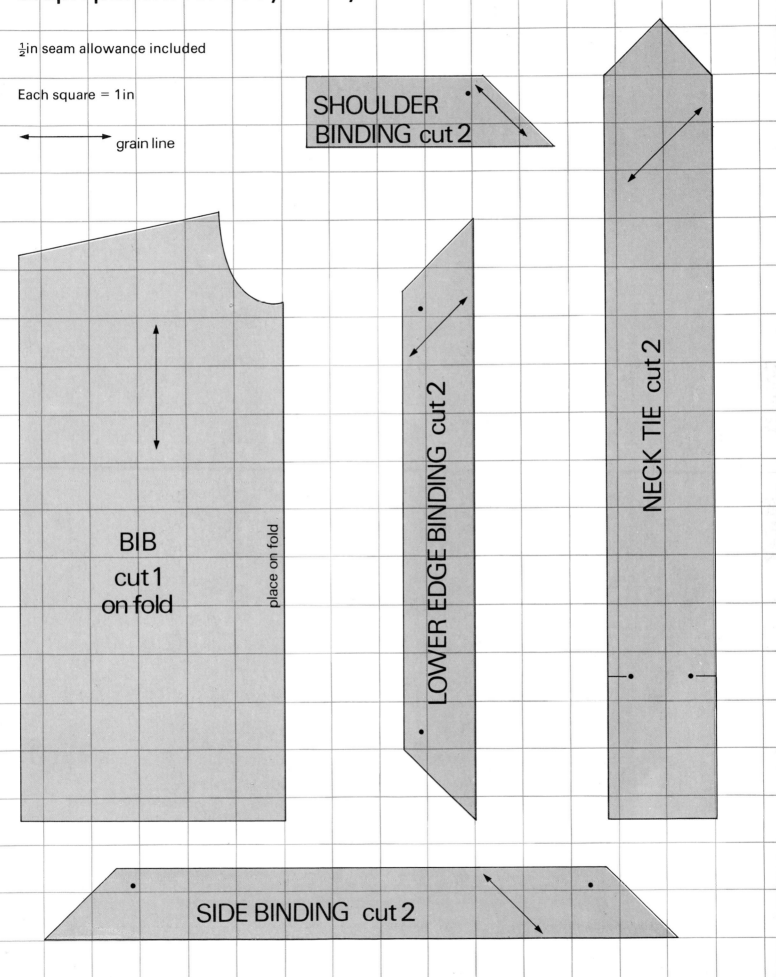

$\frac{1}{2}$in seam allowance included

Each square = 1in

←——→ grain line

SHOULDER BINDING cut 2

BIB cut 1 on fold

place on fold

LOWER EDGE BINDING cut 2

NECK TIE cut 2

SIDE BINDING cut 2

Smocked Dress

Smocking gives extra charm to this easy-to-make dress. Make it in lightweight cotton or in a soft, washable cotton and wool blend, such as Viyella.

Size
The pattern is sized to fit a child 1 year old, or a chest measurement of about 20in.

Materials
1½yd of 36in wide fabric

3 buttons, ¾in in diameter
1 skein each of 4 shades of stranded embroidery floss
a crewel needle, size 6 or 7
43 small round beads
graph paper marked in 1in squares
tracing paper
dressmaker's carbon paper

Making the pattern
Using graph paper enlarge each pattern piece to the correct size. Each square on the page represents 2 square inches on your paper – except for the insert, which is on a 1in grid for ease in enlarging. A seam allowance of ⅜in and a hem allowance of 2in are included.

Cut out the pattern pieces and transfer markings to them. Using tracing paper trace the grids for the smocking.

Cutting out
Following the cutting layout, fold the fabric in half lengthwise and position the pattern pieces – except for the neck and sleeve guides – as indicated, making sure that the grain lines lie on the straight grain of the fabric. Pin the pieces in place and cut them out. Transfer all markings.

Making the dress
Placing *wrong* sides together and matching notches, baste and stitch the sleeves to the front and backs at the armholes, taking ¼in seams. Turn the dress wrong side out. At each seam, place the two joined pieces *right* sides together, as for an ordinary seam, with the original stitching and seam allowances to one side. Stitch along the seamline in from the first stitched edge, thus enclosing the raw edges to form a French seam. (Fig. 1)

Lay the dress on a flat surface, right side up. Transfer the smocking grid onto the fabric using the dressmaker's carbon and a sharp pencil or ball point pen. Begin ⅜in from the center-back edge, with the curved line on the neck edge. Re-position the pattern and continue around the neck edge, making 12 tracings in all, making sure that the pattern repeats match exactly. (Fig. 2)

Using the same method transfer the smaller smocking grid to the lower edge of each sleeve, using the pattern seven times and beginning and ending at the seamlines. (Fig. 3)

Work six rows of gathering stitches, by hand, around the neck edge and four along the sleeve edge, as indicated on the pattern, making a small stitch at each dot.

Pull up all the gathering threads below the neck edge. Pin the guide around the neck edge and adjust the gathering threads so that the fabric follows the shape. Secure the threads at one center-back edge by winding each around a pin in a figure-eight. These will remain in the fabric until the smocking is completed. (Fig. 4)

Using four strands of embroidery floss and alternating the colors as you like, work the smocking as instructed below, starting at the top line of gathering stitches and working downward. Make sure that the stitches are pulled up evenly but not too tightly.

Row 1 – cable stitch. Work from left to right. Join thread to left of first pleat, pass needle over two pleats and insert it from right to left under second pleat, bringing it out between the two and keeping thread below needle. Make a stitch into next pleat, from right to left, with thread above needle. Repeat these two movements to end of row.

Row 2 – outline stitch. Work from left to right. The stitch resembles stem stitch in embroidery – see page 183 – and picks up one pleat with each stitch.

Rows 3 and 4 – double cable stitch. This is simply two rows of cable stitch, worked so that the lower row is a reflection of the upper – see stitch key.

Row 5 – cable stitch.

Rows 6 and 7 – diamond stitch. Work from left to right. Join thread to first pleat in second row, then pick up second pleat, from right to left, with thread below needle. Take needle up to first row and pick up third pleat from right to left, then fourth, keeping thread above needle. Move down to second row and pick up fifth pleat, from right to left. Continue to end of work. Note: the complete diamond stitch pattern would use another row, working a mirror image of the first line of stitching.

Rows 8 and 9 – trellis stitch. This is outline stitch worked diagonally to create a diamond shape. Work from left to right, starting at the lowest point of the upper row and working first upward – inserting the needle from right to left with thread held below the needle – then downward, inserting the needle in the same way but with the thread held above it. Work the lower row in the same way, reversing the shape.

Rows 10, 11 and 12 – outline stitch, worked diagonally as shown on key.

Fasten off all threads securely on the wrong side of the dress and sew a bead in the center of each trellis between rows 8 and 9. Remove gathering threads. (Fig. 5)

Placing right sides together and matching notches, baste and stitch the center-back seam up to the dot. Press the seam open. (Fig. 6)

Placing right sides together, pin and baste the neck binding to the neck edge. Stitch. Trim the seam allowances to $\frac{1}{4}$in. Turn under $\frac{5}{8}$in on the free edge of the binding; fold the binding to the wrong side and slipstitch the turned-under edge to the stitching line. (Fig. 7)

On the lower edges of sleeves turn up

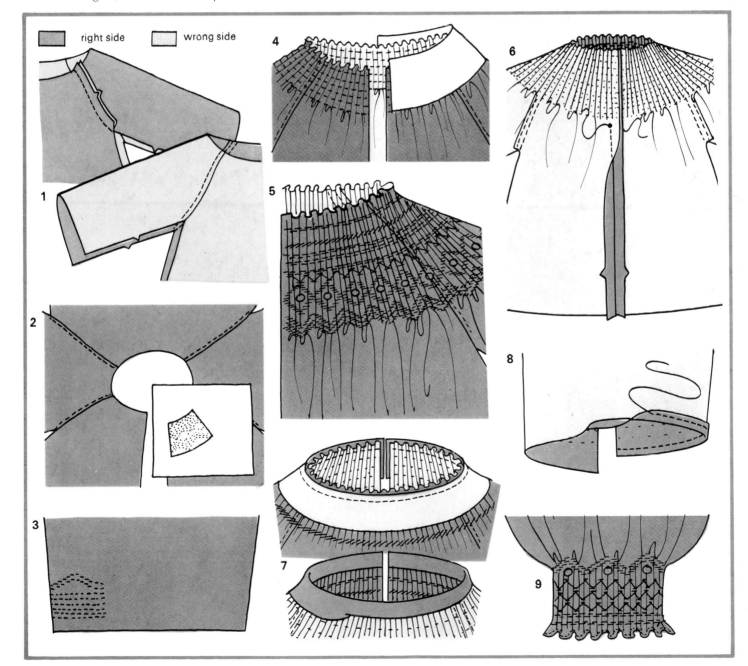

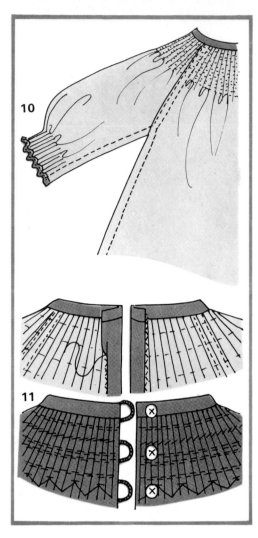

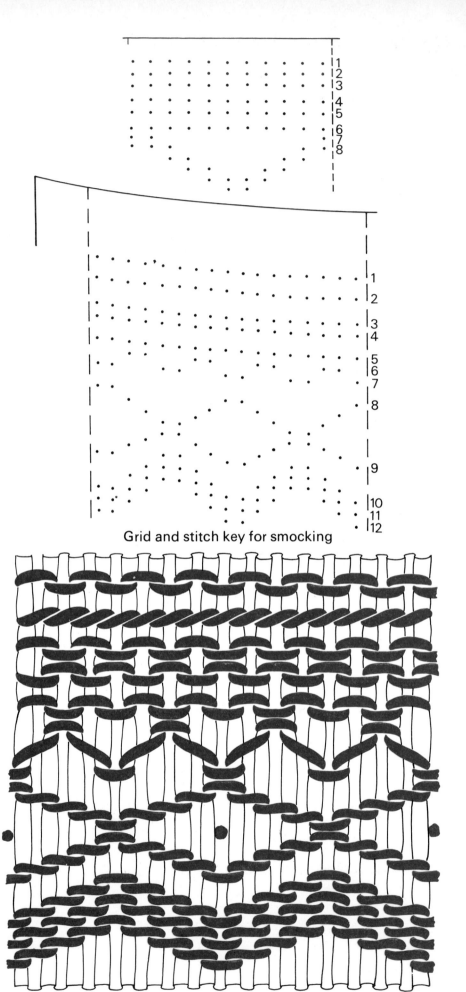

Grid and stitch key for smocking

small double hems, using $\frac{5}{8}$in of fabric, and machine stitch in place. Press. (Fig. 8)

Pull up the gathering threads to fit the sleeve guide and secure them with pins as before. Work the smocking as follows :

Rows 1 and 2 – double cable stitch.
Rows 3, 4, 5 and 6 – diamond stitch.
Rows 7 and 8 – diagonal outline stitch.

Sew a bead into each space between the last row of diamond stitch and the outline stitch. (Fig. 9)

Placing wrong sides together and matching notches, baste and stitch the side and sleeve seams, $\frac{1}{4}$in from the edge. Fold the seam to the inside and complete French seams as for armholes. Press the seams toward the back. (Fig. 10)

Turn under $\frac{1}{4}$in and then a further $\frac{3}{8}$in on remaining center-back edges and slipstitch in place. Press. Hand-work three button loops on the left-hand side as indicated on the pattern.

Sew buttons onto the right-hand side to correspond. (Fig. 11)

Check the length of the dress. Turn up the hem, fold under the raw edges, baste in place and hand-hem. Press.

Graph pattern for smocked dress

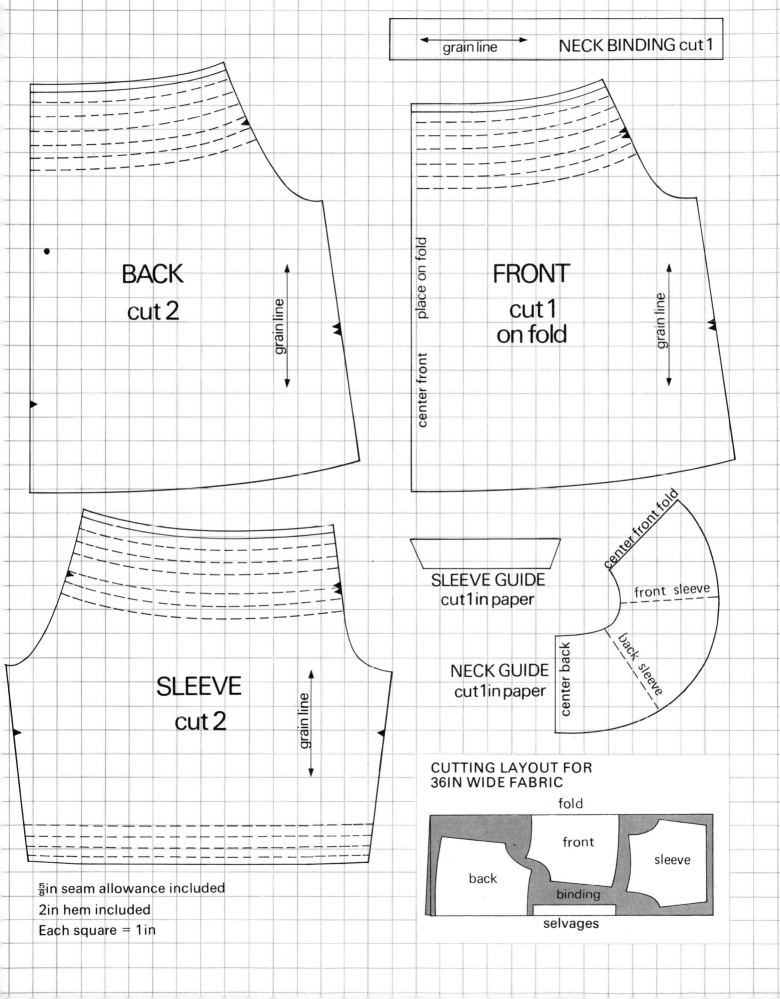

NECK BINDING cut 1

grain line

BACK
cut 2

grain line

FRONT
cut 1
on fold

center front   place on fold

grain line

SLEEVE
cut 2

grain line

SLEEVE GUIDE
cut 1 in paper

NECK GUIDE
cut 1 in paper

center front fold

front sleeve

back sleeve

center back

CUTTING LAYOUT FOR
36IN WIDE FABRIC

fold

front

sleeve

back

binding

selvages

$\frac{5}{8}$in seam allowance included

2in hem included

Each square = 1in

Quilted Coat

Raglan sleeves make this quilted jacket as comfortable for baby to wear as it is easy for you to make.

Sizes
The pattern is given in two sizes : 1 year and 18 months – or chest sizes 20in and 20½in respectively.

Materials
1yd of 36in wide quilted fabric
⅜yd of ½in wide bias binding to match the lining of the quilting
3yd of ¾ – 1in wide bias binding or braid
2 buttons
graph paper marked in 1in squares

Making the pattern
Using graph paper and following the color indicating the size required, enlarge each pattern piece. Each square on the page represents 1 square inch on your paper. A seam allowance of ⅝in is included.

Cut out the pattern pieces and transfer markings to them.

Cutting out
Following the cutting layout, fold the fabric in half lengthwise and pin the four pattern pieces in place as indicated. Make sure that the grain line on each piece lies on the straight grain of the fabric.

Cut out the pieces and transfer markings to them.

Making the jacket
Use the flat fell seam method for all seams, except the collar seam, easing the fabric at curves where necessary. First baste and stitch along the seamline, placing right sides together. Trim one seam allowance to ¼in. On the other seam allowance trim away only the outer fabric and batting, leaving the lining fabric intact. Turn under the raw edge of the lining and place this edge over the trimmed raw edge. Baste and stitch through all layers of fabric, approximately ⅜in from the seamline. (Fig. 1)

Placing right sides together and matching notches, baste and stitch the fronts to the back at the side seams. (Fig. 2)

Placing right sides together, baste and stitch the sleeve darts. Press them lightly toward the back.

Placing right sides together and matching notches, baste and stitch the sleeve seams. (Fig. 3)

Placing right sides together and matching notches, insert sleeves into armholes. Baste and stitch seams as before, easing the fabric at curves. (Fig. 4)

Placing right sides together and matching notches, baste and stitch the collar to the neck edge, using a plain seam. Trim and clip the seam allowances and press them upward. (Fig. 5)

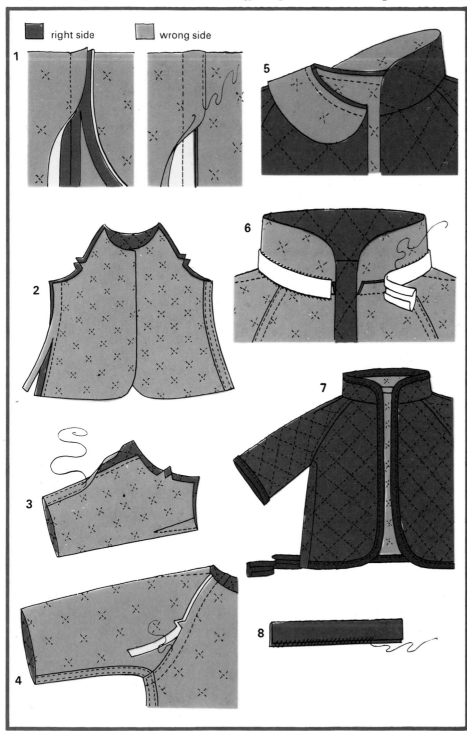

right side   wrong side

Pin and baste a strip of matching bias binding over the seam, enclosing the raw edges. Hand-hem in place along both edges. Press lightly. (Fig. 6)

Starting at a side seam, pin the folded bias binding to the edge of the coat, enclosing the raw edge. Baste the binding in place all around the edge and back to the side seam. Cut off and fold under the end. Stitch close to the edge of the binding through all thicknesses. Repeat around the lower sleeve edges. Press all edges. (Fig. 7)

Cut two lengths of bias binding 2in long. Hand-sew the long edges together to form a tube. Finish the ends by turning them in and hand-sewing. (Fig. 8)

Press. Attach both ends of each length to the wrong side of one center-front edge – right-hand side for a girl, left-hand side for a boy, – forming a loop. The upper loop should be at the neckline and the lower approximately 3in below it. The loops should be firmly overcast onto the fabric, allowing enough room for the buttons to slip through. Sew buttons to the other side of the garment to correspond to the loops.

Graph pattern for quilted coat

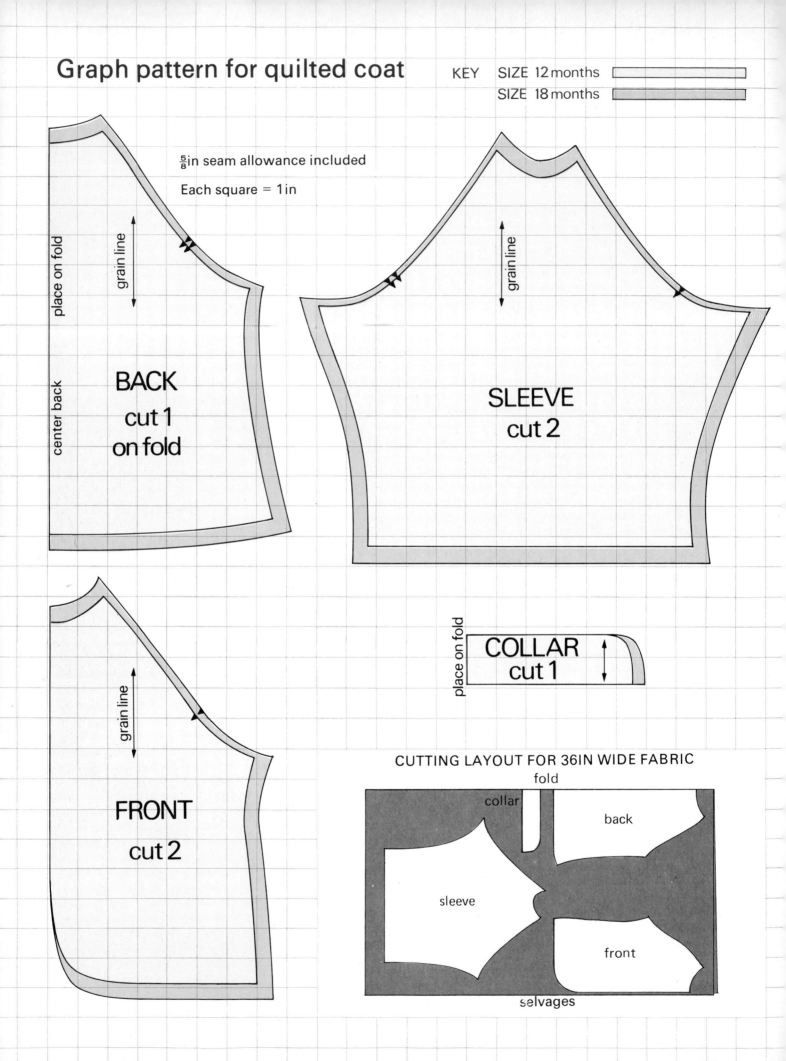

KEY   SIZE 12 months
       SIZE 18 months

$\frac{5}{8}$ in seam allowance included

Each square = 1 in

grain line

place on fold

center back

BACK
cut 1
on fold

grain line

SLEEVE
cut 2

grain line

FRONT
cut 2

place on fold

COLLAR
cut 1

CUTTING LAYOUT FOR 36IN WIDE FABRIC
fold

collar

back

sleeve

front

selvages

Stretchy Top

Fabric with "give," such as stretch terry cloth or soft jersey, makes this simple top ideal for babies and toddlers.

Sizes

The pattern is given in three sizes: 1 year, 18 months and 2 years, or chest sizes 20in, 20½in and 21in respectively.

Materials

1yd of 36in wide stretch fabric
a hook and eye
a 4in zipper
graph paper marked in 1in squares.

Using stretch fabrics

A ball point needle should be used on stretch knitted fabric. For best results stitch all seams with stretch stitch. If this is not possible, use the smallest zigzag with the stitches fairly close together. The seam should stretch slightly without the thread breaking.

Making the pattern

Using graph paper and following the color indicating the size required, enlarge the pattern pieces to the correct size. One square on the page represents 2 square inches on your paper. A seam allowance of ⅝in and a hem allowance of 1½in are included.

Transfer all markings to the pattern.

Cutting out

Following the cutting layout, fold the fabric lengthwise so that the back can be placed on double fabric and the collar on a single thickness. Pin these pieces in place, making sure to position the grain lines as indicated, and cut them out.

Re-fold the fabric evenly, pin the remaining pieces in place and cut them out.

Transfer all markings to the fabric.

Making the top

Placing right sides together and matching notches, baste and stitch the back to the front at the side and shoulder seams. Finish the seam allowances with zigzag stitching. (Fig. 1)

Placing right sides together and matching notches, baste and stitch the center-back seams up to the dot. (Fig. 2)

Placing right sides together and matching notches, baste and stitch one long edge of the collar to the neck. Trim the seam allowances and press them

upward onto the collar. (Fig. 3)

Baste the center-back seam from the dot upward and the collar seam up to the fold line. Press open. Place the zipper face

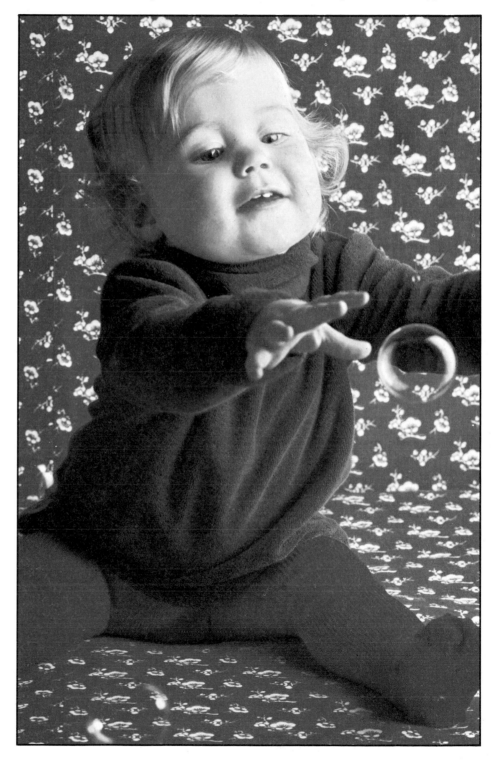

down on the seam allowances, with the center of the teeth directly over the seamline, the bottom of the teeth level with the dot and the top level with the collar fold line. Baste in place. Working on the right side, stitch along both sides of the zipper and across the bottom. (Fig. 4)

Turn under $\frac{5}{8}$in on the remaining long edge of the collar. Bring this folded edge down to meet the line of machine stitching and baste it in place so that the short ends clear the zipper teeth. Slipstitch the folded edges in place along the stitching line and on either side of the

zipper. Fold the collar to the right side to make a roll and sew a hook and eye just above the zipper on the inside. (Fig. 5)

Placing right sides together and matching notches, baste and stitch the sleeve seam. Press seam open. Repeat for the cuffs. (Fig. 6)

Placing right sides together and matching the seams, baste and stitch the cuff to the sleeve. Turn under $\frac{5}{8}$in on the cuff edge and baste and stitch this edge to the stitching line on the inside of the sleeve. (Fig. 7)

Run two rows of gathering stitches

between the notches on the sleeve cap. Placing right sides together and matching notches and side and sleeve seams, pin the sleeve into the armhole. Pull up the gathering threads and distribute the fullness evenly. Baste and stitch the armhole seam. Trim and finish the seam allowances together. (Fig. 8)

Turn under $\frac{3}{8}$in on the lower edge and then a further $1\frac{1}{8}$in. Baste in place and hand-hem. (Fig. 9)

Press the finished garment on the wrong side.

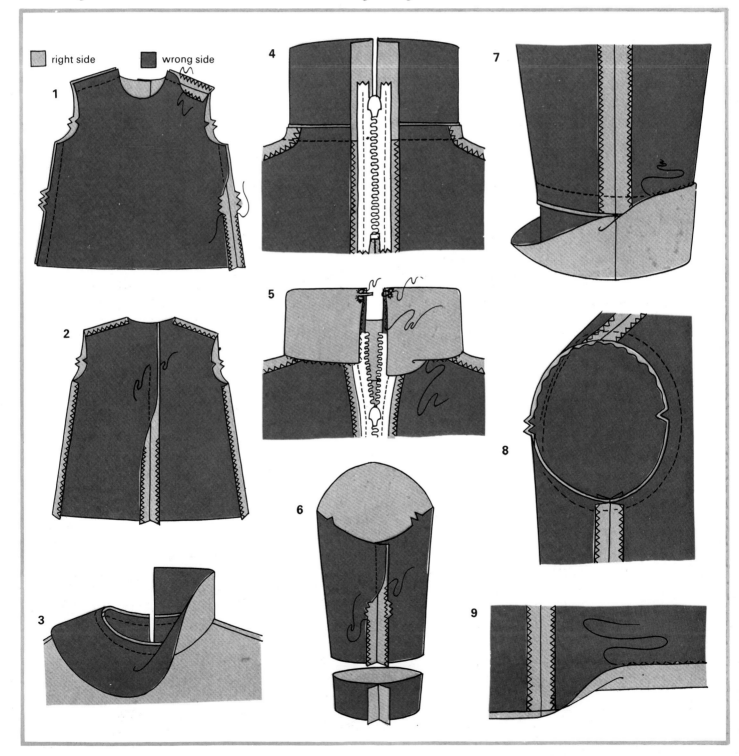

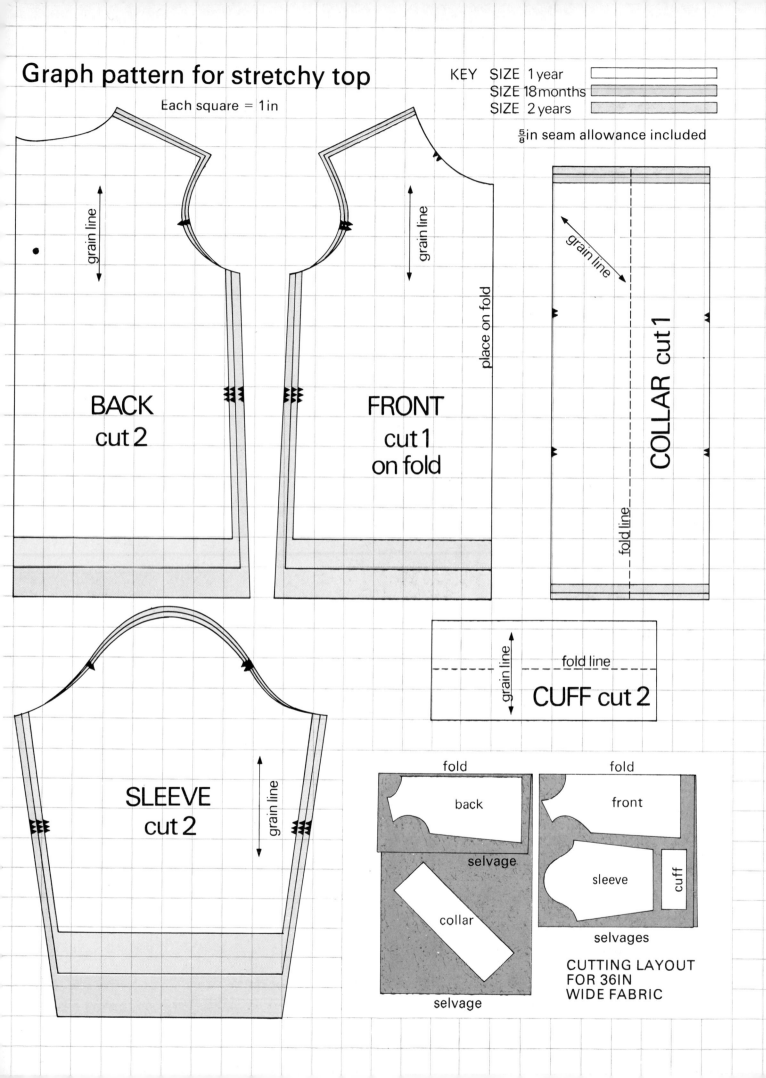

Graph pattern for stretchy top

Each square = 1in

KEY SIZE 1 year
SIZE 18 months
SIZE 2 years

$\frac{5}{8}$in seam allowance included

grain line

BACK
cut 2

grain line

FRONT
cut 1
on fold

place on fold

grain line

COLLAR cut 1

fold line

grain line

fold line

CUFF cut 2

grain line

SLEEVE
cut 2

grain line

fold

back

selvage

collar

selvage

fold

front

sleeve

cuff

selvages

CUTTING LAYOUT
FOR 36IN
WIDE FABRIC

Short Playsuit

Simple lines and stretchy fabric make this playsuit a practical, comfortable garment. Why not make several in different colors?

Sizes
The pattern is given in two sizes : 2 and 3 years – or chest sizes 21in and 22in respectively.

Materials
1yd of 36in wide stretch fabric
a 12in zipper
graph paper marked in 1in squares

Using stretch fabrics
A ball point needle should be used on stretch knitted fabric. For best results stitch all seams with stretch stitch. If this is not possible use the smallest zigzag with the stitches fairly close together. The seam should stretch slightly without the thread breaking.

Making the pattern
Using graph paper and following the color indicating the size required, enlarge the pattern pieces. Each square on the page represents 1 square inch on your paper. A seam and hem allowance of $\frac{5}{8}$in is included.

Cut out the pattern pieces and transfer the markings onto them.

Cutting out
Following the cutting layout, position the pattern pieces as indicated, making sure that the grain lines are on the straight grain of the fabric. Pin them in place and cut them out.

Transfer all markings from the pattern pieces to the fabric.

Making the playsuit
Placing right sides together and matching notches, baste and stitch the center-back seam. Trim the seam allowances to $\frac{1}{4}$in, press them to one side and finish them with zigzag stitching. (Fig. 1)

Placing right sides together and matching notches, baste and stitch the center-front seam to the dot. Trim, press and finish the seam allowances as for the center-back seam.

Placing right sides together and matching notches, baste and stitch the

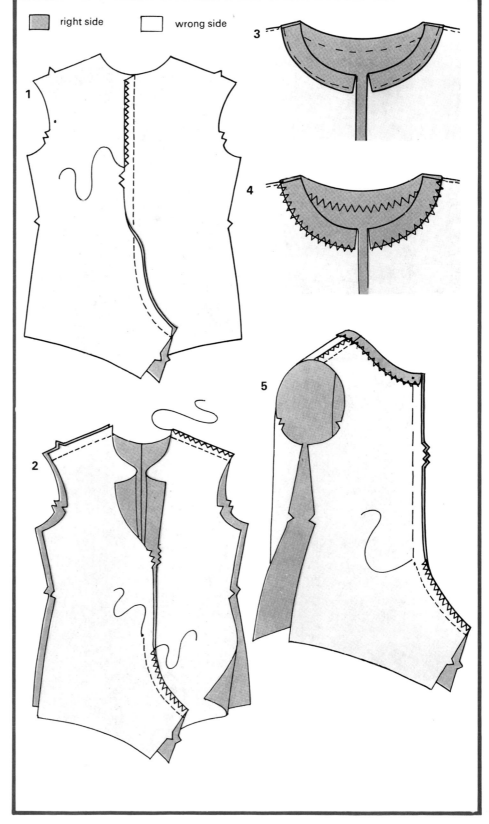

right side | wrong side

shoulder seams, easing the back to the front. Trim, press and finish the seam allowances as before. (Fig. 2)

Turn under ⅝in around the neck edge, baste and press (Fig 3). Using large zigzag stitches fairly close together, stitch the raw edge of the neck hem to the garment. (Fig. 4)

Placing right sides together and matching notches, baste the center fronts together from the dot to the neckline. (Fig. 5) Press open.

Working on the wrong side, pin and baste the zipper, face down, to the garment, placing the teeth over the seamline. Fold under the upper ends of the zipper tape and baste them in place. Working on the right side, machine stitch ¼in on each side of the center seamline and across the bottom of the zipper. Press. Remove the basting.

Placing right sides together and matching notches, baste and stitch the back to the front at the sides. Trim, press and finish the seam allowances as before.

Placing right sides together and matching notches and center seams, baste and stitch the crotch seam. Trim the seam allowances, press them toward the back and finish them as before. Catch-stitch the seam down where it crosses the center-back seam.

Turn under ⅝in around the leg edges, baste, press and zigzag as for the neckline. (Fig. 6)

Placing right sides together and matching notches, baste and stitch the sleeve seam. Trim the seam allowances, press them toward the back and finish them as before.

Turn under and finish the lower edge as for the neckline. (Fig. 7)

Run a gathering thread between the notches over the sleeve cap. Placing right sides together and matching dots and notches, pin the sleeve into the armhole, distributing the fullness evenly. Baste and stitch. Trim the seam allowances, press them toward the sleeve and finish them as before. (Fig. 8)

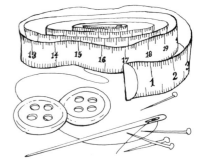

Graph pattern for playsuit

$\frac{5}{8}$in seam allowance included

Each square = 1 in

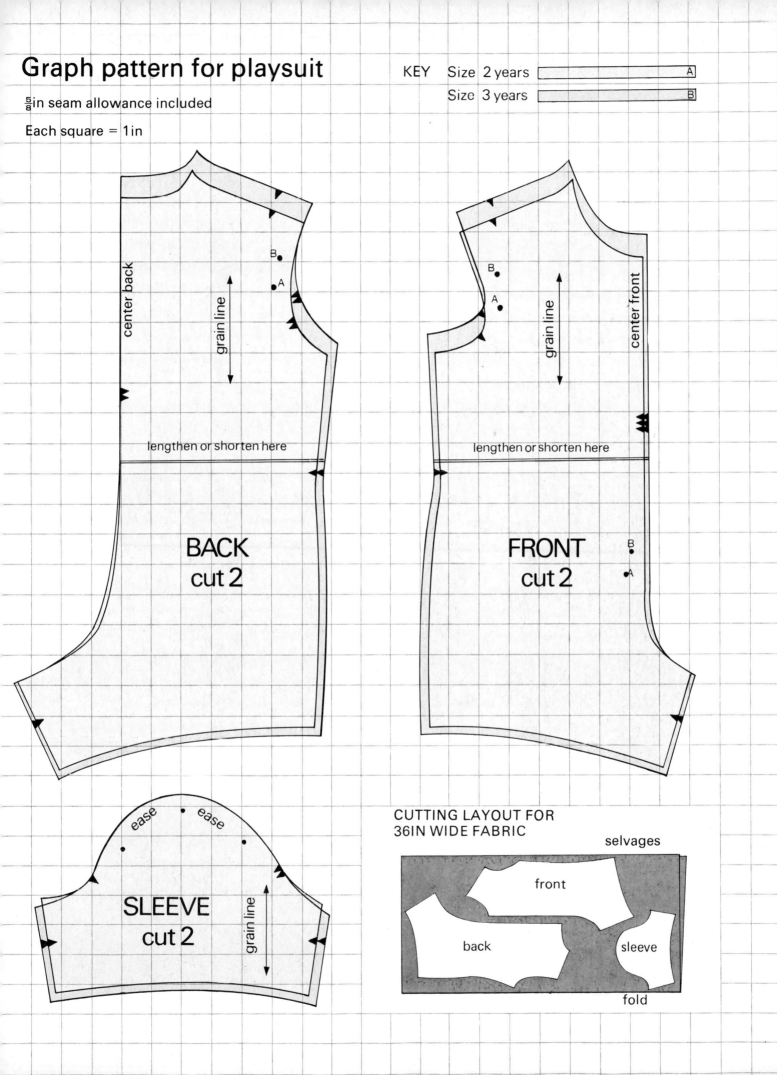

center back

grain line

B •
• A

lengthen or shorten here

**BACK
cut 2**

center front

grain line

B •
A •

lengthen or shorten here

**FRONT
cut 2**

B •
• A

ease   •   ease

•   •

**SLEEVE
cut 2**

grain line

CUTTING LAYOUT FOR
36IN WIDE FABRIC

selvages

front

back

sleeve

fold

Boy's Shorts

Just right for a toddler's active life, these shorts have a stretchy waist and handy pockets. They are lined for a good shape and extra durability.

Sizes

The pattern is given in two sizes: 2 and 3 years, or waist sizes 21in and 22in respectively.

Materials

$\frac{5}{8}$yd of 36in wide fabric for either size
$\frac{5}{8}$yd of 36in wide lining fabric – make sure the lining fabric is of the same type, i.e., requires the same care, as the main fabric
$1\frac{1}{4}$yd of $\frac{1}{4}$in wide elastic
graph paper marked in 1in squares

Making the pattern

Using graph paper and following the color indicating the size required, enlarge each pattern piece. One square on the page represents 2 square inches on your paper. A seam and hem allowance of $\frac{5}{8}$in is included.

Cut out the pattern pieces and transfer all markings to them.

Cutting out

Following the cutting layout, fold the fabric and position the pattern pieces as indicated, making sure that the grain lines are on the straight grain of the fabric. Pin in place and cut out.

Transfer all markings from the pattern to the fabric.

Fold the lining fabric in the same way. Pin on the pattern pieces, omitting the pocket, and cut them out.

Making the shorts

Turn under the seam allowance on the curved edge of the pockets and baste, clipping at intervals as shown so that it lies flat. Machine stitch $\frac{3}{8}$in from the edge. Press.

Turn under the seam allowance on the remaining unnotched edges, baste and press. (Fig. 1) Place one pocket on each front where indicated, matching notches at sides. Baste pockets in position. Working on the right side, topstitch close to the edges, omitting notched sides. Topstitch again $\frac{1}{4}$in in from the edges. Press. (Fig. 2)

Placing right sides together and matching notches, baste and stitch the center front and center back seams. Clip crotch curve and press seams open. (Fig. 3)

Placing right sides together and matching notches, baste and stitch the side seams. Press open. (Fig. 4)

Placing right sides together and matching center seams, baste and stitch the crotch seam. Clip curve and press the seam open.

Similarly stitch the center, side and crotch seams of the lining. (Fig. 5)

Place the lining inside the shorts, right sides facing and notches and seams matching, and baste and stitch the lining to the shorts around the leg edges. Clip the curves almost to the stitching.

Turn the shorts right side out and press them.

Tack the lining to the shorts. To do this, hand-sew the center, side and crotch seam allowances of the shorts and lining together, using small stitches, as close to the seamline as possible.

Turn down the waist edge along the fold line; press. Turn under the seam allowance on the raw edge and baste this edge in place through lining and main fabric.

Machine stitch close to the turned-under edge. (Fig. 6) Add another row of stitching $\frac{3}{8}$in above the first and another

the same distance from the waist edge. (Fig. 7)

Cut two lengths of elastic, each the circumference of the waist.

Unpick the center back seam on the inside only where it crosses the elastic casings. Insert the elastic and hand-sew the ends together securely. Overcast the openings in the center back seam. (Fig. 8)

Fold the shorts on the right side so that inner and outer leg seams touch at the lower edge and the crotch. Press in the front and back creases.

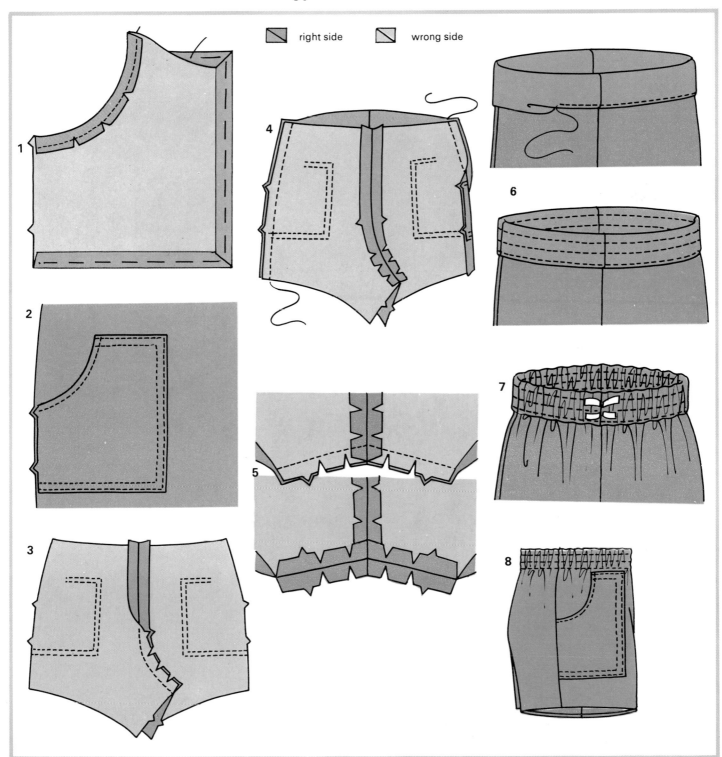

right side   wrong side

Graph pattern for shorts

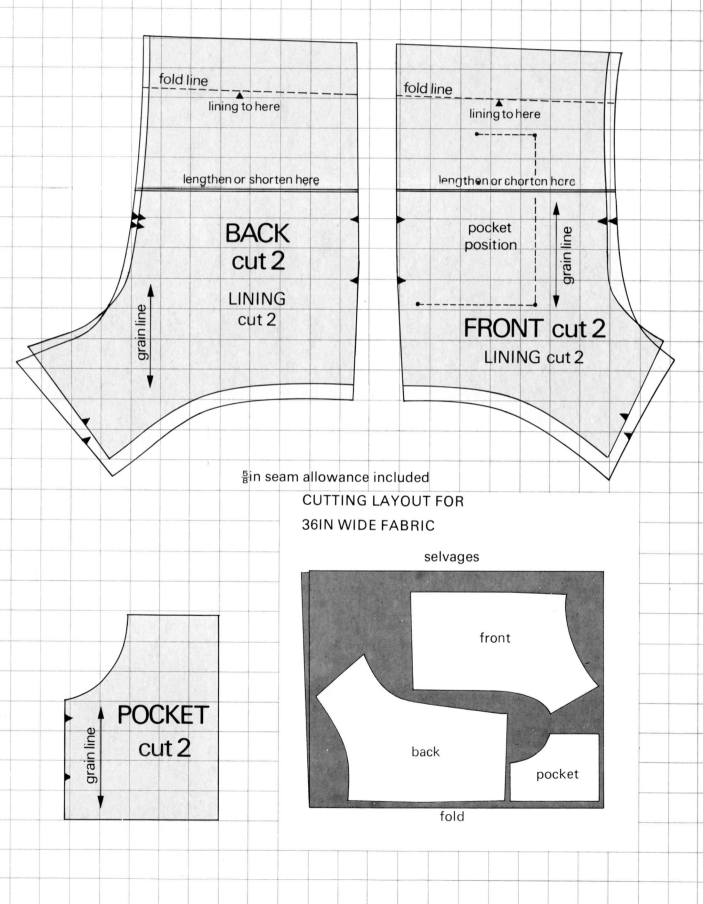

KEY   Size 2 years
      Size 3 years

Each square = 1 in

fold line
lining to here

lengthen or shorten here

BACK
cut 2

LINING
cut 2

grain line

fold line
lining to here

lengthen or shorten here

pocket
position

grain line

FRONT cut 2

LINING cut 2

$\frac{5}{8}$ in seam allowance included

CUTTING LAYOUT FOR

36IN WIDE FABRIC

selvages

front

back

pocket

fold

POCKET
cut 2

grain line

Patch Jumper

The simple lines of this jumper make it easy to wear, and the patches give it a jaunty look.

Sizes
Pattern in three sizes: 3, 4 and 5 years – or chest sizes 22in, 23in and 24in.

Materials
1yd of 36in wide fabric

an assortment of fabric scraps of the same fiber content as the main fabric, e.g. cotton scraps for a cotton dress
a medium-sized button
graph paper marked in 1in squares

Making the pattern
Using graph paper and following the color indicating the size required, enlarge each pattern piece. One square on the page represents 2 square inches on your paper. An allowance of ⅝in is included on all seams and an allowance of 2in for the hem.

Cut out the pattern pieces and transfer the markings to them.

Cutting out
Following the cutting layout, fold the fabric and position the pattern pieces as indicated. Make sure that the grain lines lie on the straight grain of the fabric. Pin the pieces in place and cut them out. Transfer markings to the fabric.

From the assortment of fabrics cut squares measuring 4in.

Making the jumper
Placing right sides together and matching notches, baste and stitch the side seams. Finish the seam allowances with zigzag stitching and press them open. (Fig. 1)

Turn under the seam allowances on the patches, mitering the corners, and baste around the edges.

Lay the dress flat, right side up, and arrange the patches on it as you like. Baste and stitch them in place. Note: if you prefer you can zigzag stitch them in place, first trimming away the seam allowances and then stitching over the raw edges.

Pockets may be made by using the patches double, with wrong sides together, and stitching them to the dress along three sides only – the upper edges being folded and topstitched together first, by machine or by hand. (Fig. 2)

Placing right sides together, baste and stitch the center-back seam as far as the notch. Finish the seam allowances with zigzagging and press the seam open.

Placing right sides together, baste and stitch the shoulder seams. Finish the seam allowances and press them open. (Fig. 3)

Placing right sides together, baste and stitch the underarm seams of the armhole facings. Press the seams open. Finish the outer edges of the facings with zigzag stitching. (Fig. 4)

Placing right sides together and matching notches, baste and stitch the armhole facing to the armhole. Trim and clip seam allowances and turn facing to wrong side. Baste around the stitched edge. Catch-stitch facing to dress at shoulder and side seams. Press. Remove basting threads. (Fig. 5)

Placing right sides together, baste and stitch the back neck facings together at the center back up to the notch. Press seams open. (Fig. 6)

Placing right sides together, baste and stitch back neck facing to front neck facing at shoulder seams. Press seams open. Finish the outer edge of the facing with zigzag stitching. (Fig. 7)

Placing right sides together and matching notches, baste and stitch facing to neck and back opening. Trim and clip the seam allowances, cutting across corners at center-back neck. Turn the facing to the wrong side; baste around stitched edges as before. Press; remove basting thread. (Fig. 8)

Catch-stitch facing to dress at shoulder seams and center-back seam. (Fig. 9)

Sew the button to the right-hand side of the back neck opening and work a button loop on the left side to correspond. (Fig. 10)

Adjust the hemline. Finish the raw edge with zigzagging, turn up the hem allowance, baste and hem by hand. (Fig. 11)

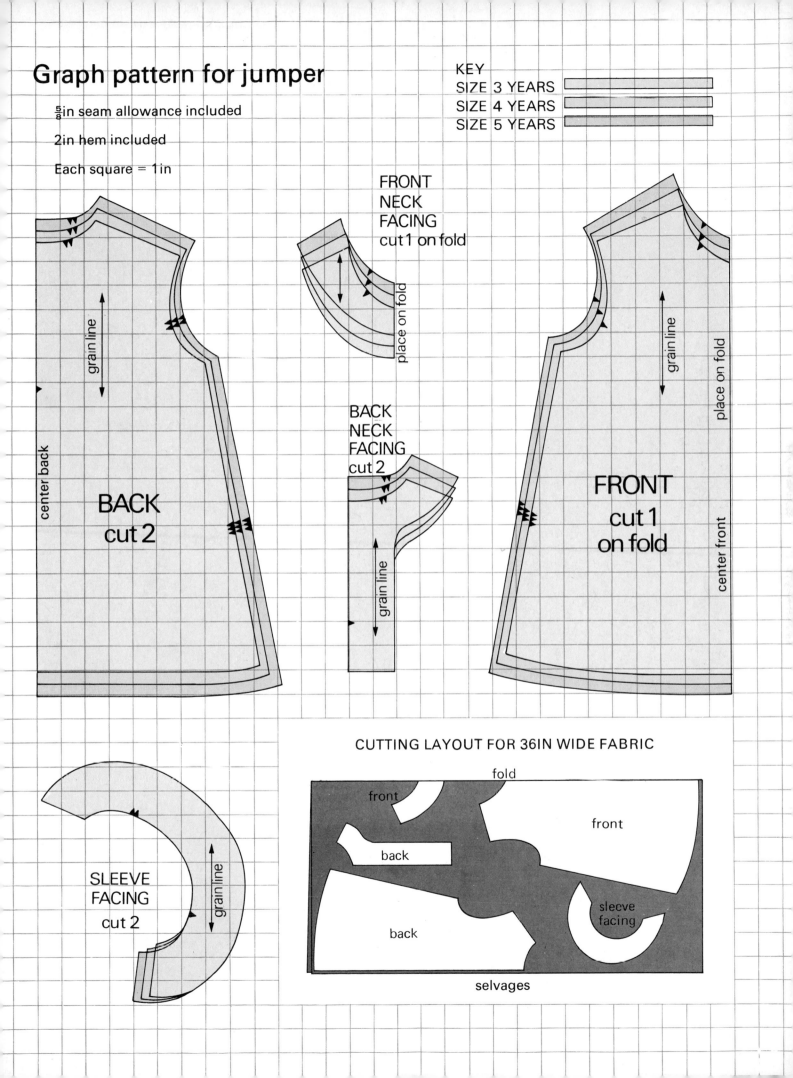

Graph pattern for jumper

$\frac{5}{8}$in seam allowance included

2in hem included

Each square = 1in

KEY
SIZE 3 YEARS
SIZE 4 YEARS
SIZE 5 YEARS

grain line

center back

**BACK
cut 2**

FRONT
NECK
FACING
cut 1 on fold

place on fold

BACK
NECK
FACING
cut 2

grain line

grain line

**FRONT
cut 1
on fold**

place on fold

center front

**SLEEVE
FACING
cut 2**

grain line

CUTTING LAYOUT FOR 36IN WIDE FABRIC

fold

front

front

back

back

sleeve
facing

selvages

Simple Sundress

Nothing could be simpler to make than this charming sundress. The top is shaped with two lengths of elastic threaded through casings, so that the width can be adjusted for a perfect fit. For extra style add an apple patch pocket.

Sizes

The cutting measurements (see diagram) are given for three sizes: 2-3 years, 6-7 years and 9-10 years. Finished lengths are 14½in, 21½in and 25½in respectively.

Materials

(Amounts given in [ ] refer to the larger sizes.)
1⅛yd [1½yd : 1¾yd] of 36 in wide fabric
2⅞yd [3⅛yd : 3½yd] of ½in wide seam binding
2¼yd of narrow elastic
a bodkin or tapestry needle
scraps of red fabric for pocket (optional)
green stranded embroidery floss in two
    shades (optional)
tracing paper (optional)
dressmaker's carbon paper (optional)
a medium-sized crewel needle (optional)
an embroidery hoop (optional)

Cutting out

Cut the fabric in half crosswise and pin the two pieces together, with wrong sides facing. Measure and cut the front/back pieces, following the measurement diagram for the size required and cutting the shorter sides on the lengthwise grain of the fabric.

From the remaining fabric cut two straps, with the longer side running lengthwise.

Making the dress

Place the front and back pieces together, right sides facing, and pin, baste and stitch along the two shorter sides, taking ⅝in seam allowance (Fig. 1). Press open the seam allowances and finish them with zigzag stitching.

Turn down ⅜in on the upper edge, then turn down a further ⅜in. Pin, baste and stitch close to the inner, folded edge. Remove basting and press. (Fig. 2)

Cut two lengths of seam binding, each long enough to go all the way around the dress, plus ¾in for turning under.

Pin one length of binding to the

underside of the dress, ¾-1¼in down from the upper edge, starting and ending at one side seam and turning under ⅜in on each end. Stitch it in place close to each edge.

Similarly pin and stitch the other length of binding in place about 1¼-1½in below

the first. (Fig. 3)

Fold each strap in half lengthwise, wrong sides facing, and pin and stitch the long edges together taking ⅜in seam allowance. Press the seams open.

Turn the straps right side out (Fig. 4). Position the seam so that it lies in the

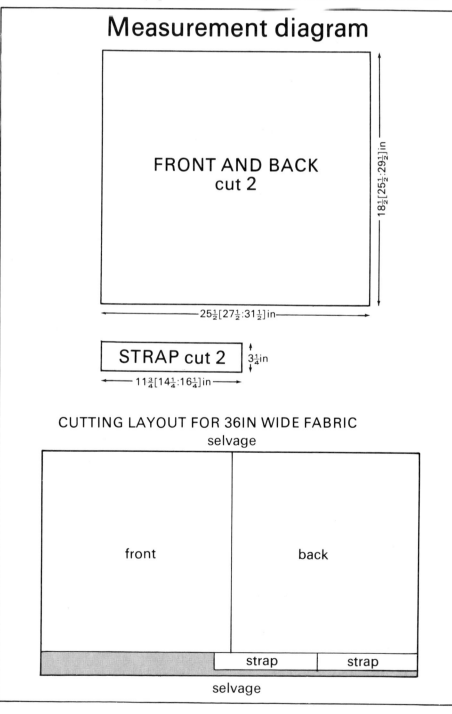

Measurement diagram

FRONT AND BACK
cut 2

18½[25½:29½]in

25½[27½:31½]in

STRAP cut 2   3¼in

11¾[14¼:16¼]in

CUTTING LAYOUT FOR 36IN WIDE FABRIC

selvage

front

back

strap   strap

selvage

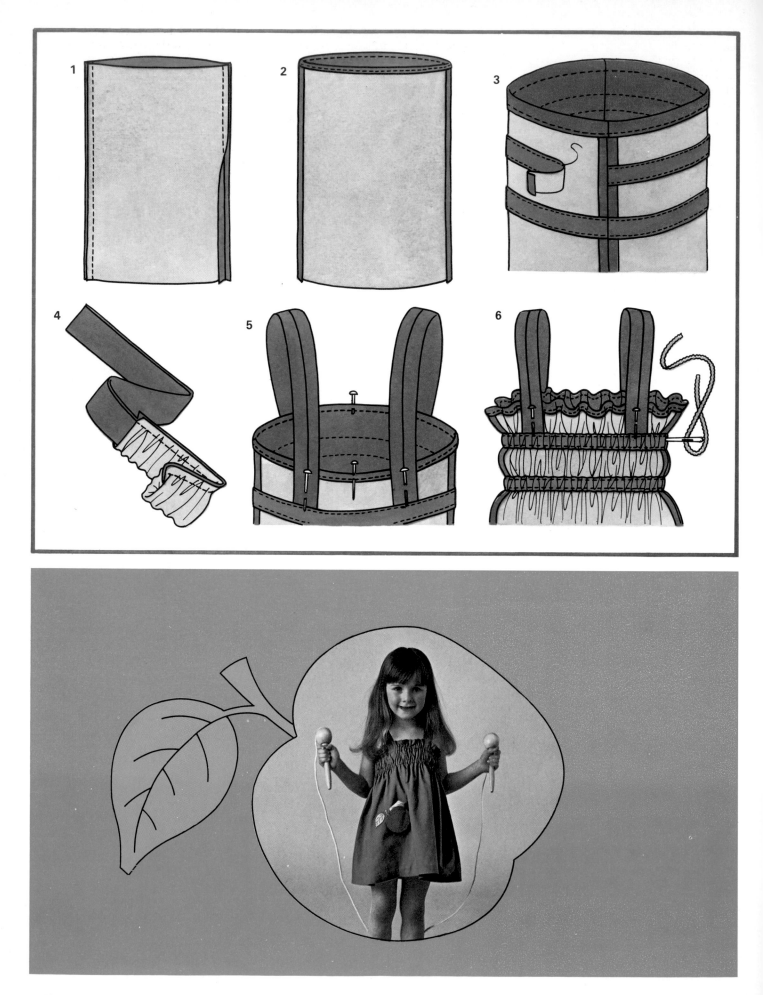

center of the strap, as shown, and press each strap flat.

Insert a pin in the center of the front and the back sections. Pin the straps in place on the underside, positioning them halfway between the pin and the side edges. (Fig. 5)

Cut the elastic in half. Using the bodkin or tapestry needle, thread one length through each casing. Draw up elastic to fit chest measurement and knot the ends together temporarily. (Fig. 6)

Try the dress on the child. Adjust the elastic and check the length and position of straps, adjusting them if necessary. Turn up the hem and mark the desired length with tailor's chalk or pins.

Turn under the ends of the straps and hand-sew them securely to the seam binding.

Trim off surplus elastic and sew the ends together securely.

Fold up $\frac{3}{8}$in along lower edge; machine stitch. Turn up the hem along the marked hemline. Pin, baste and hand-hem it in place. Press. Add a patch pocket, if desired.

Making the patch pocket

(The method described below can be adapted for any other shape you prefer.)

Trace the apple shape given on page 120, omitting the stem and leaf. Cut out the pattern and pin it to a double thickness of fabric (right sides facing). Cut out the shape adding $\frac{3}{8}$in seam allowance all around.

Pin the two shapes together, still with wrong sides facing, and baste and stitch $\frac{3}{8}$in in from the edges, leaving a 1$\frac{1}{4}$in opening along the lower edge. Trim seam allowances and clip and notch them as necessary. (Fig. 7)

Turn the pocket right side out. Work the seam to the edges and baste, turning under the raw edges at the opening. Press; remove basting thread.

Pin and baste the pocket to the dress on the right-hand side at the level desired. Topstitch it in place close to the edge (thus also closing the gap) and leaving a 2$\frac{1}{4}$in wide opening at the top. Add another line of topstitching inside the first.

Trace the leaf and stem from the photograph and, using dressmaker's carbon, transfer them to the dress fabric in the correct position. (Fig. 8)

Embroider the leaf and stem in any stitch you like – such as long and short stitch, with lines of backstitch in darker green, or entirely in lines of chain stitch.

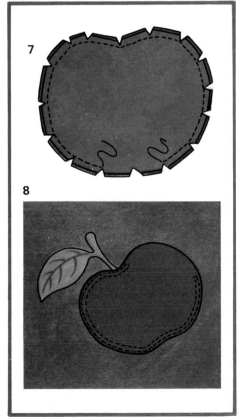

Raincoat and Hat

On gray days a bright red raincoat and sou'wester, made in water-repellent plastic or vinyl fabric, do a lot to raise the spirits – as well as keeping a little girl warm and dry.

Sizes
The pattern is given in two sizes : 18 months and 3 years – or chest sizes 20½in and 22in respectively.

Materials
1⅛yd of 60in wide plastic or vinyl fabric, or
    1¾yd of 36in wide fabric – for either size
5 gripper fasteners
carpet or fabric adhesive
transparent tape
graph paper marked in 1in squares.

Using plastic or vinyl fabric
Attach pattern pieces and hold edges together with transparent tape, rather than pins, which leave marks. Do not baste. Mark any position lines on the wrong side with pencil. If the sticking continues, place a piece of tissue paper on both sides of the fabric and remove after stitching.

Making the pattern
Using graph paper and following the color indicating the size required, enlarge the pattern pieces. Each square on the.page represents 2 square inches on your paper. A seam allowance of ¼in is included and a hem allowance of 1in on the lower edge and sleeves.

Cut out the pattern pieces and transfer all markings to them.

Cutting out
Following the appropriate cutting layout, position the pattern pieces as indicated, making sure that the grain lines are parallel to the selvage. Attach the pieces with transparent tape and cut them out.

Cut another collar section and two more crown sections.

Transfer all markings from the pattern pieces to the fabric.

For the sou'wester strap cut a strip of fabric 1½in wide and 18in long.

Making the raincoat
Placing right sides together and matching

notches, stitch the side seams. Fold the seam allowances toward the back, and, working on the right side, add a line of topstitching ⅛in from each seamline.

Turn under ¼in along the facing edges and stitch. (Fig. 1)

Turn under ¼in along the lower edge of the coat ; turn up a further ¾in and tape the hem in place. Machine stitch. (Fig. 2)

Fold the facing to the right side along the fold line and stitch along the neckline to the center front. Repeat for other front facing. Clip at center points almost to the stitching. Turn the facings to the inside and glue them to the wrong side of the coat with carpet or fabric adhesive. (Fig. 3)

Fold the sleeve darts to the inside and

stitch. Fold each dart toward the back of the sleeve and topstitch, working on the right side, approximately ⅛in from the dart seam.

Placing right sides together and matching notches, stitch the sleeve seam. Open the seam flat and glue the seam allowances to the wrong side. (Fig. 4)

Turn up and stitch the lower edge of the sleeve as for the coat hem. (Fig. 5)

Placing right sides together and matching notches and side and sleeve seams, stitch the sleeve into the armhole. (Fig. 6) Fold the seam allowances toward the sleeve and topstitch, working on the right side ⅛in from the seamline. (Fig. 7)

Placing right sides together and matching notches, stitch the two collar

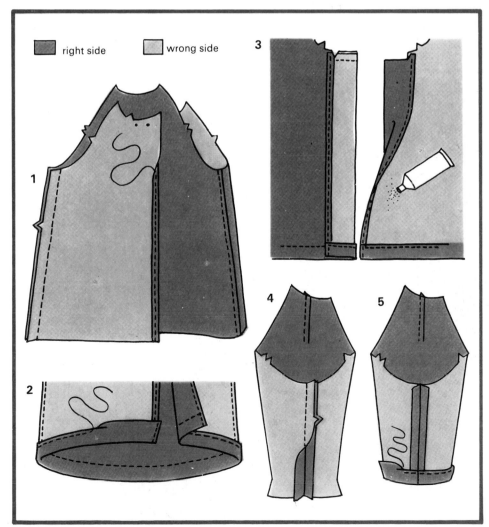

right side   wrong side

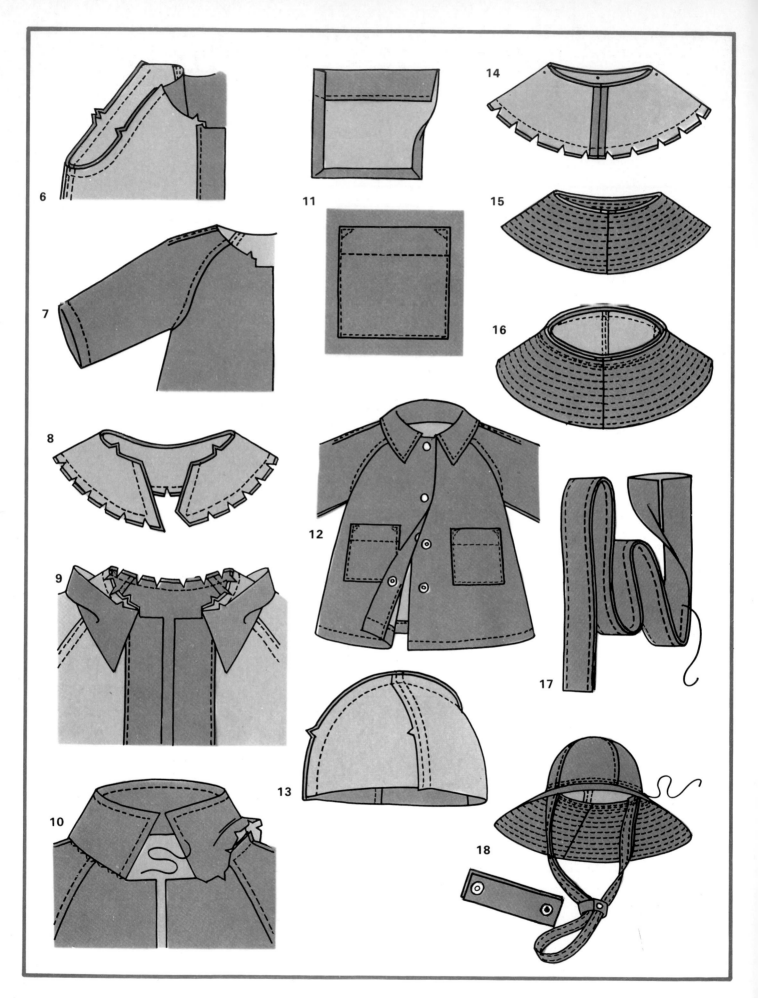

pieces around the outer edges. Clip the curve, trim off corners and turn collar right side out. (Fig. 8)

Place the right side of the top collar on the wrong side of the coat at the neck edge, matching notches and with front edges of collar at center front of coat. Stitch. Clip seam allowances almost to the stitching. (Fig. 9)

Make small clips on the neck edge of the under-collar, fold under the seam allowance and hand-sew the folded edge to the neckline seam. Topstitch around the outer edges of the collar $\frac{1}{8}$in from the edge. (Fig. 10)

Turn under 1in on the upper edges of the pockets and stitch.

Turn under $\frac{1}{4}$in on the other edges and topstitch to the front of the coat in the position indicated. Machine stitch a triangle at each corner for extra strength. (Fig. 11)

Attach gripper fasteners to the center fronts. (Fig. 12)

Making the sou'wester
Placing right sides together and matching notches, join two sections of the crown. Fold the seam allowances to one side and topstitch, working on the right side, $\frac{1}{8}$in from the seamline. Join the other two sections in the same way and then join the two sets together. (Fig. 13)

Placing right sides together, stitch the center back seam of each brim. Glue the seam allowances flat on each side.

Placing right sides together and matching seams, stitch the upper to the under brim around the outer edges. Clip the curve and turn the brim right side out. (Fig. 14)

Work a continuous line of machine stitching from the outer to the inner edge, keeping the rows $\frac{1}{4}$in apart. (Fig. 15)

Placing right sides together, matching notches and aligning center back brim seam with one crown seam, stitch the brim to the lower edge of the crown. (Fig. 16)

Fold the strap lengthwise so that the edges meet at the center. Fold the strap in half again and topstitch close to the edges. (Fig. 17)

Place the ends of the strap at the inner edge of the under brim, aligned with the side crown seams, and stitch them in place.

Turn the hat right side out, and, with the seam allowances and strap ends turned upward, topstitch around the crown just above the seamline. Add a second line of topstitching parallel to the first and catching in the turned-up seam allowances.

Cut a small strip of fabric measuring approximately $\frac{1}{2}$in wide and 4in long. Fold it in half lengthwise and glue the wrong sides together. Fix the under section of one gripper fastener to one end, fold the band around the strap and fix the upper half of the fastener to correspond. Trim away any excess fabric. (Fig. 18)

Graph pattern for raincoat

KEY   Size 18 months ▭
       Size 3 years ▭

¼ in seam allowance included   Each square = 2 in

1 in hem included

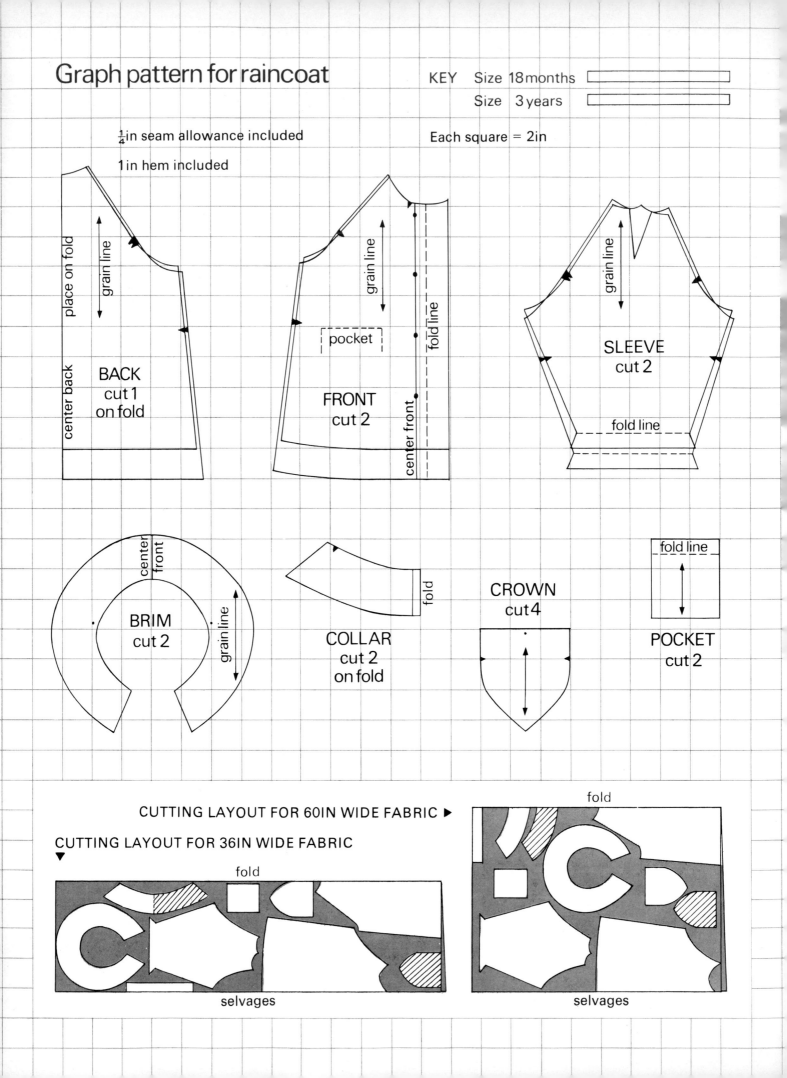

place on fold   grain line

center back

BACK
cut 1
on fold

grain line

pocket

fold line

center front

FRONT
cut 2

grain line

SLEEVE
cut 2

fold line

center front

grain line

BRIM
cut 2

fold

COLLAR
cut 2
on fold

CROWN
cut 4

fold line

POCKET
cut 2

CUTTING LAYOUT FOR 60IN WIDE FABRIC ▶

CUTTING LAYOUT FOR 36IN WIDE FABRIC
▼

fold

fold

selvages

selvages

Bean Bag Cushion

Children love these comfortable, colorful floor cushions – just like giant bean bags. Filled with polystyrene beads, they adapt instantly to any posture.

Size
Unfilled, the bag measures approximately 58in in diameter.

Materials
$3\frac{7}{8}$yd of 48in wide patterned fabric – sturdy cotton or cotton-polyester blend, corduroy or leather-like vinyl are good choices
$3\frac{7}{8}$yd of 48in wide lining fabric
16 cubic feet of polystyrene beads
a large sheet of paper for patterns (see measurement diagrams)
strong sewing thread
a yardstick
a right-angled triangle (optional)

Making the patterns
For the top pattern first draw four lines to the measurements shown in diagram A. Use a triangle or some other right-angled object to make sure the lines intersect at right angles. Next draw lines from the ends of the center horizontal line to the ends of the other two horizontal lines, forming a hexagon.

In the same way, following the measurements in diagram B, draw a larger hexagon for the base pattern.

For the side section pattern draw four intersecting lines to the measurements given in diagram C. Draw curved lines joining the horizontal lines, as shown in the diagram. For symmetry, draw one side, then cut out this half of the pattern, fold it along the center vertical line and use this edge in drawing the other curved line. Cut out all three patterns.

Making the cushion
From patterned fabric cut one top, one base and six side sections.

Place two side sections together, right sides facing. Pin, baste and stitch the seams, $\frac{1}{2}$in from the edge, ending the stitching $\frac{1}{2}$in from the two ends. (Fig. 1)

Stitch down the seam again, inside the seam allowances and close to the first line of stitching, for added strength. Press the seam allowances to one side. (Fig. 2)

Join the remaining sections in the same way to form a ring.

Leave the bag wrong side out. Place the top section, wrong side up, over the smaller opening and pin it in place, matching raw edges and with right sides facing, aligning side seams with corner points. Baste and stitch a $\frac{1}{2}$in seam; add a second line of stitching as before. (Fig. 3)

Join the base in the same way, but leave two sides open. Turn the bag right side out.

Make up the lining in the same way as the cover, but leave only one side open.

Using a saucepan or pitcher as a scoop, fill the lining with beads. The beads will not fill the bag completely; this allows room for them to move when someone sits on the cushion.

Turn in the opening edges of the lining and overcast them firmly together.

Push the filled lining into the cover. Turn in the opening edges of the cover and slipstitch them firmly together. (Fig. 4)

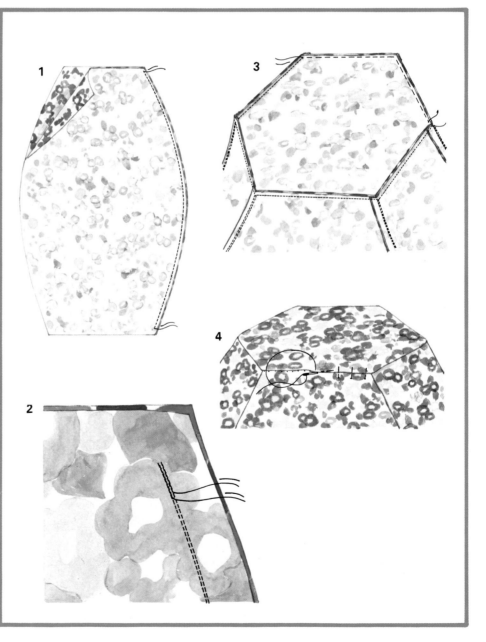

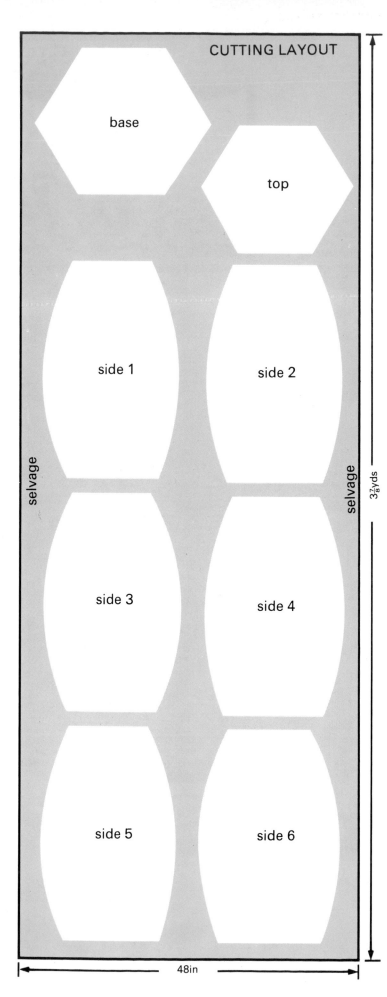

CUTTING LAYOUT

base

top

side 1

side 2

side 3

side 4

side 5

side 6

selvage

selvage

$3\frac{7}{8}$yds

48in

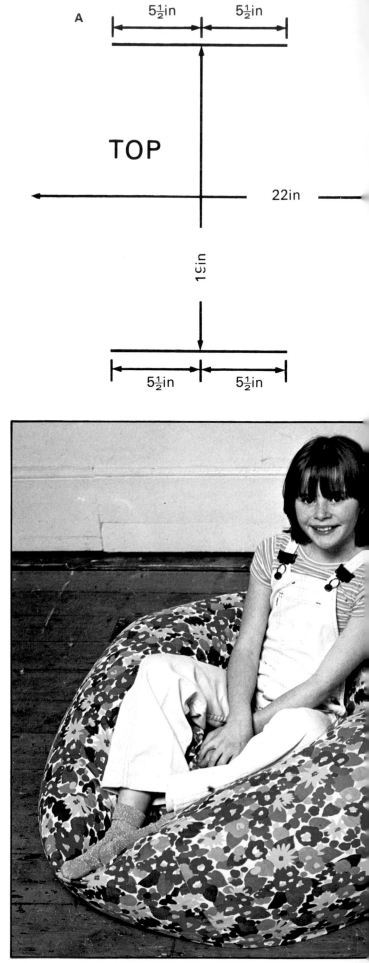

A

$5\frac{1}{2}$in $5\frac{1}{2}$in

TOP

22in

16in

$5\frac{1}{2}$in $5\frac{1}{2}$in

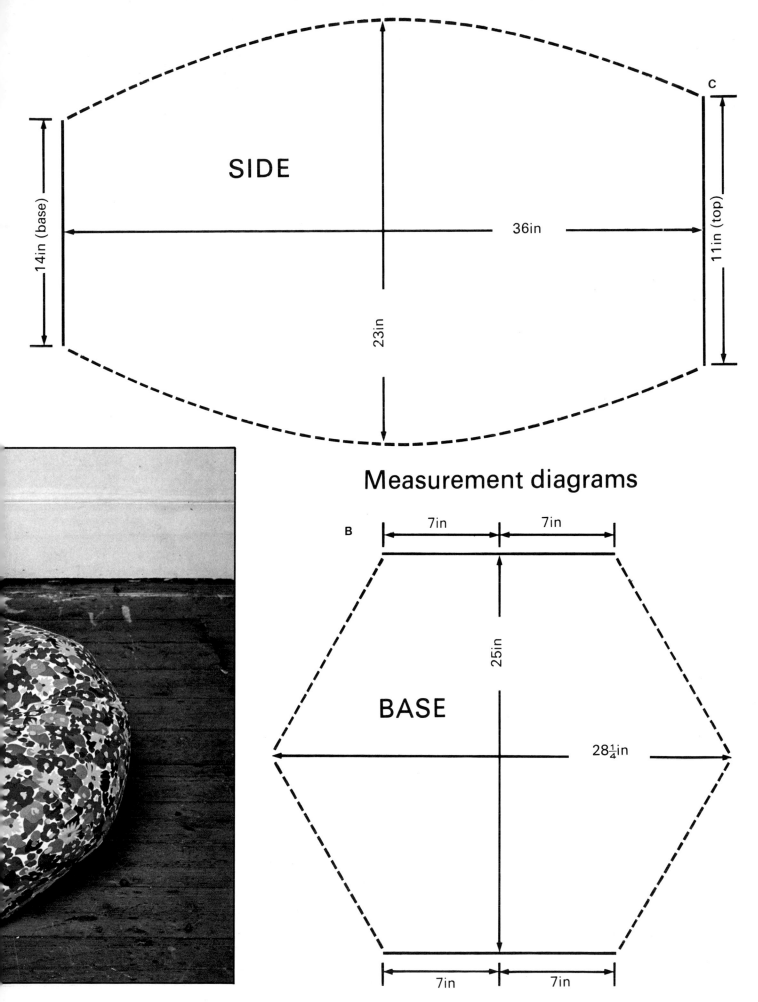

SIDE

14in (base)

36in

11in (top)

23in

C

Measurement diagrams

B

7in

7in

25in

BASE

$28\frac{1}{4}$in

7in

7in

TOYS

Old-fashioned Rag Doll

She is a model of perfection, from her beautifully embroidered face to her neat buttoned shoes. A toy that could well become an heirloom.

Size
The doll measures 20½in in height.

Materials
⅝yd of 36in wide soft, closely-woven fabric in pale pink
⅝yd of 36in wide floral printed cotton fabric
⅝yd of 45in wide white lawn
stranded embroidery floss in pale pink, peach, brown, blue, black, and white
a crewel needle, size 7
5 small pearl buttons
a ball of mohair-type yarn in light brown
1⅛yd of ⅜in wide velvet ribbon to harmonize with printed fabric
⅝yd of ¼in wide pink satin ribbon
2¾yd of ⅝in wide lace edging
¾yd of 3in wide eyelet lace edging
5in of narrow white woven tape
⅞yd of ¼in wide elastic
2 sprigs of artificial flowers
scraps of soft black leather
suitable stuffing
tracing paper
dressmaker's carbon paper
a 6in diameter embroidery hoop

Cutting out
Trace the pattern pieces given on pages 136–139. Using dressmaker's carbon paper, transfer the pattern outlines to the appropriate fabrics as follows: the body from the soft pink fabric, the shoes from the black leather and the bodice from the floral fabric – all double thickness. Cut the head pattern, once only, from the pink fabric, for the back; for the front head cut two 10in squares of pink fabric.

From white lawn cut two 5in diameter circles for the mob cap, two pieces each 10½ by 10in for the bloomers, one piece 39½ by 8½in for the petticoat, and one 3in square for the handkerchief.

From floral printed fabric cut one piece 35½ by 8in for the skirt and two pieces each 9 by 6in for the sleeves.

Making the doll
Transfer the facial features and head outline to one of the squares of pink fabric, using dressmaker's carbon. Note: to keep the fabric smooth, pin it to an ironing board or other working surface. Lay the marked square over the plain one and stretch both in the embroidery hoop.

Using two strands of embroidery floss, work the features. Then remove embroidery from hoop and press it on the wrong side. Cut away the excess fabric outside the cutting line. (Fig. 1)

Place back and front heads together, right sides facing. Pin, baste, and stitch, leaving neck open. Clip curves, turn head right side out and fill it firmly. Pin the neck edges together.

Place the body pieces together, right sides facing, and pin, baste, and stitch the edges together, starting and finishing at the neck opening. Clip curves, turn right side out and stuff, starting with feet and hands and ending with the torso. Pin the neck edges together.

At ankles, knees, tops of legs, wrists, and elbows, squeeze the filling to either side and work a line of running stitches through both layers to form a joint. (Fig. 2)

Hand-sew neat lines of stitching on hands to give the appearance of fingers and thumbs, and gently bend the hands into shape. (Fig. 3)

Unpin the neck edges and firmly insert the neck down into the neck opening of the body; pin in place. Turn under the raw edge of the neck opening and carefully and firmly slipstitch this to the neck.

For the hair cut lengths of yarn about 20in long. Cut a strip of white tape 5in long. Place the yarn across the tape at right angles. Carefully stitch the yarn to the tape, using matching thread. (Fig. 4)

Place the hair piece on the head with the stitching running down the center to

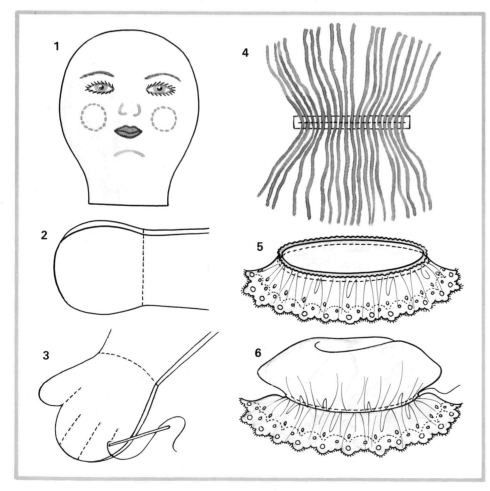

suggest a parting. Tuck under the raw edges of the tape and stitch the hair to the head along the previous line of stitching.

Cut the satin ribbon in two and tie a small bunch of hair at each side of the face. Sew the bunches to the head with small invisible stitches. Decorate each bunch with a small sprig of flowers slipped into the hair just above each bow.

Making the choker and mop cap
Cut a length of velvet ribbon to fit around the neck; turn in the ends and sew them together at the back of the neck to form a choker hiding the neck seam.

Stitch the ends of the eyelet lace together. Run a line of gathering stitches along the raw edge. (Fig. 5)

Draw up the gathering thread to fit around the mob cap circle. Pin, baste and stitch the eyelet lace to the mob cap circle, placing right sides together. Run another line of gathering stitches around the mob cap circle and draw them up to give the effect of a puffy cap. (Fig. 6) Pin (continued on page 140)

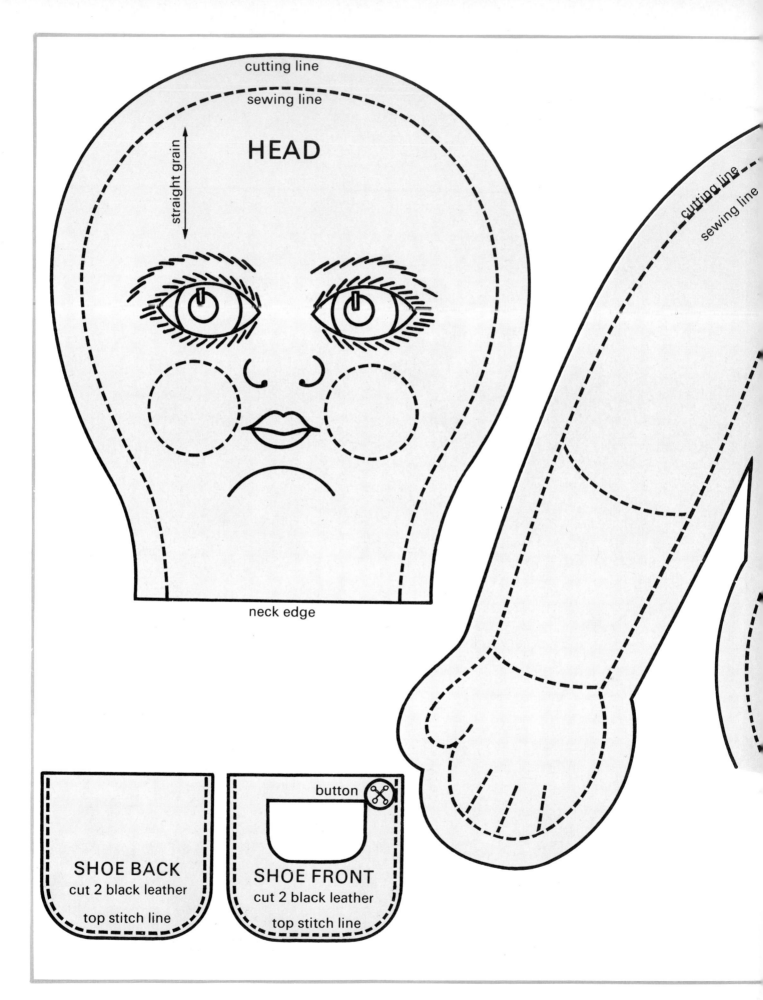

cutting line

sewing line

straight grain

HEAD

neck edge

cutting line

sewing line

SHOE BACK
cut 2 black leather

top stitch line

button

SHOE FRONT
cut 2 black leather

top stitch line

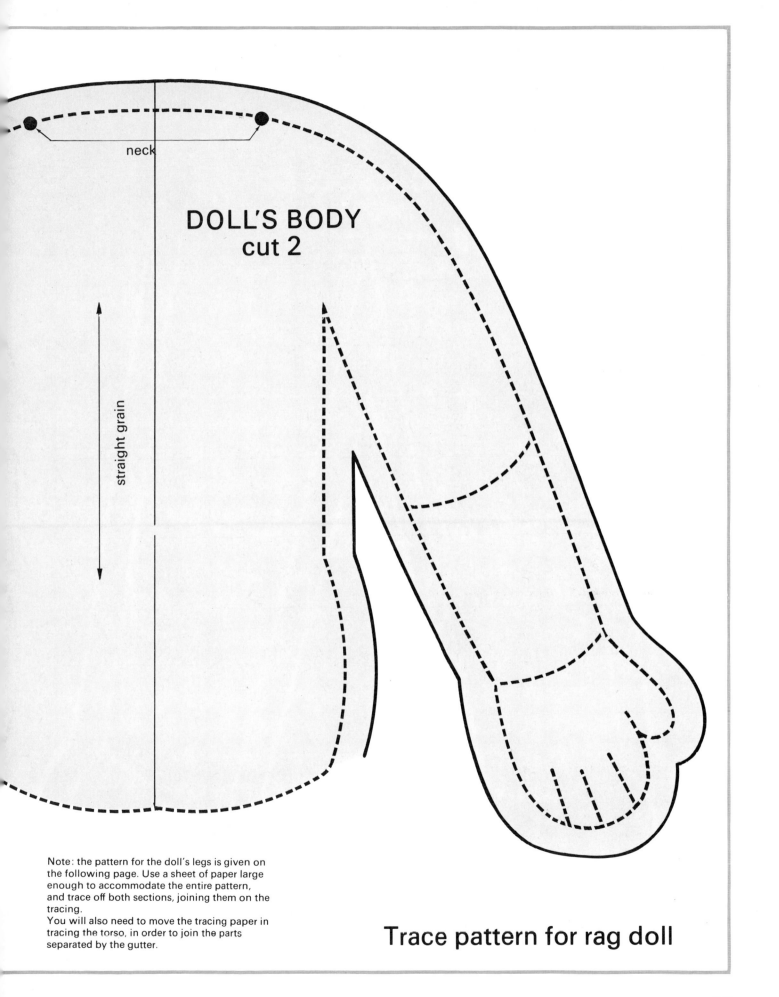

**DOLL'S BODY
cut 2**

neck

straight grain

Note: the pattern for the doll's legs is given on the following page. Use a sheet of paper large enough to accommodate the entire pattern, and trace off both sections, joining them on the tracing.
You will also need to move the tracing paper in tracing the torso, in order to join the parts separated by the gutter.

Trace pattern for rag doll

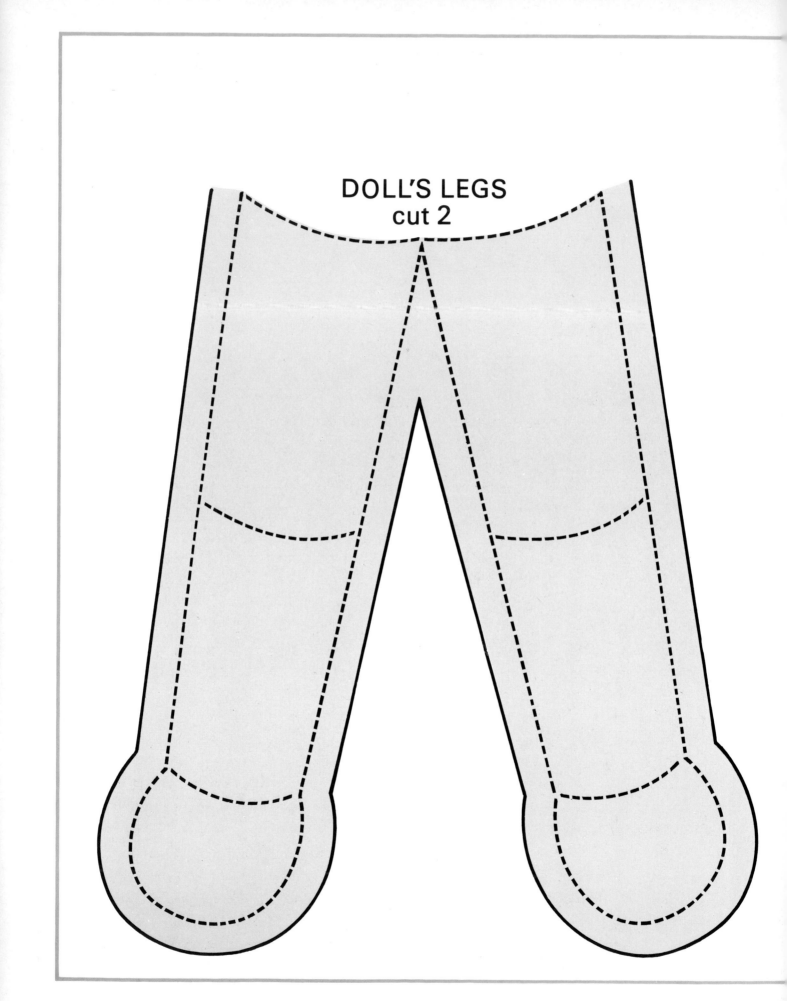

DOLL'S LEGS
cut 2

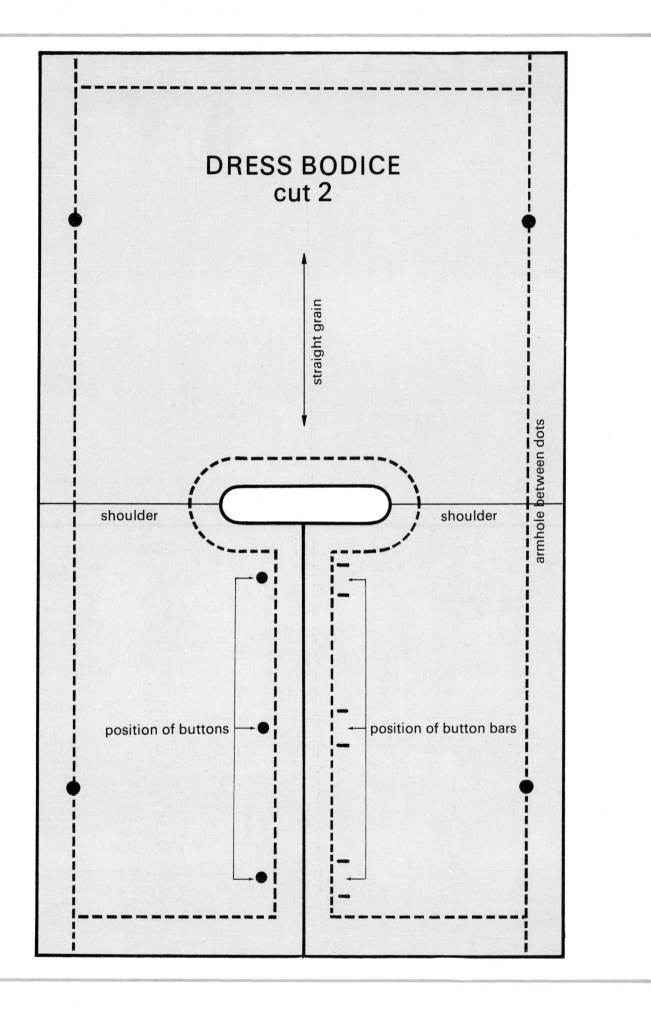

DRESS BODICE
cut 2

straight grain

shoulder

shoulder

armhole between dots

position of buttons

position of button bars

and sew the cap to the doll's head around the seamline.

Making the underclothes

Place the two bloomer pieces together, right sides facing. Pin, baste and stitch a 4½in seam down each of the long sides. Press seams open. (Fig. 7)

Fold the fabric so that seams lie on top of each other. Pin, baste, and stitch the leg seams, matching the crotch point. (Fig. 8)

Make a casing for the waistband by turning under first ¼in then ⅜in. Pin and baste in place, then topstitch close to the turned-under edge, leaving a small opening for the elastic. Thread elastic through the casing, cut it to fit doll's waist and sew the ends together firmly.

Finish the leg openings of the bloomers in the same way.

Fold the petticoat piece in half width-wise with right sides together; pin, baste and stitch the short edges together to make the center-back seam.

Turn up a double ¼in hem on the lower edge; pin, baste and topstitch.

Pin, baste and stitch lace edging to the hem.

Finish waist of petticoat as for waist of bloomers.

Making the dress

Fold the skirt piece in half widthwise with right sides together; pin, baste and stitch the short edges together to make center-back seam. Press seam open.

Turn up a double ¼in hem; pin, baste and hand-hem in place. Pin, baste and hand-sew the upper edge of the lace just under the lower edge of the skirt.

Run two gathering threads along the upper edge of the skirt.

Place the two bodice pieces together, right sides facing. Pin, baste, and stitch around the neck and back opening. Clip curves; turn bodice right side out and press.

Sew three buttons close to the edge on the left side of back opening in the positions marked. Work three button loops on the right edge to correspond. (Fig. 9)

Run a gathering thread along one long side of each sleeve piece. Draw up gathering to fit between dots on bodice. Adjust gathers evenly. Pin, baste, and stitch gathered edge of each sleeve to bodice, right sides facing. (Fig. 10)

Fold bodice and sleeves in half along the shoulder lines, right sides facing. Pin, baste and stitch sleeve and side seams. Press seams open. (Fig. 11)

Pin bodice to skirt with right sides facing, placing back opening at center back of skirt. Draw up skirt gathers to fit bodice and adjust them evenly. Baste and stitch waist seams; press seam upward.

Make a casing in lower edges of sleeves, as for waist of bloomers. Insert elastic.

Pin, baste, and hand-sew lace edging to neck edge.

Turn the dress right side out. Dress the doll. Tie the remaining length of velvet ribbon around the waist and tie a bow in front. Neaten the ends of the ribbons by snipping a "V" shape in each. (Fig. 12)

Making the handkerchief and shoes

Hand-roll and sew a tiny hem along the edge of the handkerchief. Embroider a small sprig of flowers in one corner. Fold and press the handkerchief and hand-sew it to the right hand.

Place back and front shoe pieces together, wrong sides facing. Topstitch around the curved edges. Sew a button to each shoe at outer side of bar. Carefully ease shoes onto doll's feet. (Fig. 13)

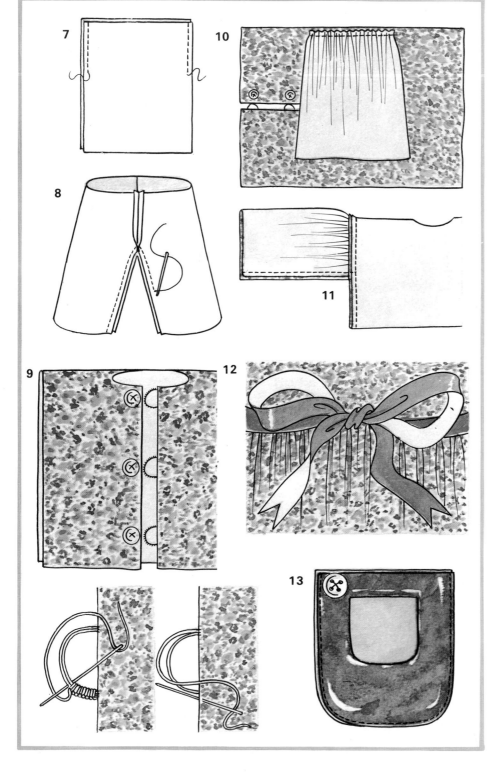

Stuffed Stegosaurus

This prehistoric monster is more friendly than fearsome. Made of bright-colored felt, he is a toy with a difference.

Size
The toy measures 4ft in length.

Materials
1½yd of 36in wide bright green felt
½yd of 36in wide dark green felt
a 12in square of orange felt
a 6in square of yellow felt
5lb of synthetic stuffing
two toy eyes – or scraps of black felt if
    the toy is for a very small child
graph paper marked in 1in squares

Making the pattern
Using graph paper, enlarge the pattern pieces to the correct size. Each square on the page represents one 2in square on the paper. A seam allowance of ⅜in is included where required. Enlarge each spot pattern separately.

Cut out the pattern pieces and transfer all markings to them.

Cutting out
From a single thickness of bright green felt cut out the main body piece twice. Fold the fabric double and cut out the front foot twice, each back foot once and the large eye shield once.

Fold the dark green felt in half lengthwise and cut out the gusset, placing it on the fold. Also cut out the head decoration, the small eye shield, the mouth, and each of the larger spots. Open out the fabric and cut one of platelet A, three of platelet B, two of C, and one each of D and E.

From the orange felt, folded double, cut out both horn pieces and the same number of each platelet as in the dark green felt; note that as the fabric is double there will be twice as many.

From the yellow felt, folded double, cut out each small spot and the eye piece. Open the fabric and cut out one mouth.

Transfer all markings to the pattern pieces.

Making the stegosaurus
Baste and stitch two front foot pieces together close to the edge, leaving a small opening at the heel for stuffing. Stuff the foot firmly and stitch the edges together. Repeat for other front foot. (Fig. 1)

Baste and stitch the back seam on the (continued on page 145)

Graph pattern for dinosaur

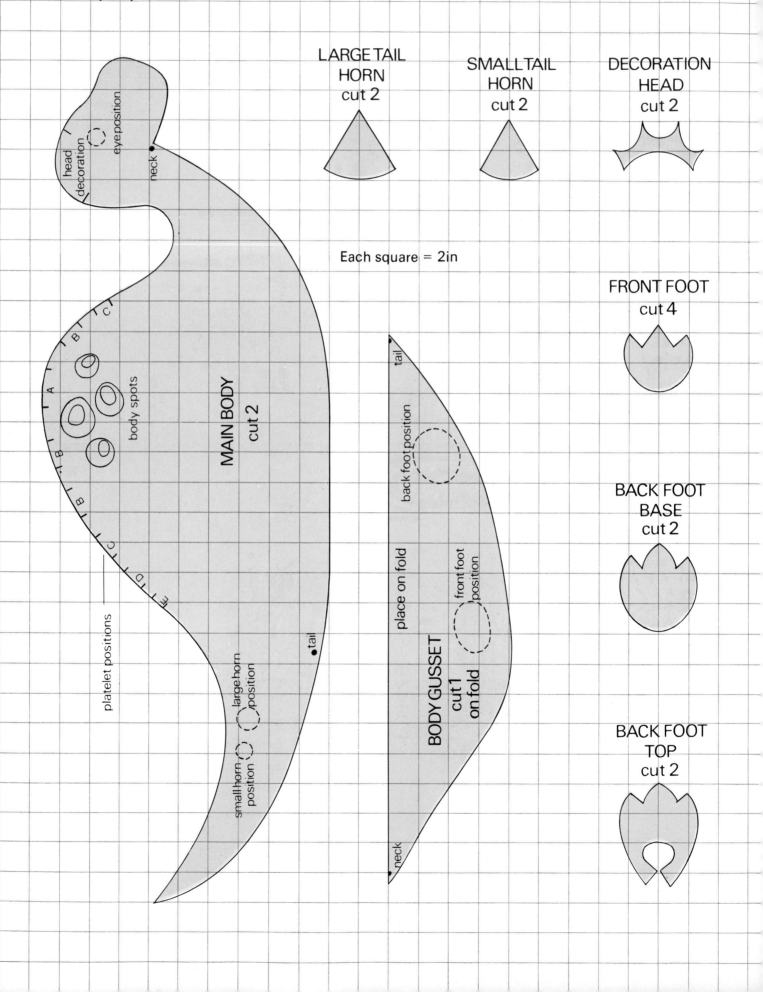

LARGE TAIL HORN cut 2

SMALL TAIL HORN cut 2

DECORATION HEAD cut 2

Each square = 2in

FRONT FOOT cut 4

BACK FOOT BASE cut 2

BACK FOOT TOP cut 2

head decoration

eye position

neck

C
B
A
B

body spots

MAIN BODY cut 2

platelet positions

B
C
D
E

large horn position

small horn position

tail

tail

back foot position

place on fold

front foot position

BODY GUSSET cut 1 on fold

neck

Trace patterns

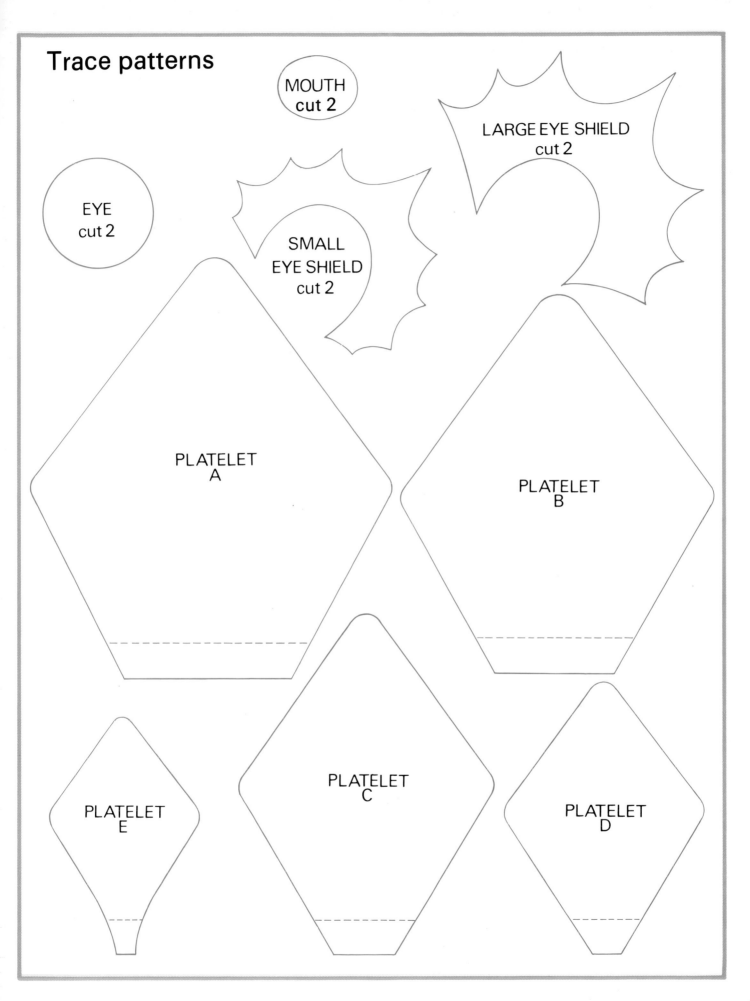

MOUTH
cut 2

LARGE EYE SHIELD
cut 2

EYE
cut 2

SMALL
EYE SHIELD
cut 2

PLATELET
A

PLATELET
B

PLATELET
E

PLATELET
C

PLATELET
D

right side   wrong side

1

2

3

4

5

6

7

8

9

back foot top. Place the top on the base, with seam allowances concealed, and stitch the two sections together close to the edges. Stuff firmly. Repeat for other back foot. (Fig. 2)

Catch-stitch the front and back feet firmly to the gusset in the positions indicated. (Fig. 3)

Baste and topstitch the yellow spots to the dark green spots. Baste and topstitch these spots to the main body sections where indicated.

Baste the yellow eye pieces in place on head.

Place smaller eye shield on the larger, with lower edges matching, and baste and stitch eye shields to head above eyes, stitching through short ends and pointed edge on small shield only. (Fig. 4)

Trim the edges of the orange platelets, trimming $\frac{3}{8}$in on the largest size and progressively less on the smaller ones.

Baste and topstitch one orange platelet to each side of the larger green platelets, with lower edges together.

Baste the completed platelets to the right side of one body section along the seamline with the points inward as shown.

Baste the head decoration in the position marked, with points downward. (Fig. 5)

Placing right sides together, baste and stitch the main body sections together from neck dot to tail dot, sandwiching the platelets and head decorations between the layers. (Fig. 6)

Baste and stitch each horn section together along the two straight edges. Turn it right side out and push out the point with the blunt end of a pencil. Topstitch around the base of the horn and stuff. (Fig. 7)

Catch-stitch each horn to the tail in the positions indicated. (Fig. 8)

Turn the main body section wrong side out. Placing right sides together, baste and stitch the gusset to the body, leaving an opening of 8in for stuffing. Clip curves and turn the body right side out. (Fig. 9)

Partly stuff the head. Secure the toy eyes in position on the yellow eye pieces – or sew on small circles of black felt. Remove basting thread from yellow eye pieces. Stuff the other parts of the toy, starting farthest from the opening and working toward the center of the body. Make sure that the stuffing is firmly and evenly packed. Slipstitch the opening edges together.

Sew the green and yellow mouth pieces onto the front of the head, slightly overlapping them as shown in the photograph.

Teddy Bear Family

These teddy bears would make ideal companions for a day in the country. They are all made from the same pattern – which can also be adapted for a dog and a rabbit (see page 150).

Sizes
The pattern is given in three sizes, measuring, in length : 26in, 22in, and 16$\frac{1}{2}$in. The three costume patterns are also sized to fit the three sizes of bear and so can be used interchangeably.

Materials
For making the patterns
graph paper. Note that the squares on the pattern correspond to different sizes of grid, depending on the size bear you are making. If you are unable to obtain paper ruled in the appropriate size grid you can either convert finely ruled graph paper, using a colored felt tip pen to mark in the principal lines, or make your own grid on blank paper.

For making the bears
fur fabric 54in wide : $\frac{3}{4}$yd for large size, $\frac{1}{2}$yd for medium size, $\frac{3}{8}$yd for small size
a 9in square of black felt *or* a piece of simulated leather, bonded velvet or similar fabric measuring 4$\frac{1}{2}$in by 13in for large size, 11in for medium size and 8in for small size
a small amount of black knitting yarn
carpet or button thread in black and in a color matching the fur fabric
carpet or fabric adhesive
a pair of eye buttons
a yarn needle
a small piece of black felt for nose tip
a small piece of dark pink felt for tongue

For dressing the bears
Vest
felt or similar fabric : 12 by 24in for large size ; 9 by 19in for medium size ; 15 by 7in for small size
contrasting thread
3 small buttons
a length of ribbon

Apron
checked cotton or similar fabric : 12 by 31in for large size ; 9 by 23in for medium size ; 7 by 17in for small size

seam binding, $\frac{1}{2}$in wide : 2$\frac{1}{8}$yd, 1$\frac{3}{4}$yd and 1$\frac{1}{8}$yd for large, medium and small sizes respectively
lace to trim apron bib and skirt

Dress
checked cotton or similar fabric : 33 by 12in for large size ; 29 by 10in for medium size ; 22 by 7in for small size
narrow ribbon : 1$\frac{5}{8}$yd, 1$\frac{3}{8}$yd and 1yd for large, medium and small sizes respectively
shirring elastic
narrow lace to trim hem of dress

Making the bears
Using graph paper of the appropriate scale, enlarge the pattern pieces as required – see key to sizes on pattern, page 149. A seam allowance of $\frac{1}{4}$in is included. Cut out the pieces and transfer the markings onto them.

Fold the fur fabric in half lengthwise. Place the center head on a single thickness of fabric. Place the back, front, foot, side head, and ear on double fabric, aligning the grain lines with the straight grain of the fabric. Cut out these pieces, then cut out the ear in double fabric once more. Open out the fabric and cut one nose piece.

Cut two soles and front paws from the black fabric. Cut a nose tip from black felt and a tongue from pink felt.

Transfer all markings from the pattern pieces to the fabric.

Body
Placing right sides together and matching notches, baste and stitch the center-front and center-back seams.

Placing right sides together and matching notches, baste the front paws to the front arms. (Fig. 1).

Placing right sides together and matching notches, baste and stitch the back to the front on the inside leg seam, stretching the back to fit the front.

Placing right sides together and matching notches, baste and stitch the front to the back from the neckline down the arms, around the paws and side seams to the lower edges of the legs. (Fig. 2)

Placing right sides together, baste and

stitch the center-front seam of feet. Clip the curve. Placing right sides together and matching notches and the center-front seam of the foot to the dot on the sole, baste and stitch the foot to the sole. Turn the foot right side out. (Fig. 3)

Push the foot inside the leg. (Fig 4)

Place right sides together and match notches and the center-front seam of the foot to the dot on the leg, baste and stitch the foot to the leg. Turn body right side out.

Head

Placing right sides together and matching notches, baste and stitch the side head sections to the center head.

Placing right sides together and matching notches, baste and stitch the nose piece to the head. (Fig. 5)

Placing right sides together and matching notches and nose seam, baste and stitch from the dot, around the nose and under the jaw to the neckline. (Fig. 6)

Fold the nose (as shown in Fig. 6) so that the center line is aligned with the seam just stitched, and baste and stitch across as shown.

Turn the head right side out and attach the eyes, either by sewing them on with strong thread, if they have shanks, or by placing them in position on the right side and pressing on the metal holder from the back.

Stuff the body and the head, pushing the stuffing well into the feet, paws and nose first.

Placing right sides together and matching notches, baste and stitch the curved edge of the ears. Turn the ears right side out. Turn in $\frac{1}{4}$in on the straight edge and slipstitch the folded edges together.

Place the ear on the line indicated on the head and securely slipstitch it in place using strong thread. (Fig. 7)

Using strong black thread and leaving the end free, work large overcasting stitches over the edge of the nose tip. Place a small amount of stuffing in the center, (Fig. 8) and pull up the thread to form a ball. Place the ball on the nose with the gathered edge where the two seams meet and sew it securely in place using strong black thread.

Using black knitting yarn, work two straight stitches, $\frac{1}{2}$in to 1in long, to form a "V" on the seamline under the nose tip.

Fold the tongue in half crosswise. Place this fold across the nose seam, between the ends of the two black stitches. (Fig. 8)

Backstitch along it, attaching the tongue to the head. Apply glue to one half of the tongue and press the two halves together.

Match the center fronts of the head and body and the center-back point of the head to the center-back seam of the body, and sew the head and body together using strong thread and small stitches. Take the needle through the fabric $\frac{1}{8}$in from the edges of first the head and then the body. Pull up the thread every two or three stitches. For extra strength it is advisable to work at least two rows of stitching here. Fasten off securely.

To fluff up the pile, brush the whole body very gently, especially on the seamlines to hide the stitching.

Making the costumes

Using the graph paper, enlarge the pattern pieces to the required size and cut them out. The scale is the same as for the body pieces.

Cut the pieces in the appropriate

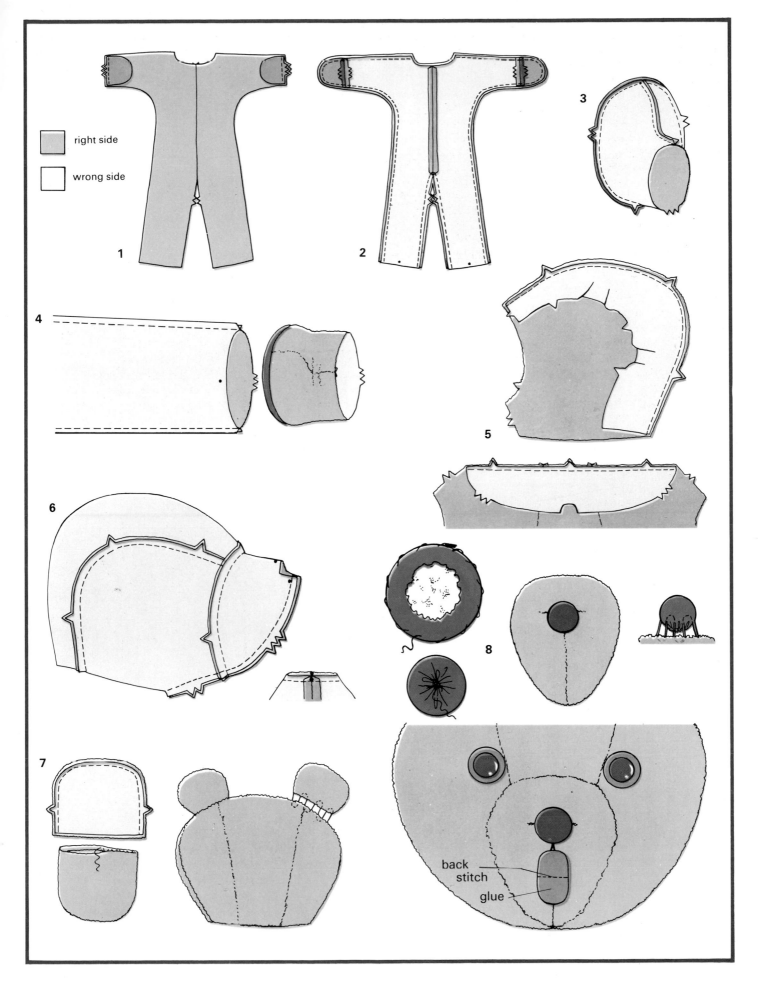

right side

wrong side

1

2

3

4

5

6

7

8

back stitch

glue

fabrics and transfer the pattern markings
to them.

Vest

Placing right sides together, stitch the
shoulder seams ¼in from the edge.

Working on the right side, topstitch
around all edges, ¼in from the edge, using
contrasting thread and either straight
stitch or zigzag. Zigzag stitch the edges.

Cut buttonholes on the left front and
sew buttons on the right front to match.

Tie the ribbon in a bow around the
bear's neck.

Apron

Turn up 1¼in on the lower edge and
machine stitch in place. Sew lace on the
right side, over the stitching line.

Turn under small hems on the sides of
the apron skirt and bib and machine
stitch.

Run a line of gathering stitches along
the upper edge of the skirt and pull up to
half the bear's waist measurement. Adjust
the gathers evenly.

Cut a length of seam binding twice the
waist measurement and mark the center
point. Pin the binding over the gathers on
the right side and stitch it in place, using
either straight or zigzag stitch.

Turn under 1⅛in on the upper edge of
the bib. Machine stitch and trim with lace
as for the skirt.

Cut the remaining seam binding in half.
Place each piece on the right side of the
bib, ¼in from the edge, and stitch in place
using straight or zigzag stitch.

Place lower edge of bib under the
gathered skirt, the center front matching
the center point of the seam binding.
Machine stitch in place.

Dress

Placing right sides together, stitch the
center-back seam, ¼in from the edge.
Finish the raw edges together, using
zigzag stitch or hand overcasting.

Turn up a small hem on the lower edge
and stitch close to the folded edge. Stitch
narrow lace over the hem, catching in the
raw edge underneath.

Stitch lace over the raw edge at the
top of the dress.

Work several rows of shirring, starting
¼in from the lace and continuing to the
required length. Fasten the ends securely
on the wrong side.

Cut the ribbon into three equal lengths.
Sew two lengths to the top of the dress to
form straps. Tie a bow in the third and
sew it to the front of the dress.

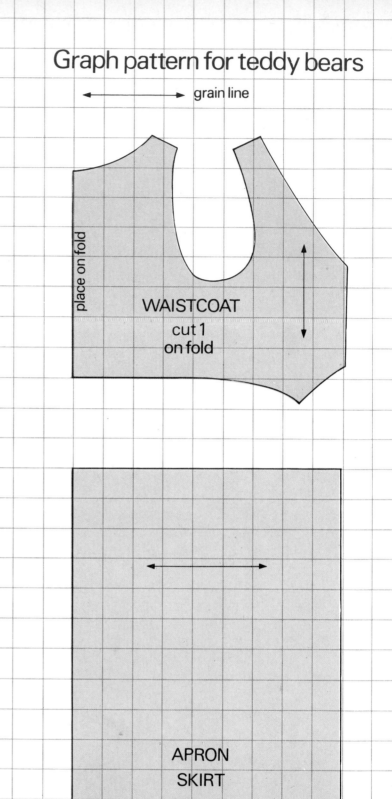

Graph pattern for teddy bears

←————————→ grain line

place on fold

WAISTCOAT
cut 1
on fold

APRON

SKIRT

cut 1

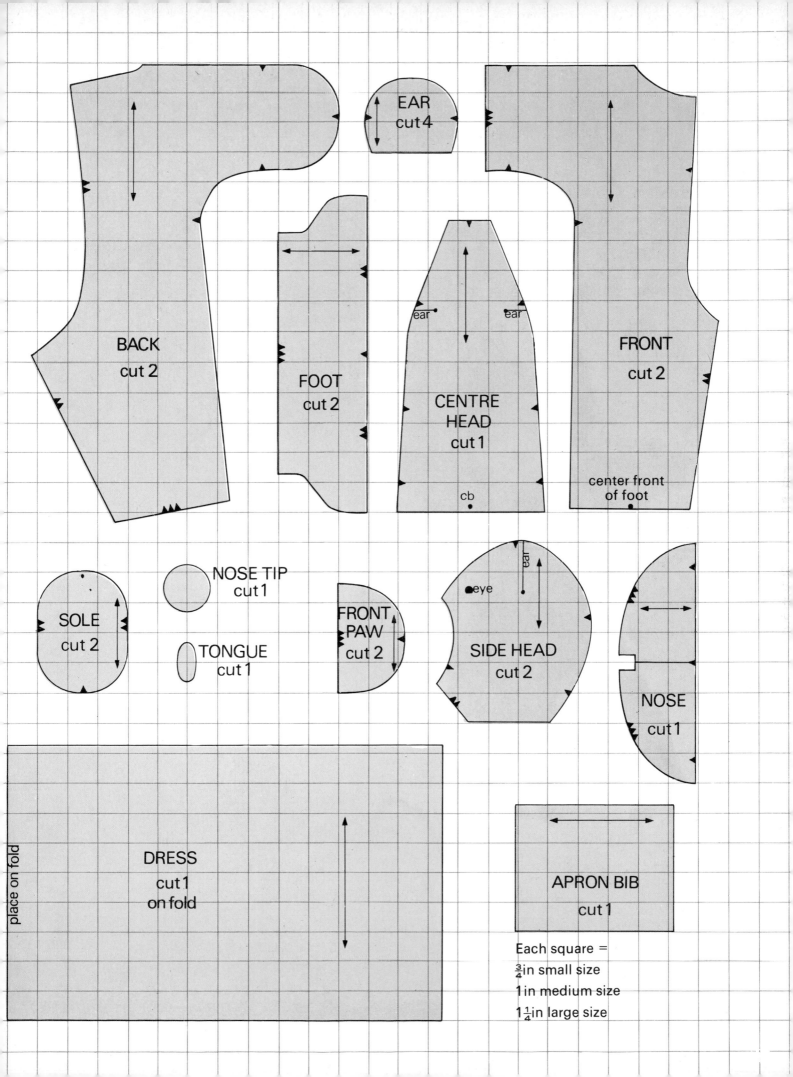

BACK
cut 2

EAR
cut 4

FRONT
cut 2

FOOT
cut 2

CENTRE
HEAD
cut 1

ear

ear

cb

center front
of foot

NOSE TIP
cut 1

SOLE
cut 2

TONGUE
cut 1

FRONT
PAW
cut 2

ear

eye

SIDE HEAD
cut 2

NOSE
cut 1

place on fold

DRESS
cut 1
on fold

APRON BIB
cut 1

Each square =
¾ in small size
1 in medium size
1¼ in large size

Dog and Rabbit

Unlike their real-life counterparts, this cuddly dog and rabbit are ideal companions. They are made of soft fur fabric and can be dressed, if you like, using the bear costumes on page 149.

Sizes
The pattern – which is the same as for the bear (page 149) with modifications given

here – can be used to make three sizes : 26in, 22in, and 16½in long.

Materials
Materials needed are the same as for the teddy bears (page 149) but omitting the fabric for soles and paws. The materials required for costumes, if desired, are also the same. In addition you will need :
½yd of fur fabric in a contrasting color for each toy
a small piece of thin cardboard for nose tip for the dog
1yd of 1in wide ribbon for each toy

Making the dog
Using graph paper, enlarge the teddy bear body pieces given in the graph pattern on page 149, omitting the ears and nose tip. Then enlarge the ear, nose tip, and two tail pieces for the dog given in the graph pattern below.

Cut out the pattern pieces in the two fur fabrics, using the main fabric for the body back, front, side head, top tail, and two of the ear pieces and the contrasting fabric for the center head, soles, paws and two other ear pieces.

Make and stuff the body and head in the same way as for the bear.

Placing right sides together and matching notches, baste and stitch the top tail to the lower tail, leaving the straight edges open.

Turn the tail right side out and stuff. Turn in the raw edges and slipstitch the folds together. Stitch the tail to the back of the dog using strong thread.

Finishing the head
Slipstitch the ears to the head seams so that the front edge of the ear is 2½in, away from the nose seam.

Using the pattern piece for the nose tip, cut a piece of cardboard. Cut a piece of felt using the same pattern but adding ¼in all around.

Work a line of gathering stitches around the edge of the felt. Place the cardboard piece on the center felt and pull up the gathering thread so that the edge of the felt overlaps the cardboard tightly. Fasten the thread securely. Slipstitch the nose tip to the nose where indicated.

Cut out and attach the tongue and eyes as for the bear.

Sew the head and body together as for the bear. Finish by tying a bow around the neck. Or make one of the costumes given for the bear.

Making the rabbit
Using graph paper, enlarge the teddy bear body pieces given in the graph pattern on page 149, omitting the head pieces and ears. Then enlarge the center and side head pieces, the ear, and the tail for the rabbit given in the graph pattern below.

Cut out the pattern pieces in the two fur fabrics, using the main fabric for the front and back body, side head, nose, tail, and two of the ear pieces and the contrasting fabric for the center head, front paws, feet, soles, and the other two ear pieces.

Make and stuff the body in the same way as for the teddy bear. Make the head in the same way as for the bear, using the head pieces as given for the rabbit.

Using strong matching thread and leaving the end free, work large overcasting stitches around the edge of the tail piece. Place a wad of stuffing in the center of the tail and pull up the thread to form a ball. Sew the tail in place, using strong thread.

Finishing the head
Stitch the ear pieces together around the curved edges, taking ½in seam allowances. Turn ears right side out.

Turn under the raw edges on the ear and slipstitch them together. Fold the ear in half along the lower edge and slipstitch it to the head so that the inside edge of the ear is aligned with the seamline of the head.

Cut out, make, and attach the tongue, eyes, and nose tip as for the bear.

Sew the head and body together as for the bear. Finish by tying a bow around the neck, or make one of the costumes given for the bear.

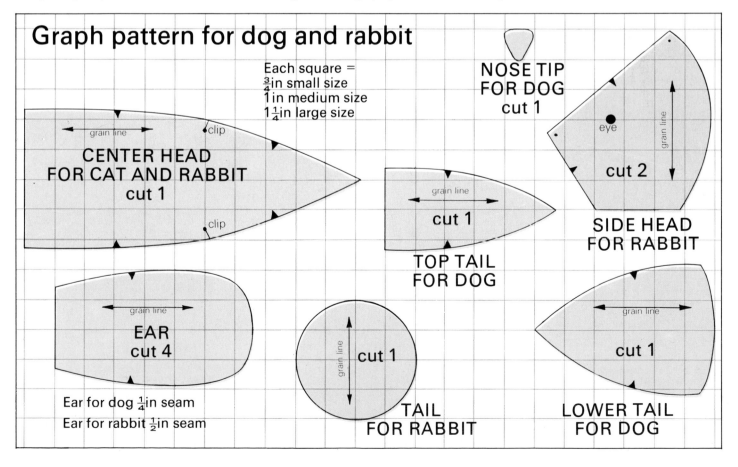

Graph pattern for dog and rabbit

Each square =
¾in small size
1in medium size
1¼in large size

CENTER HEAD FOR CAT AND RABBIT
cut 1
grain line
clip
clip

NOSE TIP FOR DOG
cut 1

eye
cut 2
grain line
SIDE HEAD FOR RABBIT

grain line
cut 1
TOP TAIL FOR DOG

EAR
cut 4
grain line
Ear for dog ¼in seam
Ear for rabbit ½in seam

cut 1
grain line
TAIL FOR RABBIT

cut 1
grain line
LOWER TAIL FOR DOG

Knitted Playmates

Soft knitted toys have a natural appeal for tiny hands. All of these toys are adaptations of one basic knitted shape.

Size
The knitted tube measures about 8½in long when finished and stuffed.

Materials
(The yarn used for the basic shape is a knitting worsted such as Pingouin Confortable.)
a pair of size 2 needles, or any size that will give the correct gauge
synthetic stuffing
a French knitting spool (horse rein) and yarn needle for some of the toys

Bird
1 ball of blue yarn for basic shape
a small amount of navy yarn
scraps of blue and navy felt

Frog
1 ball of green yarn for basic shape
scraps of dark green, pale green, and black felt

Lion
1 ball of honey-colored yarn for basic shape
a small amount of gold yarn
scraps of honey, green, and black felt
a small amount of black embroidery thread
white crochet cotton
tracing paper
dressmaker's carbon paper

Gnome
1 ball each of dark green, red, and pale pink yarn for basic shape
small amounts of white and gray yarn
scraps of dark green, light green, white, and red felt
a bell for hat

Soldier
1 ball each of royal blue, red, pale pink, and black yarn for basic shape
scraps of red and black felt
gold sequins and rickrack for trimming – or, if the toy is for a very small child, omit the sequins and sew "buttons" on using gold stranded embroidery floss and satin stitch.

Indian squaw
1 ball each of medium brown, dark brown, sand, and pale peach yarn for basic shape
small amounts of red and orange yarn
scraps of dark brown, medium brown, and tan felt

Gauge
24 sts and 36 rows to 4in over st st on size 2 needles. This may be deviated from slightly – if substituting a different yarn, for example – but note that the shape produced will consequently be larger or smaller.

Basic shape
Using size 2 needles and color required, cast on 27 sts for base.
Next row *K1, pick up loop lying between cast-on sts and K tbl – called "make 1" or M1 – rep from * to last 2 sts, K2. 52 sts.
Beg with a P row, work 68 rows st st.
Next row *P2 tog, rep from * to end. 26 sts.
Cut off yarn leaving a long end.
Thread yarn through rem sts and draw up very tightly to close top of head.

Making up
For all shapes except the lion, run a gathering thread through the 40th row from the base to shape neck at a later stage.
    Join the side edges with backstitching. Insert stuffing through base opening. Close the opening by running a gathering thread through cast-on loops and drawing it up tightly.
    Draw up gathering thread to shape neck.

Working French knitting
Thread the end of the yarn through the spool and hold it in place with your left hand while working.
    Wind yarn in counterclockwise direction around each nail.
    Now working in a clockwise direction, take yarn around outer edge of next nail and, using a blunt-ended yarn needle, lift the lower loop over the yarn and over the nail.
    Continue working around each nail in this way in a continuous circle to form a tubular cord. To bind off, pass each loop

over next nail, still in a clockwise direction. When one loop remains, pass end through last loop and draw up firmly.

Bird

Make up basic shape, using purl side as the right side of the fabric.

Using navy yarn, make four lengths of French knitting: two 8in long to form wing shapes at sides, one 11in long for feet and one 10¼in long for comb on top of head. Sew the braid in place as shown in the photograph.

Cut eyes and beak from felt, using the trace pattern below, and sew them in place.

Trim wing tips with short lengths of blue and navy knotted fringe.

Frog

Using green yarn make four lengths of French knitting: two 8in long for back legs and two 6¾in long for front legs. Trim ends of legs with knotted fringe and sew them in place.

Cut facial features from felt, using the trace pattern below, and sew them in place as shown in the photograph.

Lion

When making up the shape omit the gathering thread for the neck.

Cut a circle of honey-colored felt about 4in in diameter. Using tracing paper and dressmaker's carbon, transfer the facial features given in the trace pattern onto the felt circle.

Embroider the facial features as shown in the photograph, make eyes from green felt, and sew the circle to one end of the tube.

Using honey-colored yarn, make three lengths of French knitting: one 16in long to frame face, one 4¾in long for tail and one 9in long to sew on side of tube to represent back legs. Sew the braids in place.

Using honey and gold yarn, knot a fringe through the braid framing the face. Trim end of tail with honey knotted fringe.

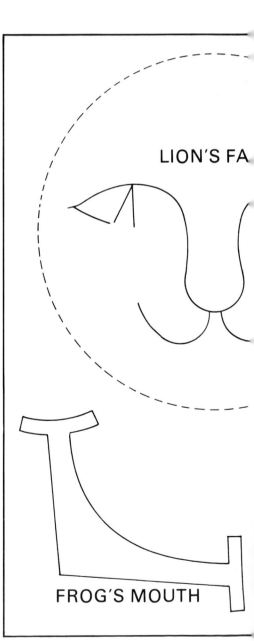

LION'S FA

FROG'S MOUTH

Gnome

Work the basic shape in three colors as follows: 16 rows dark green, 24 rows red, and 30 rows pale pink.

Pattern for hat Using size 2 needles and dark green, cast on 54 sts. Work 12 rows st st. Change to red. Work 4 rows. Dec one st at beg of next 12 rows. 42 sts. Dec one st at each end of next 18 rows. 6 sts. Cut off yarn, thread through rem sts and fasten off.

Join side seams. Allow cast-on edge to roll up on right side of hat. Sew bell to hat.

Sew hat onto head, then embroider straight stitches in gray yarn above face and around back of head.

Make facial features in felt, as shown in the photograph, and sew them in place.

Make a white beard with knotted fringe.

Soldier

Work the basic shape in four colors, as follows: 16 rows royal blue, 24 rows red, 12 rows pale pink, then 18 rows reverse stockinette stitch in black.

Cut facial features in felt and sew them in place. Trim uniform with rickrack and sequins as shown.

Indian squaw

Work the basic shape in four colors as follows: 16 rows medium brown, 24 rows sand, 12 rows pale peach and 18 rows dark brown.

Make lengths of French knitting 9in long: one each of red, orange, and medium brown. Sew them around face and head to form headdress. Trim the headdress with a knotted fringe in orange, red, dark brown, medium brown, and pale peach.

Trim the lower edge of costume with knotted fringe in sand-colored yarn and embroider large cross stitches in orange above the fringe as shown in the photograph.

Cut facial features in felt and sew them in place.

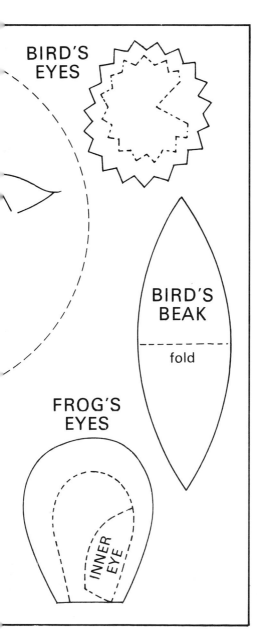

Portly Owl

A jaunty bow tie complements the self-assured air of our feathered friend. His portly shape is made of corduroy and felt.

Size
The toy measures approximately 12in in height.

Materials
¾yd of 36in wide wide-wale brown corduroy

a piece of brown felt 12 by 16in
a piece of white felt 10 by 12in
a piece of orange felt 10 by 12in
a piece of black felt 4in square
¾yd of 1½in wide checked ribbon
synthetic stuffing
tracing paper

Cutting out
Using the tracing paper, trace all the pattern pieces and cut them out.

Cut each piece in the appropriate fabric, following the instructions given on the pattern. A dashed line on the outer edge indicates that the piece is to be cut on the fold. Cut the wing pattern twice on double fabric so that you have a right and a left wing.

Transfer all markings to the fabric.

Making the owl
Pin the front feather piece to the right

side of one of the main body pieces. Place the bib and eye rim pieces on top of it. Baste these pieces in place and stitch around the edges of the bib and eye rims, close to the edges as shown. (Fig. 1)

Pin and stitch black circles onto brown circles. Slipstitch white crosses onto circles as shown. Pin eyes to eye rims and topstitch in place close to the edge, first inserting a small amount of stuffing for a slightly raised effect. (Fig. 2)

Pin and stitch the darts in the two beak pieces. Place the two pieces together, with darts on the outside, and stitch them together along the two outer edges as shown. Stuff the beak and sew it securely to the face. (Fig. 3)

Place feather strip along lower curved edge of one wing piece on right side of fabric as shown. Pin and baste in position. Place the corresponding wing piece, right

side downward, over the first piece. Machine stitch along the curved edges, catching in the feather strip. (Fig. 4)

Turn wing right side out and topstitch close to seamline. Stuff the wing and stitch across the open end to hold stuffing in place. Repeat for other wing.

Fold one foot piece in half down the middle. Stitch a narrow dart along the fold, tapering toward the point of the center claw. Repeat on one other foot piece. These form the upper foot pieces. (Fig.5)

Place the upper foot pieces, dart side upward, onto the lower foot pieces and stitch them together close to the curved edges. Stuff and stitch along open edge to hold stuffing in place. (Fig. 6)

Pin and baste the wings in position on seamline of front body piece, right sides facing. (Fig. 7)

Place right sides together, pin, baste and stitch the three main body pieces together, making sure the seamlines meet neatly and accurately at the top.

Pin and baste the feet in position on the base seamline of the front body piece.

Pin the body base to the main body section, placing right sides together and matching the "corners" of the base with the body seams. Baste and stitch in place, leaving an opening of about 6in. (Fig. 8)

Turn the owl right side out and stuff firmly, making sure all the curves, particularly along seams, are well packed and shaped. Slipstitch the opening edges together securely.

Tie a bow in the ribbon and sew it in place on the bib.

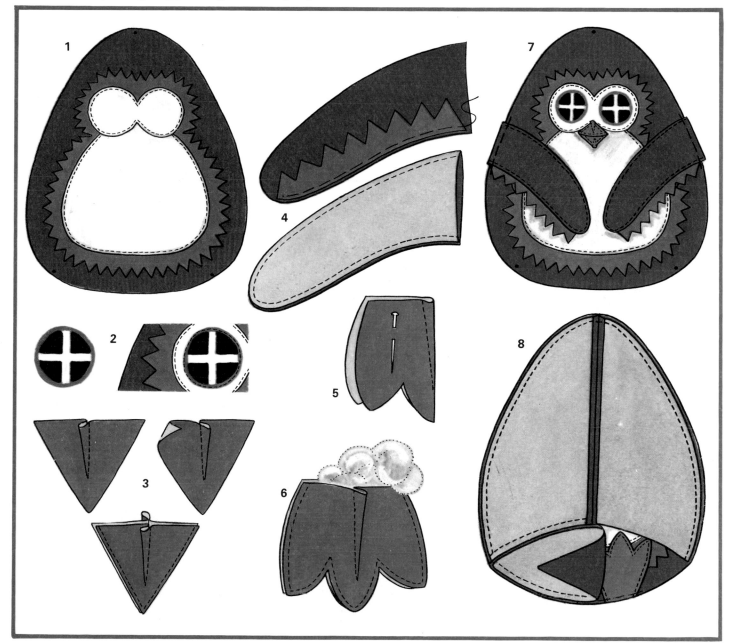

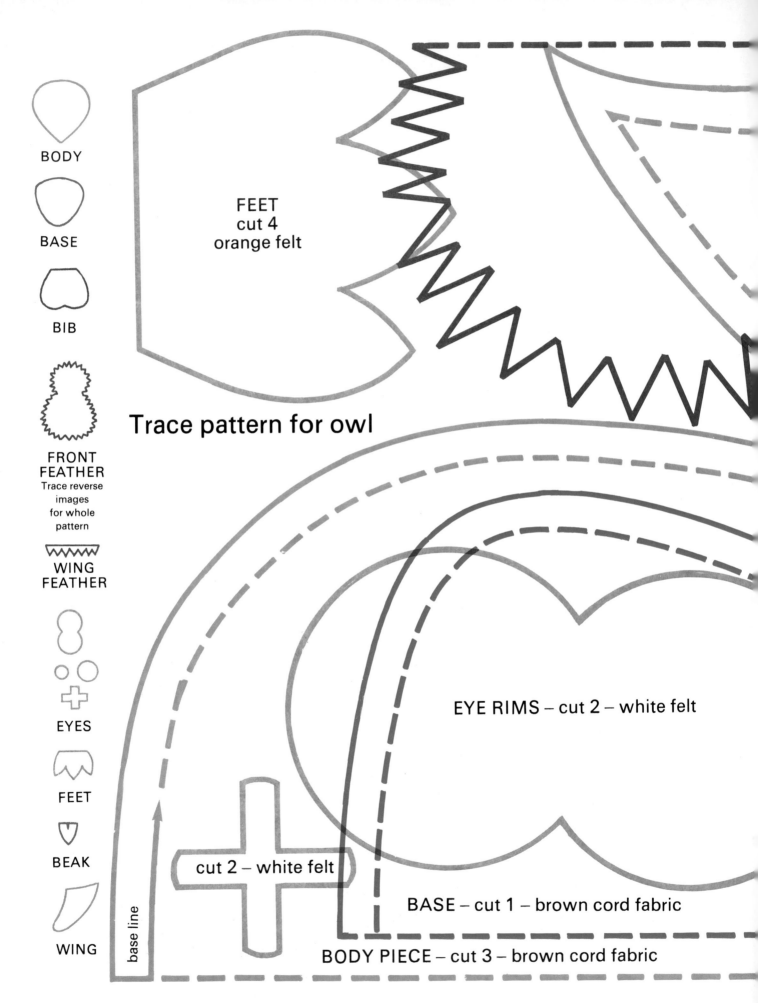

BODY

BASE

BIB

FRONT
FEATHER
Trace reverse
images
for whole
pattern

WING
FEATHER

EYES

FEET

BEAK

WING

FEET
cut 4
orange felt

Trace pattern for owl

EYE RIMS – cut 2 – white felt

cut 2 – white felt

base line

BASE – cut 1 – brown cord fabric

BODY PIECE – cut 3 – brown cord fabric

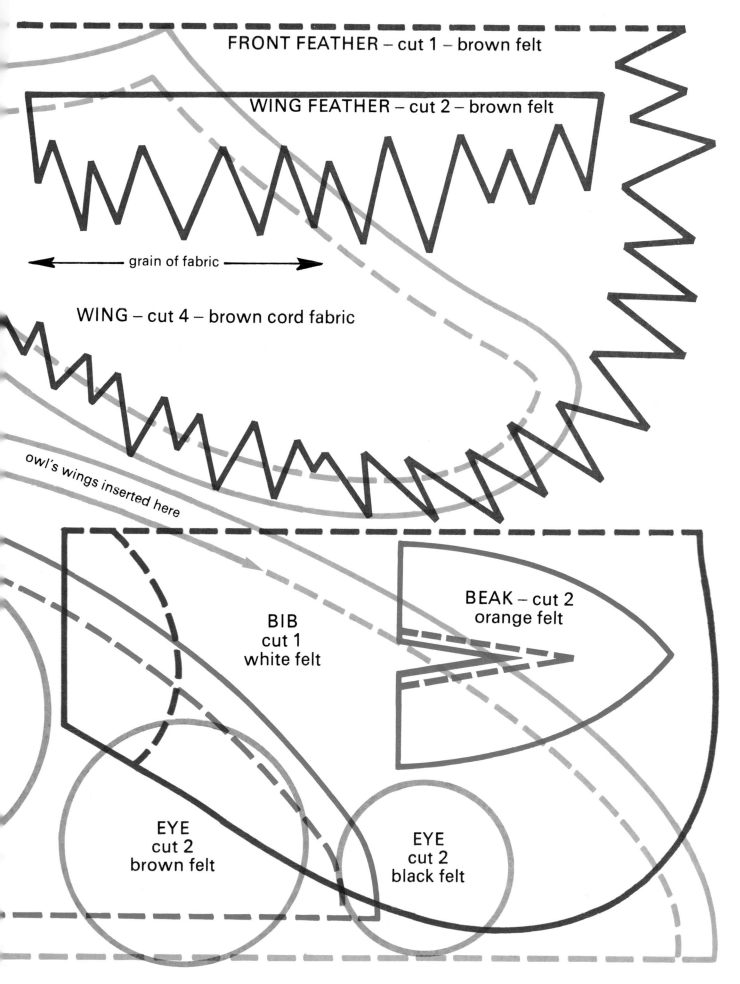

FRONT FEATHER – cut 1 – brown felt

WING FEATHER – cut 2 – brown felt

← grain of fabric →

WING – cut 4 – brown cord fabric

owl's wings inserted here

BIB
cut 1
white felt

BEAK – cut 2
orange felt

EYE
cut 2
brown felt

EYE
cut 2
black felt

Felt Pony

A few scraps of felt, some yarn, and stuffing make this endearing pony. You can vary the basic design to make a cart horse, circus pony, or zebra.

Size
The pony measures about 10in in height.

Materials
2 pieces of felt 12in square
a scrap of felt in a contrasting color for the saddle
scraps of black and white felt for the eyes
about 12in of rickrack
about 18in of cord for the bridle
a ball of thick yarn
$\frac{1}{2}$yd of $\frac{1}{2}$in wide woven tape
a small amount of synthetic stuffing
fabric adhesive
tracing paper

Making the pony
Trace the pattern pieces printed opposite, tracing the head in position on the neck – i.e. matching lines A – B.

Cut out the pattern twice in felt. Measure the curved edge of the neck and cut a piece of woven tape to this measurement.

Unwind a small amount of yarn, wind it around three fingers several times, and cut it off.

Remove the yarn, still in loops, from your fingers and place it on the sewing machine, just under the foot, with the tape on top and to one side. (Fig. 1) Stitch. Continue in this way until yarn is attached to the whole length of the tape.

Cut the loops on the long ends of the yarn to form a fringe.

Make the tail in the same way, using a 1in length of tape.

Place the two body pieces together with the tail between them so that the tape is covered. Leaving the curved neck edge open, baste and stitch the pieces together $\frac{1}{8}$in from the edge.

Stuff the pony fairly firmly, pushing the stuffing down into the legs with a knitting needle.

Place the mane in the open neck edge so that the tape is covered and baste it in place. Machine stitch, using a zipper foot, through all thicknesses.

For the eyes, cut two $\frac{3}{4}$in diameter circles from white felt and two $\frac{1}{2}$in diameter circles from black felt. Glue these onto face. Glue a few strands of the mane in front of the eyes as shown in the photograph.

Cut two pieces of cord for the bridle and tie these over the head. (Fig. 2) Cut off any excess and put a spot of glue on each knot.

From contrasting felt cut a piece for the saddle measuring $4\frac{1}{2}$ by $1\frac{3}{4}$in. Round off the corners. Stitch rickrack around the edges, overlapping the braid by about $\frac{1}{2}$in at the join.

Glue the saddle in place.

Make foot fringes on 3in lengths of tape as for the mane, but winding the yarn around two fingers instead of three.

Glue the foot fringes around the bottoms of the pony's legs.

Variations
Circus pony Give your pony a long flowing mane and a decorative saddle and harness – perhaps with bells – and omit the foot fringes.

Cart horse Plait the pony's mane and tail and give it longer and even more luxurious foot fringes.

Zebra By making the pattern in a boldly striped cotton fabric and by cutting the mane much shorter and omitting the foot fringes, you can make a zebra. Note : it is necessary to add on seam allowances of $\frac{1}{4}$in all around the pattern when cutting out. Stitch the body together with right sides facing, then turn it right side out through the gap left along the neck.

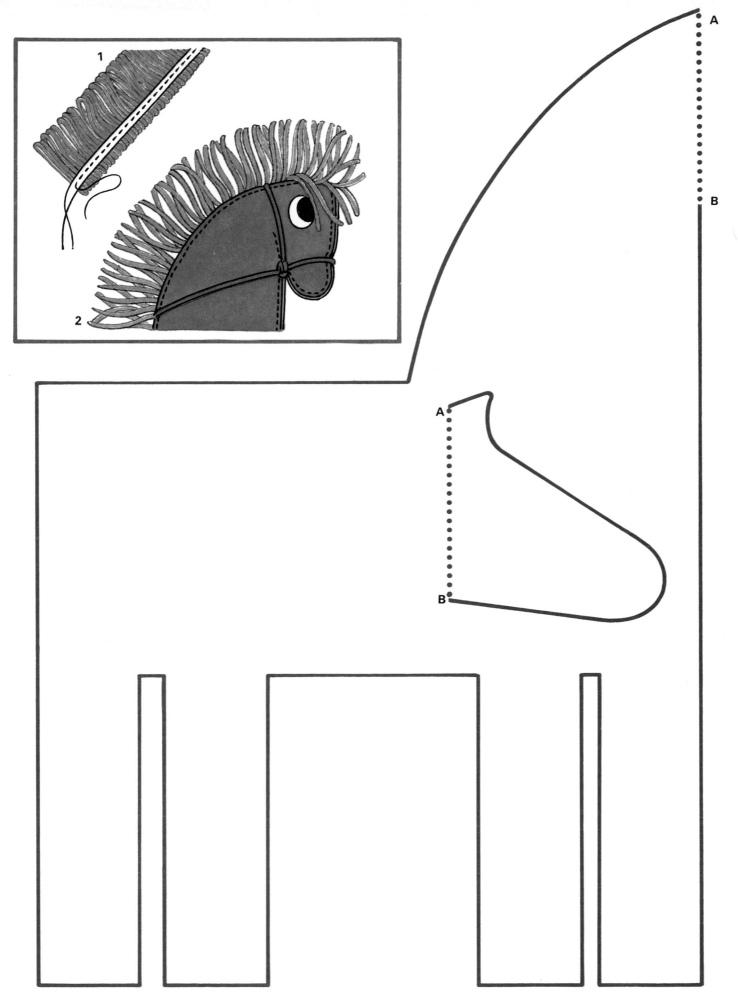

A

B

1

2

A

B

Knitted Penguins

Picture these lovable penguins peeping out from someone's Christmas stocking. They are sure to be favorites.

Size
The largest penguin measures approximately 8in in height, depending on the yarn used and the gauge obtained.

Materials
Large penguin
2½oz of black sport yarn
1¾oz of white sport yarn
yellow and orange sewing thread
a piece of black felt 4 by 8in
a piece of orange felt 4in square
a small piece of white felt for eyes
2 sequins or 2 small circles of felt for eyes

9oz of white synthetic stuffing
a pair of size 6 knitting needles

Small penguin
1oz of black sport yarn
1oz of white sport yarn
a piece of orange felt 4 by 8in
2 sequins or 2 small circles of felt for eyes
3½oz of white synthetic stuffing
a pair of size 2 knitting needles

Chick
1oz of gray medium weight fluffy or
   random yarn
a small amount of medium weight
   charcoal gray yarn of similar type
small scraps of pink, white, and yellow felt
2 sequins or 2 small circles of felt for eyes
1¾oz of white synthetic stuffing
a pair of size 2 knitting needles

For all three penguins: tracing paper

Gauge
The gauge will vary slightly according to
the yarn used and so, consequently, will
the size of the toy.

Pattern – large and small penguins
The large and small penguins are knitted
from the same instructions. Use the yarn
double for the large penguin and single
for the small one. The shading on the
front may be omitted on the small
penguin.

Back
*Using appropriate needles and black
yarn, cast on 7 sts for base. Working in st
st inc one st at the end of next 12 rows
ending with a P row. 19 sts.*
Cut off yarn and leave sts on a holder.
Repeat from * to *.
Next row K to end, then K across the sts
of first piece. 38 sts. Work 11 rows st st
across both sets of sts.
Dec one st at each end of next and every
foll 6th row until 22 sts rem.
Work 5 rows without shaping.
Next row K9, (K2 tog) twice, K9. 20 sts.
Next row P8, (P2 tog) twice, P8. 18 sts.
Next row K7, (K2 tog) twice, K7. 16 sts.
Next row P6, (P2 tog) twice, P6. 14 sts.
Work 2 rows st st over 14 sts. Bind off.

Front
** Using appropriate needles and white
yarn cast on 7 sts for base.
Working in st st inc one st at end of next
12 rows ending with a P row. 19 sts. **
Cut off yarn and leave sts on a holder.
Repeat from ** to **.
Next row K to end, then K across the sts
of first piece. 38 sts.
Work 3 rows across both sets of sts.

Dec one st at each end of next and
every foll 6th row until 28 sts rem; work
1 row.

Shading
Next row K9, strand in both colors of
sewing thread over next 10 sts by knitting
them together with the white yarn, K9.
Next row P9, strand next 10 sts, P9. Cont
stranding in this way but work 1 more st
of stranding at each side on every K row
and *at the same time* cont shaping by dec
one st at each end of every 6th row as
before until 24 sts rem. P 1 row.
Next row Cont to strand (K1, K2 tog) to
end. 16 sts.
Cut off yarns and threads. Change to
black yarn.
P8, turn and leave rem sts on a holder. Inc
one st at beg of next row and at this same
edge on foll 5 rows. 14 sts.
Work 7 rows in st st.
Dec one st at beg on next row and at this
same edge on foll 7 rows. 6 sts.
Work 1 row and bind off.
Rejoin yarn to rem sts and work to match
first side, reversing shaping.

Tail
Using black yarn, cast on 18 sts. Work 3
rows st st. Dec one st at each end of next
6 rows.
Bind off.
Make another piece in the same way.

Wings (alike)
Using black yarn, cast on 8 sts for outside
and work 6 rows st st. Inc one st at each
end of next row. 10 sts. Work 5 rows st st.
Inc one st at each end of next row. 12 sts.
Work 9 rows st st.
Dec one st at each end of next and every
foll 3rd row until 4 sts rem.
Work 1 row st st. Bind off.
Make one more wing piece in black yarn
and two wing pieces in white yarn.

Assembling
Using backstitch, sew the seam at the top
of the head and the two side seams. Stuff
the penguin evenly and sew the base
seam.
   Sew a white wing piece to the inside of
a black wing piece and slipstitch the
finished wing to one side seam 1in below
the change of yarn at neck. Repeat for
other wing.
   Sew the two tail pieces together along
the curved edges; stuff the tail evenly.
Sew the cast-on edges of the tail to the
back of the penguin.
   Work loops of double yarn through the
outer edge of the tail as shown in the
drawing. Trim ends to 1in. (Fig. 1)
   Trace the patterns for the feet, beak,
and eye pieces. Cut each piece twice
from the appropriate colored felt.
   Stitch the two beak pieces together on
the long edges, using stab stitch. Stuff the

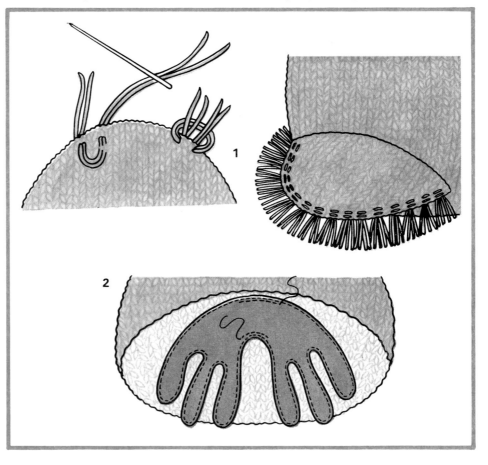

Trace patterns

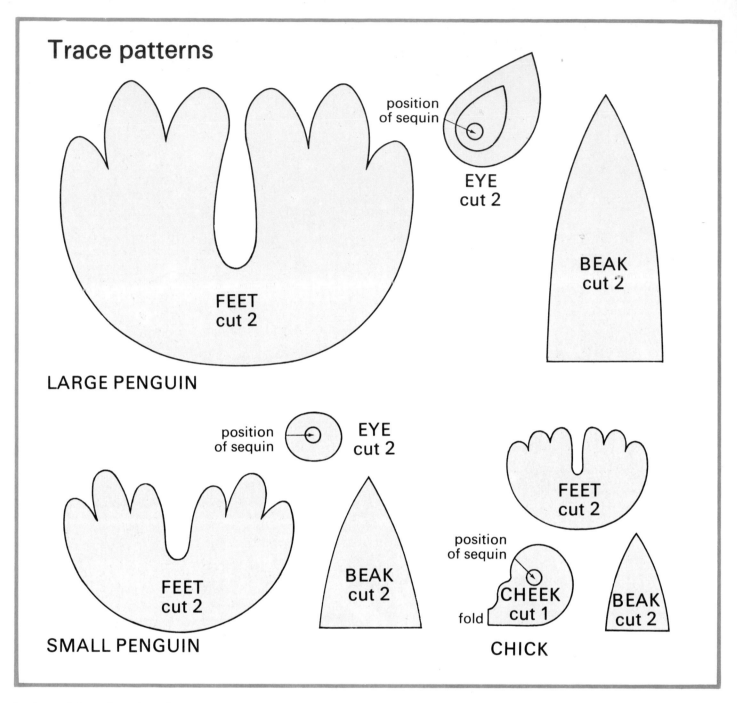

LARGE PENGUIN

position of sequin

EYE
cut 2

BEAK
cut 2

FEET
cut 2

position of sequin

EYE
cut 2

FEET
cut 2

FEET
cut 2

BEAK
cut 2

position of sequin

CHEEK
cut 1

fold

BEAK
cut 2

SMALL PENGUIN

CHICK

---

beak carefully and sew it in place.

Sew the two feet pieces together all around, using stab stitch, and sew the feet to the base of the body with the back edge at the base seam. (Fig. 2)

Sew or glue the felt eye pieces and sequins in place. Note: if toy is for a very small child, sew pieces on, rather than gluing, and use felt circles instead of sequins.

Pattern – chick
Body
Using size 2 needles and gray yarn, cast on 38 sts for neck edge. Work 21 rows rev st st, ending with a P row.
Next row K1 * (K2 tog) twice, K5, rep from * to last st, K1.

Next row P to end.
Next row K1, (K2 tog) 14 times, K1. Bind off.
Using charcoal yarn and with wrong side facing, K up 26 sts evenly along cast-on edge of body. Work 14 rows rev st st.
Next row P1, * (P2 tog) twice, P2, rep from * to last st, P1. 18 sts.
K 1 row.
Next row (P2 tog) 9 times. Bind off.

Wings
Using size 2 needles and gray yarn used double, cast on 4 sts. Work 12 rows in garter st.
Next row K2 tog, K2.
Next row K2 tog, K1.
Next row K2 tog and bind off.

Make another wing in the same way.

Assembling
Using backstitch sew the back seam, leaving a small opening at the base. Stuff body evenly and sew up the opening.

Trace the pieces for feet, cheeks, and beak and cut them out from the appropriate colored felts. Sew the wings to each side of the body ½in from the change of yarn at the neck. Make up the beak and feet as for the larger penguins and sew them in place. Sew or glue the cheeks in place and glue sequins in place for eyes. Note: if toy is for a very small child, sew on all features and use felt circles, rather than sequins, for eyes.

Versatile Toy Bag

Opened flat it's a colorful sheet to play on. Pull up the cords and it's a handy bag for carrying toys home.

Size
The completed sheet/bag measures approximately 34in in diameter.

Materials
1yd of 36in wide sailcloth
$\frac{5}{8}$ to $1\frac{1}{8}$yd of a bold animal or toy printed fabric from which large motifs can be cut
18 $\frac{3}{4}$in diameter white plastic curtain rings
$4\frac{3}{8}$yd of white piping cord
a wooden embroidery hoop
a thumbtack, string and chalk

Making the bag
Fold the square of sailcloth in half and then in half again the opposite way. Pin the edges together to hold them.

Place the folded square on the floor. Tie one end of the string around the thumbtack and the other around a piece of chalk so that the distance between pin and chalk is the same as one side of the fabric. Hold the pin in place where the folds cross (the center of the fabric) and, holding the string taut, draw an arc from one folded edge to the other. (Fig. 1)

Remove thumbtack and chalk. Pin the four layers of fabric together just inside the chalk line. Cut along the line, through all layers. Remove pins and open out fabric, which is now a circle.

Turn under $\frac{3}{8}$in twice around the edge. Pin, baste and stitch in place.

From the printed fabric cut out various motifs, allowing $\frac{3}{4}$in extra on each one.

Arrange the motifs around the edge of the circle, positioning them about $1\frac{1}{2}$in from the outer edge. Pin and baste them in place, making sure they lie flat against the background fabric. (Fig. 2)

Set your sewing machine to the closest possible zigzag stitch with a stitch width of about $\frac{3}{16}$in. Place the first motif to be stitched in the embroidery hoop. The fabric layers in the hoop need not be very taut but must be held in equal tension. Stitch around the outlines of the motif, just inside the edges (Fig 3). When necessary, remove the fabric from the machine and reposition it in the hoop to include previously omitted parts of the motif.

In the same way attach the remaining motifs.

Draw all loose thread ends to the wrong side and tie them securely.

With sharp-pointed scissors very carefully cut away the excess fabric at the edge of each motif. (Fig. 4)

Sew the curtain rings to the edge of the cloth, spacing them evenly.

Thread the piping cord through the rings and knot the ends together.

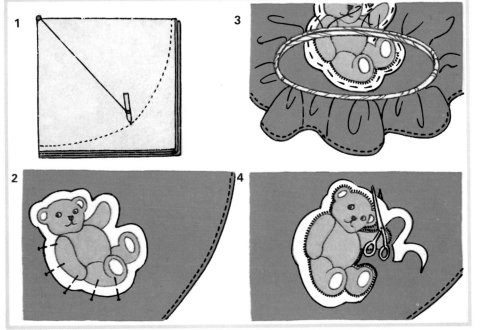

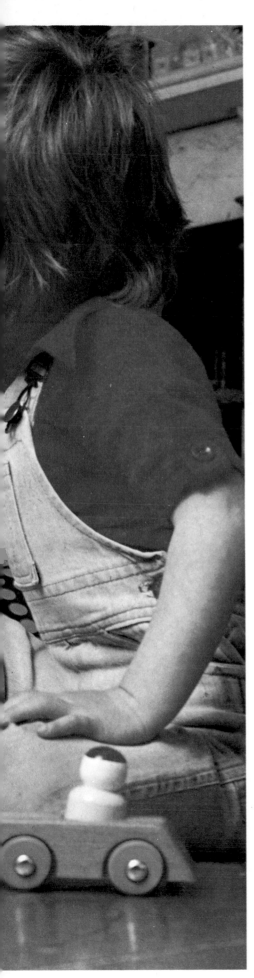

Toy Town

Three soft little pillows, decorated to suggest a house, a thatched cottage and a produce market, make a colorful pretend village for a toddler.

Size
Each building measures about 10in in height.

Materials
(for the three buildings)
⅜yd of 36in wide white, plain-woven cotton fabric for backing
a piece of white felt 23½ by 8in
a piece of brown felt 10 by 6in.
three pieces of felt, each 31½ by 12in, in red, blue and yellow
tapestry wool in brown, red, yellow and green
stranded embroidery floss in blue, green and red
suitable stuffing
a large and a medium-sized crewel needle
tracing paper

dressmaker's carbon paper

Making the cottage
Using tracing paper and a sharp pencil, trace the patterns for the cottage given on page 168, tracing the solid black lines only. (Fig. 1)

Using dressmaker's carbon paper, transfer the entire outer shape onto the white backing fabric. Cut out this piece.

Mark and cut an identical piece in yellow felt for the back (Fig. 2). Also from yellow felt cut a strip 31½ by 4in for the gusset.

Using dressmaker's carbon paper mark the remaining pieces on the appropriate colored felts. Mark a rectangle of white felt for the front wall of the house, up to the roof, and a solid blue rectangle for the door – the curtains go on top of it. Cut out all pieces.

Lay the white felt front wall over the lower part of the backing piece and pin and baste it in place. (Fig. 3)

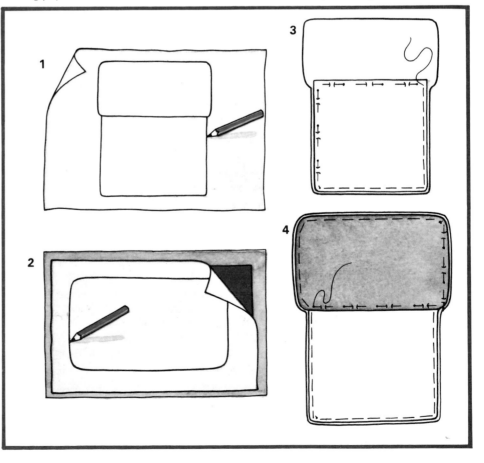

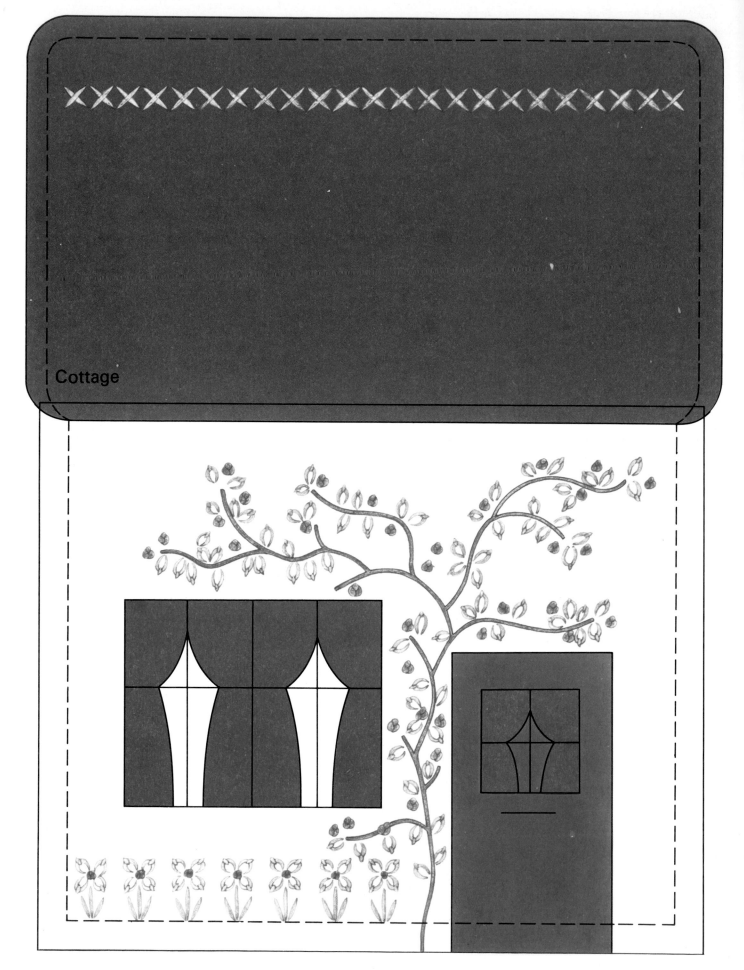

Cottage

Lay the brown roof piece over the backing piece with the lower edge overlapping the white felt wall. Pin and baste it in place. (Fig. 4)

Using matching sewing thread, topstitch across the lower edge of the roof, catching in the front wall. Similarly topstitch around all outer edges, $\frac{3}{8}$in from the edge, measuring as you go to keep the stitching straight.

Using the pattern on page 168 as a guide, pin the door and windows in their correct positions. Baste and topstitch them in place using matching thread.

Using black thread and with the machine set at satin stitch, width about $\frac{3}{16}$in, stitch around edges of windows in wall and door. Repeat, stitching across windows in both directions to complete frames. (Fig. 5)

Stitch a short bar under the door window to suggest a mail slot.

Using pencil and following the pattern on page 168, mark the vine on the front wall. Stitch over the lines, again using satin stitch, with brown thread. (Fig. 6)

Draw all thread ends to the underside and tie them off or darn them into the fabric.

Using three strands of green embroidery floss, embroider the leaves in detached chain stitch. For the flowers embroider French knots using red tapestry wool. (Fig. 7)

To suggest decorative thatching, work a row of cross stitch in brown tapestry wool across the top of the roof. (Fig. 8)

Embroider a row of flowers across the lower edge of the cottage, using the line of stitching as the base. Use three strands of embroidery floss, in red, blue and green, working the stems and leaves in straight stitch and the petals in detached chain stitch, with French knots for the centers. (Fig. 9)

Pin the gusset strip to the front of the cottage as shown along the line of topstitching around the edge, with the ends of the gusset meeting at the center of the base. Pin, baste and stitch the ends together to fit (Fig. 10). Trim seam allowances, if necessary, to $\frac{3}{8}$in and press seam open. Baste all around the edges, exactly over the existing stitching line.

Pin, baste and stitch the back of the cottage to the gusset, right sides facing, leaving a 4in opening in the base.

Turn the cottage right side out and stuff it firmly. Turn in the raw edges and slipstitch them together neatly.

Making the produce market
Trace the pattern on page 170.

Cut the main shape in the backing fabric and in blue felt. Also from blue felt cut a gusset strip $31\frac{1}{2}$ by 4in.

Mark and cut out a front wall, roof, awning, door and curtains from the appropriate colored felts.

Attach the front wall and roof pieces as instructed for the cottage, and topstitch around the outer edges $\frac{3}{8}$in from the edge.

Using the pattern as a guide, position and stitch down the awning, door and curtains, using matching thread, close to the edges.

Using satin stitch on the machine and constrasting thread, stitch around door and window frames. Add a line below the door window for the mail slot.

Using yellow tapestry wool, work a row of cross stitch across the top of the roof. Using red tapestry wool work a row across the top of the awning.

For the fruit work French knots in yellow, green and red tapestry wool.

Embroider a row of flowers beneath the window, above the stitching line, using red and green tapestry wool, working cross stitches for the flowers and straight stitches for leaves and stems.

Finish the produce market as instructed for the cottage.

Making the house
Trace the pattern on page 171.

Cut out the main shape in the backing fabric and in red felt. Also from red felt cut a gusset strip $31\frac{1}{2}$ by 4in.

Mark and cut out the front wall, roof, door, shutters and curtains from the appropriate colored felts.

Attach the front wall and roof pieces as described for the cottage and stitch around the outer edges $\frac{3}{8}$in from the edge.

Using the pattern as a guide, position and stitch the door, curtains and shutters to the front wall, using matching thread, close to the edges.

Using satin stitch on the machine and matching and contrasting thread as appropriate, stitch around door, shutters and window frames. Add lines of satin stitch in red to suggest slits in shutters and one line in contrasting thread to suggest a mail slot in the door.

Using six strands of blue embroidery floss, work a row of cross stitch along the lower edge of the roof.

Mark the vine as for the cottage and go over the lines with machine satin stitch. Embroider leaves and flowers as instructed for the cottage.

Work a row of flowers along the base line of stitching, using the same stitches as for the cottage flowers and using green embroidery floss for the stems and leaves, yellow tapestry wool for the petals and blue stranded floss for the flower centers.

Finish the house as instructed for the cottage.

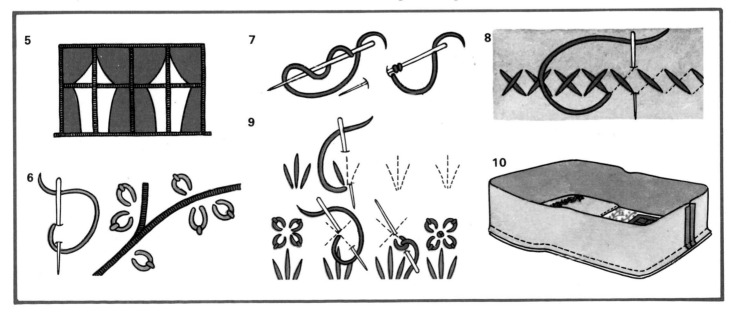

Produce market

170

House

Flower-garden Playhouse

Perfect for make-believe, this playhouse fits neatly over a kitchen table. Roses, tulips and daisies adorn the walls, and the door rolls up for easy access.

Size
The playhouse fits a table 29in tall with a top measuring 54 by 29½in. Smaller proportions can be extended by means of a piece of plywood.

Materials
4⅞yd of 36in wide strong white cotton or synthetic fabric

2⅞yd of 36in wide red fabric
1⅛yd of 36in wide blue fabric
¾yd of 36in wide brick red fabric
4⅜yd of 1½in wide blue woven tape
6½yd of ½in wide bias binding in several shades of green
scraps of cotton, corduroy, velveteen, terry cloth, etc., in yellow, mauve, orange, pink, crimson and shades of green
yellow stranded embroidery floss
a large crewel needle
2 red buttons
12in of ⅜in diameter dowel

a piece of thick cardboard 55 by 35½in
tracing paper
a yardstick

Making the playhouse
From the white fabric cut two rectangles, each 55½ by 31½in for the front and back walls and two pieces 31½in square for the side walls.

From the blue fabric cut three strips for the door frame: two measuring 26½ by 2¾in and one measuring 16 by 2¾in.

Place the shorter strip over the ends of the other two strips at right angles, with

right sides facing upward. Fold under the two ends of the shorter strip diagonally as shown and pin in place. Baste and topstitch along the folded edges. On the underside trim away the excess fabric. (Fig. 1)

Pin the right side of the door frame to the wrong side of the front wall, positioning it in the center and aligning the lower edges.

From red fabric cut two pieces for the door, each measuring 22$\frac{3}{4}$ by 12in. Pin, baste and stitch the two pieces together along one short edge (the bottom), taking a $\frac{3}{8}$in seam. Press the seam open.

Turn under $\frac{3}{8}$in along the side edges for 1$\frac{1}{4}$in to each side of the seam; pin, baste and stitch this hem in place. (Fig. 2)

Fold the door along the seam, with right sides facing. Pin, baste and stitch $\frac{3}{8}$in seams to within $\frac{3}{4}$in of the lower edge. Turn the door right side out. Pin, baste and stitch across the lower edge, $\frac{3}{4}$in up, to form a casing.

Pin and baste the top edges of the door together. Place this upper edge under the door frame, so that it is even with the inner edge of the frame. Baste and stitch this inner edge to the front wall, thus also catching in the door as you do so. (Fig. 3)

Trim away the enclosed wall section; clip into the corners. Bring the door frame through to the right side. Turn under the outer edge $\frac{3}{8}$in and pin, baste and stitch it to the front wall close to the folded-under edge.

For the window frames cut 24 strips of blue fabric, each 12$\frac{1}{2}$ by 2$\frac{3}{4}$in. Pin four strips together to form a square, folding under the ends diagonally as for the door frame. Baste and topstitch. Trim away excess fabric. Repeat for the remaining five windows. (Fig. 4)

Place two window frames onto the underside of the front wall, right side of frame to wrong side of wall, 5in down from the upper edge and 2in from the stitching line of the door frame. Pin, baste and stitch along the inner edge. Trim away the wall sections inside the window frames and clip into the corners. (Fig. 5)

Turn the window frames to the right side. Fold under the outer edges and pin, baste and stitch them in place.

Similarly join two window frames to the back wall and one to each side wall, aligning the upper edges.

For window bars cut the blue tape into 12 pieces each 9in long. Fold each piece in half lengthwise and pin and stitch close to the edges. Pin two pieces across each window frame so that they cross at the center. On the underside, turn under the short ends and hand-sew them to the

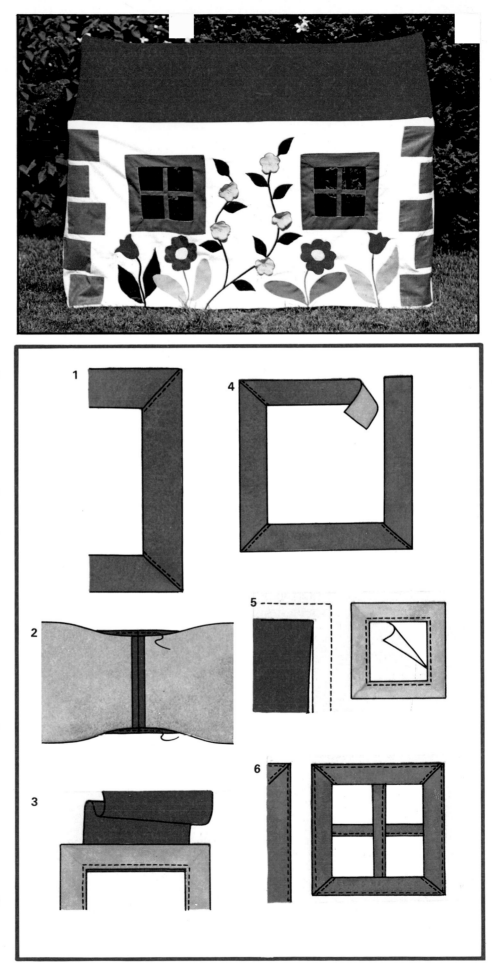

173

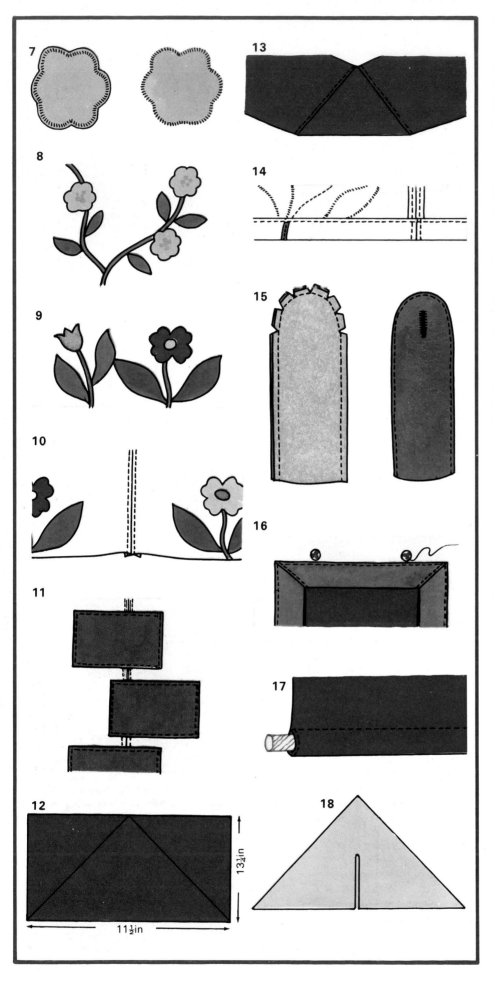

wall. Join the bars at the center with a few stitches. (Fig. 6)

Trace the patterns for the rose and small rose leaf. Cut out ten pink roses and nine dark green leaves. Pin the rose pieces together in pairs, wrong sides together. Baste and stitch them together near the edges using a close zigzag stitch. Trim off excess fabric. (Fig. 7)

Pin and baste the roses to the back wall in between the two windows as shown. Attach the roses to the wall with a few French knots worked in yellow stranded embroidery floss.

Cut two lengths of green bias binding, long enough to make stems for the roses, as shown in the photograph. Fold each piece in half lengthwise and pin and baste them in position on the wall. Topstitch down the center of the binding.

Pin and baste leaves to either side of stems. Stitch them to the wall using a close zigzag stitch around the edges. (Fig. 8)

Trace the patterns for the remaining flowers, flower centers and leaves. Cut out seven daisies, seven centers and seven tulips in assorted colors and fabrics. Cut out 11 rounded leaves and 14 pointed leaves, all in the different green fabrics. Pin and baste flowers to the walls of the house in the positions shown – or to please yourself. Cut and fold lengths of green bias binding as for rose stems and baste them in position and topstitch. Pin and baste leaves in position at the base of each stem, at least 2in above lower edges, placing them at different angles and overlapping them in some cases. Stitch all flowers, flower centers and leaves in place using close zigzag stitch. (Fig. 9)

Pin, baste and stitch the side walls to the front wall, right sides facing, taking $\frac{3}{4}$in seam allowance. Press seams open. Topstitch to either side of the seam, through seam allowances. (Fig. 10)

In the same way join the side walls to the back wall.

From the brick red fabric cut twenty rectangles for bricks, each measuring 7 by $5\frac{1}{2}$in. Turn under $\frac{3}{8}$in on all four sides of each brick; pin and baste in place.

Pin and baste five bricks in place over one corner seam, about $\frac{3}{4}$in apart, staggering them as shown (Fig. 11). Topstitch each brick around the edges. Repeat on the remaining three seams.

From the red fabric cut four pieces for the roof: two measuring $55\frac{1}{2}$ by $21\frac{1}{4}$in and two measuring $31\frac{1}{2}$ by $13\frac{1}{4}$in.

On each smaller piece – the end pieces – mark the center of one long side. Using a straightedge, draw lines from the opposite corners to this point. Cut along these diagonal lines to form two

Trace patterns

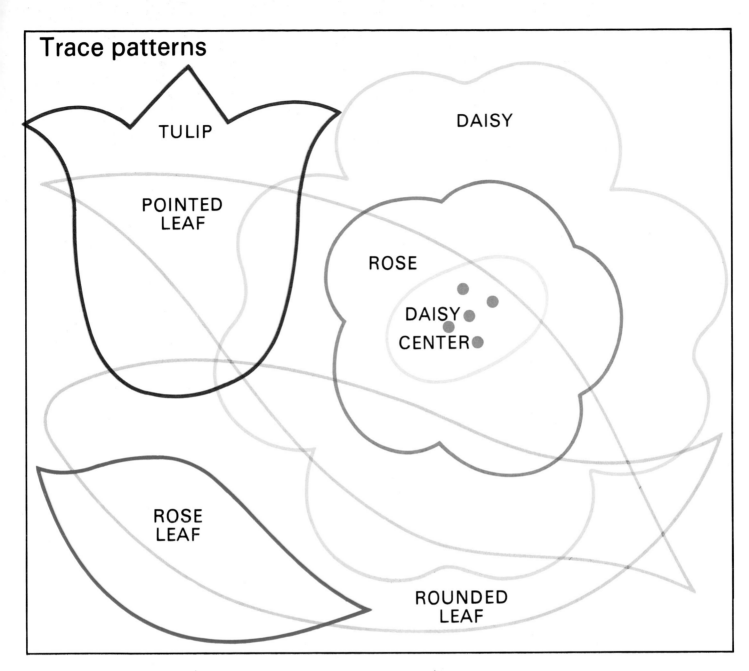

TULIP

DAISY

POINTED
LEAF

ROSE

DAISY
CENTER

ROSE
LEAF

ROUNDED
LEAF

triangles. (Fig. 12)

Pin, baste and stitch the main roof section to the roof end pieces, overlapping the main sections over the end sections and topstitching as shown. (Fig. 13)

Place the main sections together, right sides facing, and pin, baste and stitch the center seam, taking ¾in seam allowance. Press seam open.

Turn the house wrong side out. Place the roof inside it, right side facing right side of house, and pin and baste the roof edges to the upper edges of the house, matching corners and taking ¾in seam allowance. Trim excess seam allowances at corners and press seams toward roof. Turn the house right side out.

Turn up 2in along lower edge and baste along the fold. Turn under the raw edge; pin and baste it in place. Topstitch close

to the turned-under edge. (Fig. 14)

From the blue fabric cut four pieces for tabs, each measuring 6 by 2½in. Round off one end of each piece. Pin the pieces together in pairs, right sides facing. Baste and stitch them together, ⅜in from the edge, leaving the straight ends open. Turn the tabs right side out. Turn in the raw edges and baste the ends together. Topstitch around all edges. Make a buttonhole in the rounded end of each tab. (Fig. 15)

Pin each tab underneath the door frame, about ⅜in in from the edge. Hand sew in place.

Sew buttons in corresponding positions above the door frame as shown. (Fig. 16)

Insert dowel into casing at bottom of door. (Fig. 17)

To make roof supports cut three pieces of thick cardboard: one strip measuring

54 by 11¾in for the center strut and two pieces 30 by 11¾in for the ends. Cut the end pieces into triangles as described for the fabric end pieces, above. In the center of each long side cut a slit 6in long. Make each slit wide enough to accommodate the thickness of the cardboard. Make an identical slit at each end of the center strut, ¾in from the end. Slot the end pieces onto the center strut. (Fig. 18)

Place the roof support on the table and drop the house over it.

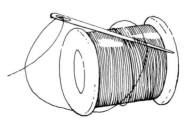

Pajama Case Clown

Sometimes he's happy, sometimes he's blue. But whichever way you turn him, he's useful – keeping a child's pajamas neatly tucked away till bedtime.

Size

The pajama case measures approximately 43in in length.

Materials

¾yd of 36in wide red and white striped cotton fabric
¾yd of 36in wide blue and white striped cotton fabric
a piece of white felt, 20 by 16in
pieces of blue, red and black felt, each measuring 10 by 12in
2¼yd of 2in wide eyelet lace edging
1⅛yd of 3in wide eyelet lace edging
10in dress zipper
black rug yarn or very thick knitting yarn for hair
polyester stuffing
¼yd of ½in wide white woven tape
tracing paper
dressmaker's carbon paper
tailor's chalk
a yardstick

Making the pajama case

Following the measurements given on page 179 and, using tailor's chalk and the yardstick, draw the main body piece on the red striped fabric. Mark in the positions of the zipper, the legs, the arms and the three felt circles. Cut out this piece. Repeat, using the blue striped fabric.

For the arms, measure and cut four rectangles, each measuring 9 by 12in – two in the red fabric and two in the blue.

From the remaining pieces of striped fabric cut out two triangles for the hat, one in each color, following the measurements given in the diagram.

Trace the patterns for the head, feet, hands, features and decorations given on pages 180–181. Using the dressmaker's carbon paper, transfer these onto the appropriate colored felts. Cut out the shapes.

Pin and baste the features onto the two head pieces in their correct positions, as shown. Topstitch close to the edges of the features. Press on the wrong side.

Place the two head pieces together, right sides facing. Pin, baste and stitch around the curved edges only, taking a ⅜in seam. Clip the seam allowances. (Fig. 1)

Turn the head right side out and fill it firmly with the stuffing. Stitch across the neck edges, either by hand or by machine, using the zipper foot.

Cut the yarn into 24 lengths, each 12in long, and divide it into two equal bunches. Tie each bunch very securely in the middle. Hand sew each bunch firmly in the position shown on each side of the head. (Figs. 2 and 3)

Pin and baste two of the large red felt circles in place (see photograph) on the blue striped hat piece and two blue circles on the red piece. Topstitch close to the edges of the circles. (Fig. 4)

Place the hat pieces together, right sides facing, and pin, baste and stitch the side seams, ⅝in from the edges. Press the

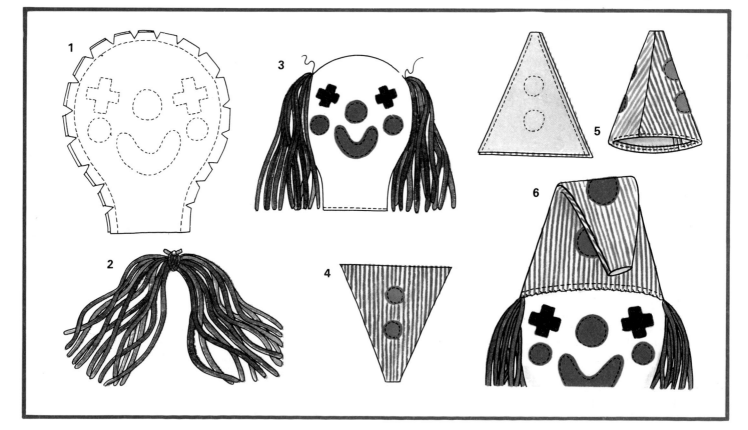

seams open and turn the hat right side out. Turn under ⅝in along the open edge and press. Run a line of gathering stitches close to the folded edge. (Fig. 5)

Pin the hat to the head, matching head and hat seams, just above the hair. Draw up the gathering thread to fit the head. Hand sew the gathered edge neatly to the head, using white thread and stitching through the white stripes only. (Fig. 6)

Fold the length of tape in half and place it between the two white felt circles for the pompom as shown. Pin, baste and stitch around the edges of the circles,

incorporating the tape and leaving a small opening where the tape emerges. Clip the seam allowances. (Fig. 7)

Turn the pompom right side out and stuff it softly. Turn in the edges of the opening and slip the point of the hat between them. Hand sew the pompom edges to the hat. (Fig. 8)

Pin and baste one red and one blue hand piece together to form the left hand. Stitch around the curved edges only. Clip the seam allowance. (Fig. 9)

Turn the hand right side out and stuff it. Stitch the straight edges together by

hand or machine. (Fig. 10)

For the right hand repeat the process, making sure that you place the two pieces together so that when turned right side out they will make a pair with the other hand.

Pin and baste the red and blue circles to each of the four foot pieces. Topstitch them in place close to the edges. Placing right sides together, pin, baste and stitch two foot pieces (one with a red circle and one with a blue one) along the curved edge. Clip the seam allowance. Repeat with the other two foot pieces. (Fig. 11)

Turn each foot right side out and stuff it. Stitch the straight edges together by hand or machine. (Fig. 12)

Place one red arm piece and one blue arm piece together, right sides facing. Pin, baste and stitch the side seams, taking a $\frac{5}{8}$in seam allowance. Press the seams open. Repeat with the other two arm pieces. (Fig. 13)

On one end of each arm turn under $\frac{5}{8}$in and press. Measure and cut a length of the narrower eyelet lace to fit each arm, allowing a little extra for a seam.

Place the edging just under the folded edge of the arm so that its wrong side is upward (i.e. facing the same way as the right side of the striped fabric). Pin, baste and stitch close to the folded edge. (Fig. 14)

Fold the lace back over the arm edge and pin it in place. Run a line of gathering stitches close to the folded edge, through the lace and the striped fabric. (Fig. 15)

Draw up the gathering thread, being careful not to break it, so that the cuff fits the hand. Pin the cuff edge in place over the hand, red and blue sides matching, and adjust the gathers. Carefully hand sew the cuff to the hand. (Fig. 16)

Pin and baste the three blue circles to the red body piece, positioning them as shown. Repeat with the red circles and blue body piece. Topstitch the circles in place.

Place the two body pieces together, right sides facing, and pin and baste them together at the sides below the armholes and along the inner leg edges. Stitch, taking $\frac{5}{8}$in seams, omitting the position marked for the zipper. Press seams open. (Fig. 17)

Insert the zipper in the position left unstitched. Remove basting thread.

Turn under the seam allowances along the unstitched armhole edges; press. Pin and baste these edges over the upper arm edges, matching colors. Topstitch close to the folded edges. (Fig. 18)

Turn under $\frac{5}{8}$in along the neck edge; press. Measure and cut a length of the wider eyelet lace to fit the upper edge of the body piece, allowing a little extra for a seam.

Attach the lace in the same way as for the cuffs. Gather the neck edge to fit the head. Adjust gathers and baste and hand sew the neck edge to the head. (Fig. 19)

Turn under $\frac{5}{8}$in on each leg edge. Trim the edge with the narrower eyelet lace and gather each edge to fit the feet. Insert the feet and hand sew them securely in place. (Fig. 20)

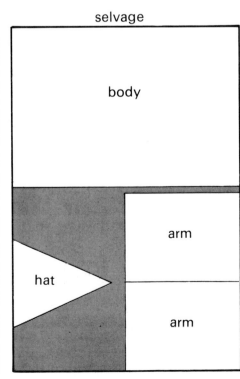

CUTTING LAYOUT FOR 24IN × 36IN FABRIC

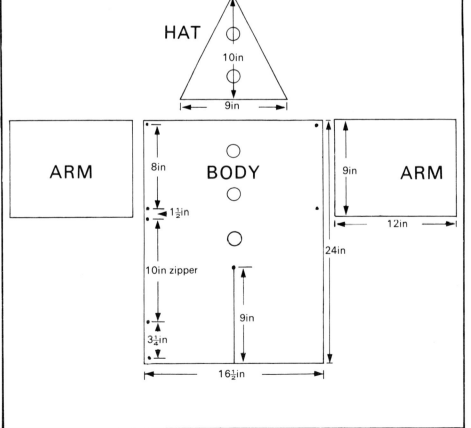

179

Trace pattern

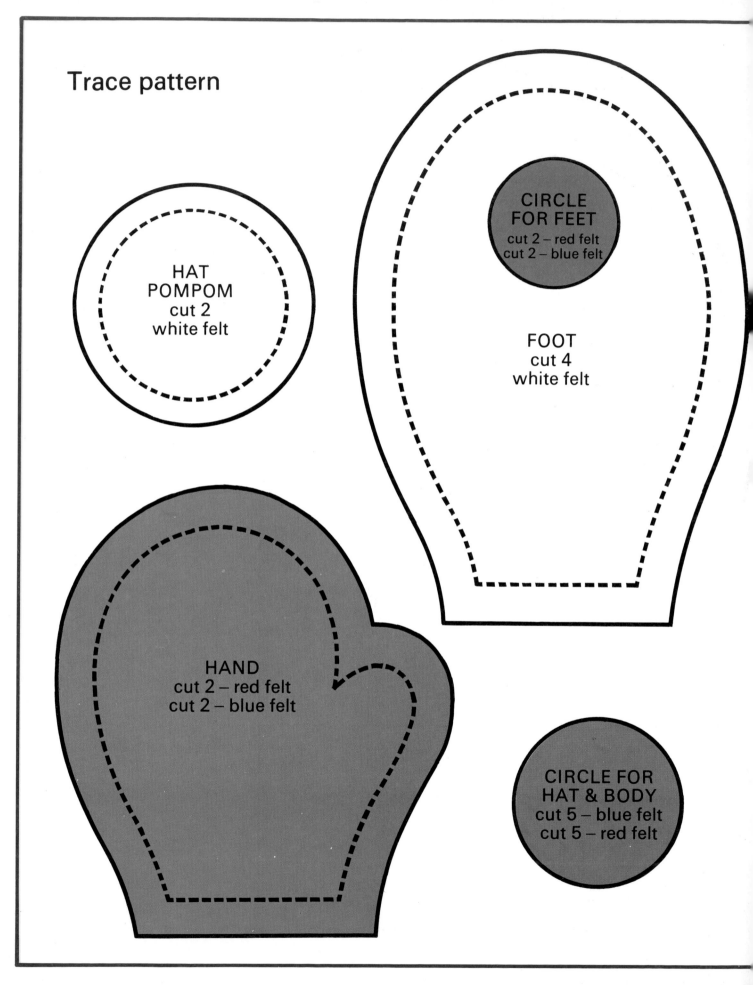

HAT
POMPOM
cut 2
white felt

CIRCLE
FOR FEET
cut 2 – red felt
cut 2 – blue felt

FOOT
cut 4
white felt

HAND
cut 2 – red felt
cut 2 – blue felt

CIRCLE FOR
HAT & BODY
cut 5 – blue felt
cut 5 – red felt

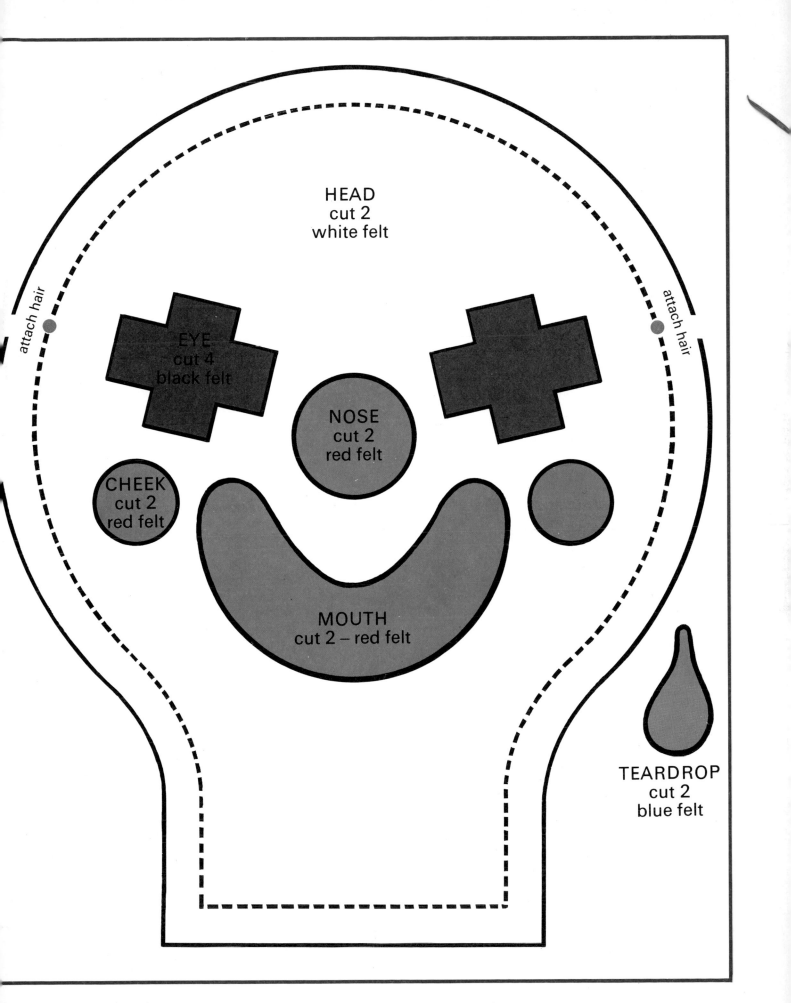

HEAD
cut 2
white felt

attach hair

attach hair

EYE
cut 4
black felt

NOSE
cut 2
red felt

CHEEK
cut 2
red felt

MOUTH
cut 2 – red felt

TEARDROP
cut 2
blue felt

GLOSSARY

Backstitch Bring needle to right side and make a small stitch backward. Then bring the needle through to the right side again, the same distance ahead of the point where it first emerged. Take another stitch back to the front of the first stitch, and continue in this way, forming a line of even stitches, touching end to end.

The stitch may also be worked with the stitches separated – a method recommended for sewing in a zipper by hand. Take the needle back over only one or two threads, but bring it up about $\frac{1}{4}$in ahead of the first stitch, and continue in this way, so producing a line of stitching that is strong, but inconspicuous on the right side.

Blanket stitch Bring needle to right side on the bottom line of the stitching – i.e. the edge along which the thread will run – take it a short distance to the right and insert it along the top line, then bring it out on the bottom line, looping the working thread under the point of the needle. Draw the thread through. Repeat.

The stitches may be worked close together, in which case it is called "closed blanket stitch" or – erroneously – "buttonhole stitch." (For true buttonhole stitch, see below.)

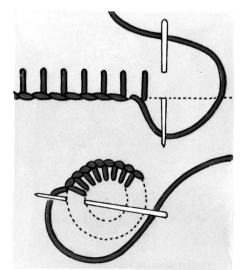

Buttonhole stitch This is similar to blanket stitch – see above – but each stitch forms a little knot along the closed edge. It is worked from right to left along the edge of the fabric. Fasten the thread with a couple of backstitches on the edge, then bring the working thread to the left and then to the right, forming a loop. Insert the needle under the edge of the fabric – over the top of the loop – and bring it out at the desired depth – over the bottom of the loop. Pull the thread through. Repeat. The stitches are illustrated spaced apart, but normally -- as on a buttonhole – they are worked close together.

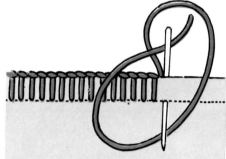

Button loops – see Thread loops.
Catch-stitch This is basically herringbone stitch and is often used on hems. Work from left to right. Make a very small stitch from right to left on the lower line of stitching, then bring the needle diagonally upward to the right and make another small stitch. Take the needle diagonally downward to the right and make another small stitch, and so on in this way.

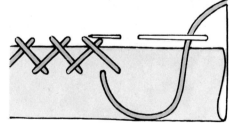

Chain stitch Bring the needle to the right side on the line of stitching and pull the thread through. Re-insert the needle in the same place and bring the point up a short distance along the stitching line, at the same time looping the thread under the point. Draw the needle and thread through – not too tightly. Repeat, again inserting the needle at the point where it emerged, inside the chain loop just formed, and bringing it out over the loop of thread that will form the next chain.

The stitches may be worked separately – in which case they are called "detached chain" – and grouped to make a flower shape – called **"lazy daisy"**.

Cross stitch Work this stitch on an even-weave fabric to keep the stitches even. It is worked simply by making two diagonal straight stitches in the form of an X. For best results work a row of stitches slanting in one direction, then turn and work the other stitches on top of the first.

French knots Bring the needle and thread to the right side and wind the working thread once or twice around the needle. Holding the thread taut, slide the needle along it to the point where thread emerges and re-insert it at that point. Hold the knot in place with your thumb while pulling the thread through.

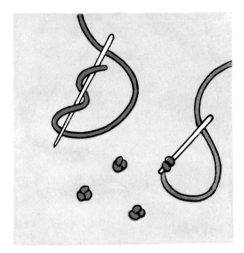

Grading seam allowances To prevent bulk, especially where several layers of fabric are joined, the seam allowances are trimmed to different depths.

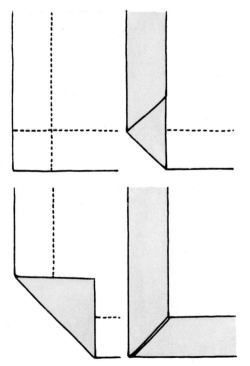

Mitering corners A method of turning a hem so that bulk at the corner is evenly distributed and the corner lies neatly.

Finishing seams This may be done in several ways. In most cases machine zigzag stitch along the raw edges is suitable. If you do not have a machine with zigzag stitch you can, instead, overcast the edge by hand. On fine fabrics the edge is sometimes folded under and straight-stitched. Firm, closely-woven fabrics may be pinked along the edges.

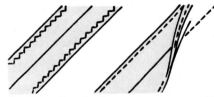

Overcasting As the name suggests, this simple stitch is worked by taking the needle diagonally over the edge of the fabric, bringing it through to the right side and then taking it over the edge again.

Satin stitch A series of straight stitches worked side by side to fill an area.

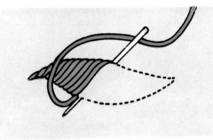

Slipstitch Often used on hems, this may be adapted for other places. Work from right to left. Pick up a thread or two in the fabric being hemmed, then insert the needle into the fold of the hem and bring it out a few threads farther on. Again pick up a thread or two of the main fabric at that point and repeat.

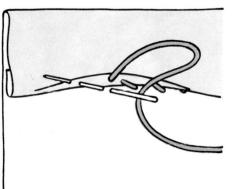

Stab stitch This is simply running stitch worked with a stabbing motion, perpendicular to the fabric, with the stitches close together.

Stem stitch A variation of backstitch, worked from left to right. Bring needle and thread to right side and insert it the desired length of stitch to the right, then bring it out halfway between the two points. Re-insert it the same distance as before to the right, again bringing it up halfway to the left. You may hold the working thread either above or below the needle, but keep it to the same side throughout a line of stitching.

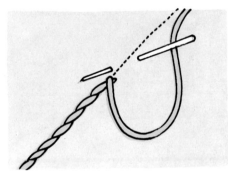

Thread loops These are used as fastenings with a button or a hook. Bring the needle up through the edge of the opening at one end of the position for the loop, then take a small stitch at the other end. Do not pull the thread tight, but leave a loop large enough for the button. Return to the first position, take another stitch and repeat until the loop contains three or four threads. Take care to keep the loops even. Now work blanket stitch – see above – over the threads, drawing the stitches close together. Fasten the thread securely on the wrong side.

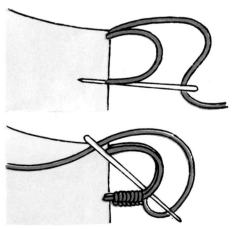

USEFUL ADDRESSES

Most of the yarns used for the projects in this book can readily be obtained in good knitting yarn shops and department stores. However, some of the imported yarns are not so widely available. If you have difficulty obtaining any of them, you may find the following addresses helpful.

Pingouin yarns

For a list of stockists in your area, American readers should write to:

Promafil Corp.
9179 Red Branch Road
Columbia, Maryland 21045

Canadian readers, write to:
Promafil Canada Ltd.
1500 rue Jules Poitras
379 St. Laurent, Québec H4N 1X7

Phildar yarns

For a list of stockists in your area, American readers should write to:
Phildar Inc.
6438 Dawson Blvd.
Norcross, Georgia 30093

Canadian readers, write to:
Phildar Ltee.
6200 Est Blvd. H. Bourassa
Montréal Nord, Québec H1G 5X3

The Twilley's Lyscordet yarn (page 66) can be obtained by mail order from:
Ries Wools
243 High Holborn
London WC1
England

3 Suisses yarns

Bucilla Yarn Co.
230 Fifth Avenue
New York, N.Y. 10001